W9-AVG-869

NICHOLAS KALDOR AND THE REAL WORLD

NICHOLAS KALDOR
AND THE REAL WORLD

Marjorie S. Turner

M. E. Sharpe

Armonk New York • London England

Copyright © 1993 by Marjorie S. Turner

Library of Congress Cataloging-in-Publication Data

Turner, Marjorie Shepherd, 1921–
Nicholas Kaldor and the Real World / Marjorie S. Turner.
p.   cm.
Includes bibliographical references and indexes.
ISBN 1–56324–147–1
1. Kaldor, Nicholas, 1908–1986. 2. Economists—Great Britain—Biography.
3. Keynesian economics. 4. Economic development.
5. Equilibrium (Economics)
I. Title.
HB103.K47T87   1993
330′.092—dc20
[B]
93-21759
CIP

Printed in the United States of America

The paper used in this publication meets the minimum
requirements of American National Standard for Information Sciences—
Permanence of Paper for Printed Library Materials, ANSI Z39.48-1984.

MV   10   9   8   7   6   5   4   3   2   1

To Merle

NK

CONTENTS

NK

PREFACE

Writing about Nicholas Kaldor recalled for me the Shandy Paradox wherein the proper telling of the tale must take longer than the living of it. Fortunately, a fine and encyclopedic biography by his literary executor, Anthony P. Thirlwall, provided a chronology of Kaldor's many and varied activities. And happily, both Thirlwall and Clarissa Kaldor encouraged me, for there is always more to tell about Kaldor. My specific task has been to stress the evolution of and the reactions to Kaldor's work in the context of the economic conditions of the times.

Nicholas Kaldor was born in Hungary in 1908 and died as Baron Kaldor of Newnham in the City of Cambridge, England, in 1986. The years between revealed no hint of scandal or psychological problems that might make Kaldor the subject of a novel. His life was, instead, a straight line of growth and achievement, of intellectual enjoyment and strong values. He enjoyed many honors. His private life was blessed by many friends and close family ties. After World War II, he, Clarissa, and their four daughters lived and entertained broadly in a large family home in Cambridge, periodically visiting their second home in Var, France. The only sadness one can detect was because of the suffering of his extended family in Hungary during World War II and under the subsequent Communist dictatorship.

Kaldor's struggles were intellectual—namely, his efforts to comprehend the economics of the real world, to fit this understanding into economic theory, and to convince his fellow citizens and economists of the accuracy of his perceptions. Kaldor forces us to ponder what the relationship between economic theory and practice should be. He started with this puzzle in his earliest work, and he was still wrestling with it at the end of his life. As are we all.

His life is also a demonstration that values, as distinguished from ideology, have a place in economics. Kaldor carried on from Adam Smith, Alfred Marshall, Allyn Young, and John Maynard Keynes, viewing economics as a moral science. He was known for his dominant personality, which could be irritating or even offensive to colleagues who tired of trying to outshout him or to Conservatives who did not share his values. He was not a man to keep his powder dry, and he did intend to challenge, but his generosity and spirit made him popular throughout his life.

To me the most endearing characteristic of this volatile intellect was his direct manner and his pattern of addressing all as his intellectual equals. His letters to the London *Times* and his speeches to the House of Lords exhibit his fundamental belief that anyone who can read can understand economics.

My grasp of Kaldor's public image was aided immensely when Thirlwall shared his huge collection of Kaldor's letters to the *Times*. While writing the manuscript, I particularly appreciated General Merrill Anthony McPeak's sending me a copy of the once secret Strategic Bombing Survey materials and Tibor Scitovsky's assisting my understanding of Kaldor's role in that survey. Clarissa Kaldor made the search of Kaldor's papers a pleasure when she welcomed me into her home where the papers were awaiting the completion of an addition to the King's College Archives. Anne Fox, librarian at Oregon State University, saved me from frustration by tracking down various materials. Both the Marshall Library at Cambridge University and my own home library at San Diego State University were helpful and indulgent.

J. William and Rosella Leasure were a team of readers, Bill for the economics, Rosella for good sense and grammar. Another team was Bob and Peggy Lucas who cast their journalistic eyes on my efforts to communicate. Economists Adam Gifford, David S. Brookshire, and Elynor Moskowitz McPeak read some of the manuscript, which benefited from their suggestions. Tony Thirlwall's efforts to straighten me out were particularly helpful. Any errors are mine.

For permission to quote I am beholden to Tony Thirlwall, as literary executor, Paul A. Samuelson, Tibor Scitovsky, Arnold Harberger, Oxford University Press, St. Martin's Press, *Banca Nazionale del Lavoro Quarterly Review, Journal of Post Keynesian Economics, Oxford Economic Papers,* and *Review of Economic Studies.*

Clarissa Kaldor granted permission for my use of the cartoon of Kaldor and Keynes and several photos in her family album. The picture of the Strategic Bombing Survey group is from the United States National Archives. The closeup photographs of Kaldor are the work of Dorothy Hahn of Cambridge, who kindly allowed me to choose from the many photos she had taken of him.

Marjorie S. Turner

NICHOLAS KALDOR
AND THE REAL WORLD

NK

INTRODUCTION

For fifty years of this century Nicholas Kaldor was known throughout the world as a master economist. His career embraced advice to more than ten countries, including his own United Kingdom, which he served as adviser to the chancellor of the exchequer during two Labour party governments. His contributions to economic theory were so vast that few economists are aware of all that he did contribute. Like Keynes, Kaldor participated in both the creation of theory and the difficult task of applying it within an economically troubled world economy.

Kaldor was first attracted to the subject of economics when, as a fifteen year old, he witnessed the German inflation in 1923. His major academic training was at the London School of Economics in the late 1920s and early 1930s, and his teaching career at LSE commenced during the early years of the Great Depression. Perhaps because of the traumatic events of that period, Kaldor never lost touch with the world around him.

Initially he was a "neoclassical" economist under the tutelage of Lionel Robbins and Freidrich von Hayek who were devoted to laissez-faire and questioned the propriety of economists' involving themselves in policy making.

He was exposed to a different approach when Professor Allyn A. Young came to LSE from Harvard. Young was skeptical of the value of the economics of equilibrium and insisted that increasing returns should be included in economic analysis. Another liberating idea was the introduction into economics of the principle of imperfect competition in the early 1930s. Finally, through study and conviction, Kaldor became a Keynesian in the late 1930s and began his many contributions to that line of reasoning. Before World War II he was almost exclusively concerned with economic theory.

During the postwar period, Kaldor left teaching briefly to participate in planning for recovery. He directed studies assessing the strengths and weaknesses of the European economy for the Economic Commission for Europe and advised numerous newly independent states on proper tax programs. He was a member of the Royal Commission on the Taxation of Profits and Income in the United Kingdom, an experience which led him to propose an expenditure tax. These activities dramatized for Kaldor the complexities of the real world.

After returning to England as a reader in economics at the University of Cambridge and a member of King's College, Kaldor systematically worked on post-Keynesian economic theory, contributing a theory of income distribution in the context of economic growth. His service to the Labour government in the 1960s led him to consider why growth rates differ among countries. Having already contributed three growth models using traditional methods, he turned to calling on economists to change their approach from the mathematically satisfying equilibrium models to an "economics without equilibrium." This ultimatum has been parried by more traditional economists, but there are signs that Kaldor's insistence on including more variables, apropos the complications of the world economy, will doubtless carry into the twenty-first century.

An account of Kaldor must include his efforts to persuade the English public on economic issues through letters to the *Times* and addresses to the House of Lords. He was eloquent in his warning of the dangers to the British economy of joining the European Common Market and of the economic foolishness of monetarism and unsupervised free trade.

Kaldor's massive body of work includes few books. Mostly it is a body of papers that is scattered to the winds—in economic journals, newspapers, and addresses. This has been remedied somewhat by the existence of eight volumes of collected papers and a special collection by F. Targetti and A.P. Thirlwall. However, even more extensive are the responses to his work. In this book I have attempted to relate Kaldor's intellectual development to the times in which he lived and to introduce the reader to the reactions of contemporary colleagues and citizens.

In carrying forward the sound traditions of Adam Smith, Alfred Marshall, Allyn Young, and John Maynard Keynes, Kaldor was, like them, an asker of big questions that he then attempted to answer. In short, Kaldor assumed the mantle of Keynes. He had his foot in both city affairs and King's College, functioning brilliantly in both the real world and academe.

The task he set for himself in his later years was that of inspiring economists to give up their comfortable views on equilibrium economics. That task was not an easy one. Kaldor staked his formidable reputation on his belief that economists must give up equilibrium first in order for economic understanding to progress. This book is a chronicle of the training, experiences, and beliefs that led him to this position.

Part I

Becoming a Theoretician

NK

Nicholas Kaldor in Retrospect

There are few master economists. Nicholas Kaldor was one, an economist who contributed to both theory and policy. Born in Hungary in 1908, he sought higher education first in Germany and then in England, absorbing a variety of experiences. While a student of economics at the University of Berlin in 1925, he displayed a flare for journalism, admitting to "a sneaking desire to become a writer." He also applied for admission to legal studies at the University of Budapest "as a sort of insurance policy," perhaps to follow his father into law. But ever since his fifteenth year, having witnessed hyper-inflation while on a family holiday in Germany, he was curious about economics.

Early experiences

Vacationing in the Bavarian Alps in 1923, Nicky Kaldor, as he was known among his friends and family, was struck by the "yawning and widening gap" between the high prices of goods in the local German currency and the much lower prices in foreign currency. Upon discovering that a branch of knowledge called economics could supposedly explain such discrepancies, he decided to become an economist.

Early experiences also introduced him to politics, for he witnessed "bewildering changes" in social regimes in the Austro-Hungarian Empire after World War I, with Hungary shedding its monarchy and then a military dictatorship for a parliamentary form of government. These events triggered an interest in "the forces which govern the political evolution of society."[1]

After finishing school in Budapest, Kaldor attended lectures at the University of Berlin, studying under such renowned German economists as Werner Sombart and Hermann Schumacher, the father of E.F. Schumacher. During this year and a half in Berlin, Kaldor spent much of his time around the Reichstag as an accredited foreign correspondent of a Hungarian newspaper. His friendships were wide and varied and included Robert Vambery, a cherished friend from childhood.[2]

But he never forgot his commitment to the study of economics. When one of his Berlin friends spoke favorably of the London School of Economics (LSE), he decided to spend a term in London as a general student. Partly in an effort to improve his English-language skills, he continued his journalistic endeavors while in England, interviewing literary figures for articles that were published in Hungary or syndicated through Europe. In Europe, he interviewed political leaders, but in England he turned toward the arts. He bought playing rights of new plays in London for a European theatrical agency, a sideline that led to his attendance at many English plays. He was supported during his student years by his father, a famous Hungarian lawyer. Kaldor's friend and colleague, Luigi L. Pasinetti, says that the deep mark of a privileged childhood remained in Kaldor throughout his life.[3]

Student life at LSE 1927–31

At the London School of Economics, Kaldor was drawn into serious study of economics, and he considered his undergraduate years at LSE as his "chief training in economics."[4]

An American from Harvard, Allyn Abbot Young, was brought to London as head of economics in 1926, the year before Kaldor arrived. Kaldor spoke enthusiastically of Young's teaching. In fact, what Young taught him regarding the impact on economic theory of the existence of increasing returns stuck with Kaldor throughout his career as an economist and became a theme to which he returned in developing his own ideas in the 1960s.[5]

Young died an untimely death from influenza in 1929, but in this limited period of exposure to his ideas, Kaldor learned from Young a "basic distrust of abstract systems *per se*, and an awareness of the need to adapt the tools of theoretical analysis to the practical problems which they are intended to illuminate." These attitudes broadened Kaldor's outlook and facilitated his becoming an influential master of economics. However, the intellectual freedom Kaldor enjoyed would eventually stimulate resistance within the profession.[6]

Young's successor at LSE was thirty-year-old Lionel Robbins whom Kaldor remembered as "flamboyant and enthusiastic." Kaldor fell "completely under Robbins' spell." Unlike Young's, Robbins's economics was that of the general equilibrium theory of Léon Walras and the Austrians, especially the Viennese economics typified by the work of Ludwig von

Mises. Through Robbins's influence, Kaldor "acquired a thorough grasp of that theory without being hampered by doubts and hesitations."[7]

In a letter to John Hicks, Kaldor recalled those early undergraduate years:

> For me it meant years of struggle (at an earlier stage) to make myself believe that the outcome of the free operation of the market, in a system such as ours, is getting the maximum out of scarce resources, that the outcome of laissez faire is some sort of rough-and-ready approximation to "maximum satisfaction."[8]

Probably seeing him as an acolyte, Robbins furthered Kaldor's attachment to the London School. After Kaldor graduated with First Class Honors, Robbins persuaded William Beveridge, director of the London School, to appoint Kaldor to the one open research position in 1930. Robbins brought other talented economists into the department including John R. Hicks and R.G.D. Allen. Hicks and Kaldor, while young bachelors, roomed near each other and became friends, establishing a lifelong professional relationship which had its ups and downs. Hicks's lectures on Walras and Vilfredo Pareto proved to be an important counterweight to Robbins's on the Austrians.[9]

Increasingly, journalism fell into the background. Kaldor's third year at LSE was devoted mostly to microeconomic theory, which he learned both from Robbins and from a young lecturer named Maurice Allen. Kaldor "benefited enormously from Oxford weekends spent in the company of a brilliant mind, Maurice Allen." Allen was at the time more left politically than Kaldor, but he became in time a conservative executive director of the Bank of England, while Kaldor moved left.[10]

This was the period when Robbins was composing his famous *Essay on the Nature and Significance of Economic Science* which defined or redefined the study of economics as that of the allocation of scarce resources, leaving politics and even policy aside.[11] Robbins raised serious questions about whether economists were capable of giving policy advice, stimulating a discussion of "welfare economics" to which Kaldor made an important contribution. It seems strange that Kaldor, with his interest in politics, was carried along even briefly by Robbins's view that economists must stand aside on policy issues, but his adoption of Robbins as mentor turned out to be temporary. It would have gone against his nature to be frozen by his earliest studies into a model that limited an economist to the consideration of the allocation of given, scarce resources in a laissez-faire setting. For one thing, the United Kingdom was in economic and social ferment. While Kaldor was still in Germany when the General Strike of 1926 occurred in England, he arrived in London just as the Great Depression was about to begin. The General Strike was the culmination of several years of post-World War I British economic decline, and serious unemployment had continued throughout the 1920s. In 1929, two years after Kaldor arrived in London, the Labour party won a general election to emerge for the first time as the largest party in Parliament. It is unlikely that Kaldor, given his early interest in politics, ignored the social and economic currents in the country he was visiting as a student.

Winds of change in economics

In courses on economic theory, Maurice Allen was leading Kaldor through the controversy raised by the application of the laws of returns to the purely competitive model. Kaldor was open to the new ideas on imperfect competition, since Young had lectured on the subject.[12] In England that doctrinal controversy, which flourished in the *Economic Journal* in the 1920s, became heated when Piero Sraffa, an Italian immigrant, dared to criticize Marshallian economics.[13] The question was, if there are increasing returns associated with expanding production, what prevents the disappearance of pure competition? If there is not pure competition, then how does the Unseen Hand work?

Intellectual currents at the London School as elsewhere ran in more than one direction. Robbins brought Friedrich von Hayek to the London School in 1931 as Tooke Professor of Economic Science and Statistics. Thus at LSE, Austrian economics also became a force challenging the Marshallian hegemony and coinciding with Robbins's efforts to erase the "political" from "political economics." Kaldor recalled that he was "much under the influence of the views not only of Robbins but also of Hayek" as late as 1932.[14]

Kaldor's command of the German language stood him in good stead. With a fellow student, Honor Croome (née Scott and niece of the editor of the *Manchester Guardian*), Kaldor translated Hayek's *Monetary Theory and the Trade Cycle*.[15] However, as a first-year research student, Kaldor began to doubt the efficacy of Hayek's analysis while translating Hayek's "Paradox of Saving." We can mark the end of Robbins's favors and Kaldor's changing allegiance by the fact that in 1934 Kaldor did not receive the accustomed promotion, which was delayed until 1938.

So his initiation into economics took place within an intellectual climate of theoretical developments imported, in part, from the United States, Italy, and Austria. The imported teaching undermined the received economic doctrines of Alfred Marshall. Faced with many contradictory ideas, Kaldor matured intellectually. He never hesitated then or thereafter to question accepted economic theory when he thought it misleading, wrong, useless, or simply out of tune with the facts around him.

From laissez-faire to Keynesianism

After a short stint of teaching, Kaldor was appointed assistant in economics in 1932. As the London School drifted toward the Austrian paradigm, Kaldor was caught up first in the value revolution precipitated by the discussions of imperfect competition and then in the Keynesian revolution, leaving the early influence of Robbins and Hayek behind.

Burgeoning unemployment engulfed the world, and both within and outside the economics profession a need was evident for the reexamination of a theory that taught there could be no prolonged depression and the government could do nothing to help. In Britain in November of 1932, nearly three million workers were unemployed, and most industries had been depressed for several of the post-World War I years.[16] Economic policy was under fire. On the advice of the Macmillan Committee, the Labour government had first reaffirmed the gold standard during the summer of 1931 and then suspended it in September. An election was called in October 1931, and Labour was replaced by a coalition, reflecting the countrywide division of opinion on what should be done. Support for laissez-faire policies diminished.

As for theory, Kaldor was in his second year of teaching when the value revolution broke open within the economic profession. Books by Joan Robinson of Cambridge and Edward H. Chamberlin of Harvard both appeared in 1933. Kaldor immediately saw the significance of the concept of imperfect competition and wrote reviews of both books. He exchanged letters with Chamberlin on whether Robinson's imperfect and Chamberlin's monopolistic competition were the same thing.[17]

About this time, Kaldor became aware of the Keynesian ideas filtering down from Cambridge through meetings between the younger staff of Cambridge and the London School research students.[18] The London School contingent tended to support Hayek's views, but the meetings were spirited exchanges. Abba Lerner of the LSE changed sides and became a supporter of Keynes. Kaldor at that time was probably more influenced by John Hicks, who had introduced him to Gunnar Myrdal's 1933 essay, "Monetary Equilibrium." In any case, Kaldor became convinced of the shortcomings of the Austrian school's "monetarist" approach and became "an easy convert to Keynes after the appearance of the *General Theory* three years later."[19]

One of the evident changes for Kaldor during this early period was his personal disillusionment with laissez-faire. Even before the appearance of Keynes's *General Theory* Kaldor proposed that the best method for reducing unemployment, though "the one most neglected by economists and politically the least favored," was simply to subsidize wages.[20]

In a letter to Kaldor answering this assertion, Keynes denied that a general subsidy of labor could increase aggregate employment.[21]

After the *General Theory* was published in 1936 Kaldor, and other like-minded economists, had, at last, a theoretical structure for interventionist policies with which to counteract the depression. Indeed, Paul Samuelson saw Keynes's theory as a denial "that there is an *Invisible Hand* channeling the self-centered action of each individual to the social optimum." In his obituary of Keynes, Samuelson called this "the sum and substance of [Keynes's] heresy."[22] Hicks said of the Robbins circle that while they earlier had shared a common viewpoint, only Hayek had kept to that "faith," while he, Kaldor, Abba Lerner, and George Shackle took various routes in departing from it.[23]

In a letter to Hicks in 1943, Kaldor said that the recent evolutions in economic theory (i.e., the Keynesian developments) showed him that laissez-faire might not produce "maximum satisfaction" after all. Kaldor added, "the 'laissez faire' system resembles the productivity of wild growth in nature, which could be increased by planning in much the same way as the yield of nature can be increased by cultivation." This appealed to Kaldor's "natural common sense." He decided that economic analysis could "be pretty useful in showing the different sources of waste and in helping to show how the problem can best be tackled."[24]

Hicks left LSE in 1935 and did not himself become identified as a Keynesian. Both Hayek and Robbins bitterly opposed Keynes's ideas, so that in adopting Keynesian modes of thought, Kaldor was swimming against the local tide. In the new Keynesian macroeconomics, the theoretical question was whether effective demand for goods was lacking and was thus responsible for the widespread depression. The major policy question was whether the government could legislate in such a way as to improve the functioning of the economy. Lines were drawn between London and Cambridge. Cambridge Keynesians said yes to both questions, and the London School (at least Hayek and Robbins) said no. Hicks was at Manchester University, which also said no. Kaldor soon became known as a Keynesian. There were costs, both professionally and personally. In 1986, he said that his close friendship with Hicks did not survive Hicks's departure from LSE. However, Kaldor did read Hicks's *Value and Capital* (published in 1939) in manuscript and accepted most of it, and their ideas converged somewhat in the 1970s.[25]

Kaldor's education from so many contradictory sources and experiences was one that left him free to argue and dispute even his own works as he learned more. And he never stopped learning—that is how he became a master of theoretical economics. He was a literary master, as well. Though he always spoke with a discernible accent, his prose is memorable; he is given credit, for example, for naming the "cobweb theorem,"[26] and for substituting the colorful term "concertina effect" for the more pedestrian "Ricardo effect."[27]

The new General Theory of Keynes put Kaldor in position to explore the making of economic policy. But this was not to happen until after World War II.

NK

CHAPTER TWO

Moral Scientist and Keynesian

Tracing the development of Nicholas Kaldor's economic thought is easier than accounting for his egalitarian values. He was the only son to survive infancy in a well-established Jewish family in Budapest. After leaving Hungary, he was supported by his father for some years while he went to school and worked as a journalist. His father died the year he was appointed to the faculty of LSE. Kaldor never lived in Hungary again, though he was an adviser to the early non-Communist post–World War II Hungarian government in 1946 and elected an honorary member of the Hungarian Academy of Sciences in 1979. He kept as close contact as possible with his relations in Hungary during the years of war and communism, and brought his mother to England after World War II.

Kaldor became a naturalized British subject in 1934, the year of his marriage to Clarissa Goldschmidt. She was a history graduate of Somerville College, Oxford University, and from an established British family. At the time of her marriage she was working for the Central Fund for German-Jewish Refugees. There is every evidence that the Kaldors shared the same values, values that led them to support the causes of working men and women and of peaceful economic development not only in England but throughout the world. Thirlwall identifies Kaldor's politics as "on the left of the political spectrum" and Kaldor as "an ardent campaigner for many causes, e.g. land nationalization, tax reform, nuclear disarmament, and the anti-Common Market campaign, to name a few."[1] On the record Kaldor is seen to desire a fair and equitable tax system and an economy which provides employment for its workers and a reasonable distribution of income and goods. But of course these are planks in the platform of the Labour party of England and Kaldor became a tax and economic adviser to three Labour governments and a pariah to Conservatives.

Belief in human equality

In the letter to John Hicks written in 1943, Kaldor set out his beliefs. He was arguing for raising the material standard of living to:

> a standard which is far above that of nine-tenths of the population, even in a rich country such as ours. For it means not only that people have enough to eat, that they are adequately protected against cold, and have a roof over their heads; it means also that they have access to all the main devices, now available to the well-to-do, of reducing the toil and trouble of daily life—such as a hot water system, or refrigerators, electric stoves, etc.—and that they can afford to have some beauty in their lives, essential for a healthy development of faculties, which means (essentially) a pretty house, with a nice garden. . . . We are all agreed that it would be a very bad thing if the material standards of the middle classes were forced down to those of the working classes; so why isn't it a good thing if the latter are leveled up to the standards of the former?

Kaldor admitted that his views were

> fundamentally . . . based on a belief in human equality—which I regard as a postulate, more in the nature of a religious tenet than the outcome of rational philosophy—that all men are born equal, and should have equal opportunities for the development of their faculties, and the leading of a full life; and because the most important condition of true equality—the inner, psychological feeling of equality—cannot be got without it.[2]

Preferring Keynes to Marx

Some further insight into Kaldor's politics is revealed in an interview by Henry R. Lieberman for the *New York Times* following the Kaldors' visit to China in 1956. Americans could not visit China at that time, so the Kaldors' remarks were of particular interest. Lieberman interviewed them in Hong Kong and found Kaldor impressed with the pace and intensity of economic development in China. Kaldor had spent three months on a tax analysis project in India before going to China, and he remarked, "I should feel relieved if United States aid to India were one-fiftieth as large as Russia's aid to China." Russian aid at the time included not only steel but technical assistance, training, and equipment. Clarissa

Kaldor added, "The whole thing is run like an English boarding school. If you conform, you're all right—and you do conform."[3]

As a state guest of China, Kaldor delivered a lecture at the University of Peking entitled "Capitalist Evolution in the Light of Keynesian Economics," in which he emphasized the importance of free communication of ideas. His interpreter was Professor Hsu, a friend and graduate of Cambridge. Kaldor found the Chinese people not as oppressed and miserable as many Westerners expected, but "experiencing a great outburst of national energy and vitality." He wanted in return to correct some misconceptions that the Chinese seemed to have of capitalist countries. It simply was not true that in the capitalist countries the standard of living of the masses was falling and that tremendous economic crises were to bring about inevitable collapse. Kaldor made it plain that he thought more of Keynes than Marx as an economist, for his lecture was mainly a fundamental criticism of the Marxist theory of capitalist development.

In China, as everywhere for Kaldor, economic analysis was related to purpose—the improvement of the material conditions of humanity. He concluded his lecture with the thought that there is "no inherent necessity in a capitalist economy or any other economy of sustained evolution" in a certain direction. All economies are subject to "social control once we understand the manner of operation of economic and social forces." But he never approved of dictatorships. He instructed the Chinese that his belief was in "a progressive social democracy."

Kaldor perceived our world as a small planet, telling the Chinese that "nothing brings home to one so much the need for mutual understanding between different peoples as a journey around the globe by air."[4]

Citizen of the world

Kaldor was a world citizen, that is, more than a loyal British subject. He was that too, but one with a uniquely international point of view, which might at times conflict with a narrower British perspective.[5] Having an international point of view did not obscure from Kaldor the nature of national interest. He was arguing British national interest when he cautioned against joining the Common Market at a time when disparate growth rates between the market countries and Britain plus the market agricultural policy could be expected to lower the British standard of living.

Instead, his international point of view allowed him to explore national interest on more than one level, domestically and internationally, in both the short and long run. As a world citizen he was fluent in Hungarian, German, and English. He had a house in Cambridge, an apartment in London, and a vacation house in Var, France. He never lived as an impecunious academic, for he never was one. One of his financial successes was the creation, with others, of two English investment trusts—Anglo-Nippon, and Investing in Success. Nor did the family's financial self-interest guide his advice to governments. He is said to have effectively damaged both trusts when he advised the Labour government in 1965 to introduce the capital gains and corporation taxes. Clarissa Kaldor found the capital gains tax very costly.[6]

While his social values were clear and directed toward the improvement of the economic conditions of people the world over, Kaldor could still think clearly about any economic problem placed before him. His personal values were that of a devoted family man with an admirable wife and four daughters, Katherine, Frances, Penny, and Mary.

Perhaps his being an expatriot during his student life set him on the course of seeking an international perspective. While completing an early research project on the economic problems of the Danubian Succession States, he spent a term at the University of Vienna. Soon after he was established in his new position at the London School, he applied for and received a Rockefeller Research Fellowship to the United States, where he spent a term at Harvard University, worked on research in Washington, D.C., and visited the Universities of Chicago, Columbia, and California at Berkeley (1935–36). This was the first of many visits to the United States and only the beginning of his wide-ranging travels for study and work.

Solidarity with the Labour party

With the Kaldors, the Labour party was a family affair. Clarissa Kaldor represented the party on the Cambridgeshire County Council for more than twenty years. Nicholas Kaldor served as a member of the Economic and Finance Committee of the Labour party's National Executive Committee even before he was an adviser to the Labour chancellor of the exchequer.[7] Given their values, there was no other party in England for them. Members of the working class had no direct part in the government of England until the franchise was extended to them in 1867. In the 1870s, Gladstone, who was a Liberal, championed the cause of working-class suffrage. Until 1892 and the formation of the last Gladstone administration, labor sympathizers generally supported the Liberals in spite of the rise of socialist thinking and the advice of the Fabians that labor should have its own party.

But after World War I the Liberal party declined, as the Labour party, with its socialist orientation, gained influence. The General Strike of 1926–27 was an effort to get the Conservative government to negotiate over the industrial relations problems in the coal industry. Historian A.J.P. Taylor calls it "the clearest display of the class war in British history." Winston Churchill denounced British workers as "the enemy" and demanded "unconditional surrender," a display of spleen that became embedded in the memory of working people and their sympathizers. Taylor claims that the General Strike marked the end of the class war, as companies began to moderate their personnel policies. However, the Conservatives in Parliament reinforced their victory in defeating the strike by passing a law making illegal any strike designed to coerce the government. This polarized British politics. The law was not repealed until Labour gained power in 1945.[8] During World War II, 1940–45, England was ruled by a coalition of the Conservatives and Labour under Winston Churchill, with Clement Attlee acting as deputy prime minister. In 1945, Labour defeated the Conservatives and Attlee became prime minister (1945–51). Kaldor then had his first public appointment, to the Royal Commission on Taxation. However, by the time the Royal Commission was to issue its report, the Conservatives had taken over, keeping power for the next thirteen years. For those years, Labour was the main opposition party and represented the only meaningful choice for intellectuals of liberal persuasion and for the working class.

Commonality with Keynes

As an economist, Kaldor had much in common with Keynes. He approached the study and practice of economics as a moral science and followed the Marshallian tradition, which eschewed mathematics. Like Keynes himself and Keynes's youthful colleague Joan Robinson, Kaldor displayed an irreverence toward received economic doctrine, always searching not for authority but for fresh ideas to be applied to theoretical and real problems. Again like Keynes, he was willing to change his mind and to abandon what seemed to be untenable positions.

While I would not call Kaldor a "convert," he was truly a Keynesian in terms of accepting the thesis of *The General Theory of Employment, Interest and Money* and early made a contribution in convincing A.C. Pigou and others of the efficacy of the Keynesian analysis.[9] Most certainly he was not an ideologue.

My assessment is that from the beginning, the youthful and inexperienced Kaldor was Keynes's equal intellectually. He studied the works of more economists than Keynes had, and from the first Kaldor, like Keynes, trod his own path, making early contributions both to traditional economics in welfare theory and to the Keynesian paradigm.

Kaldor did not start a "revolution" as Keynes had, but he took up the work that the Keynesian revolution had indicated and successfully added to it, as any fair review of his contributions will show.

As Thirlwall has argued, Kaldor took up "the mantle shed by Keynes," sharing Keynes's "urge to protest, combined with rational argument and persuasion," as witnessed by Kaldor's letters to the *Times* and addresses to the House of Lords. Both Kaldor and Keynes suffered misinterpretation and misunderstanding in their lifetime.[10]

Thirlwall has argued that both Keynes and Kaldor were interested in policy first and theory second. Keynes's path was essentially from policy to theory, but surely Kaldor was first and foremost a theorist before embarking on policy-making. Josef Steindl, who thought Keynes was at his best in developing economic policy, cites the *General Theory* as an instance of important innovations in theory being distilled from intuitive solutions of the economic problems of the day.[11] Both became master economists, in part because they insisted on trying to solve major problems. Steindl said of Keynes: "If Keynes was defeated, it was not on the plane of logic: it was on the plane of power."[12] The same may be said of Kaldor. Until we face the problems with which these men were concerned, we can put neither Keynes nor Kaldor on the back burner.

NK

CHAPTER THREE

Early Theoretical Pronouncements

Some evolution in Kaldor's early views can be shown through three selections from his work before World War II.

Stern warning to the Danubian states

Kaldor was still close to his mentors Robbins and Hayek when he decided to write about the Danubian states for the British press. Eastern Europe had not made a rapid recovery after World War I. Austria was forbidden to make alliances with other nations, and the Danube River, which flowed through more than seven countries, was internationalized. These Danubian countries had suffered throughout the 1920s from the breakup of the economic unity of the former Austro-Hungarian Empire and the general slump in agricultural and raw-material prices and had resorted to protectionist trade policies. In a series of articles in the *Economist*, published in 1932, Kaldor accused the Danubian governments of "consuming their capital" and the banking systems of "veiling" the true situation. Kaldor came out for devaluation and freer trade, as he often did, but there are discernible differences in his early and later opinions.[1]

He was probably under the influence of Hayek and his capital theory when he wrote in a scholarly article on Austria that he was interested in a "theory of economic decline." Kaldor submitted this article to Keynes, editor of the *Economic Journal*, who turned it down. Keynes asked him, "Do you seriously contend that if Austria was to restore laisser-faire conditions this would go a long way to put her right without any material change from what you describe as the two exogenous factors?" Kaldor replied, "No, but returning to laissez-faire may prevent the situation becoming steadily worse."[2]

This early faith in laissez-faire was soon lost, and his views on exchange rates and protection became much more complex than indicated in the Danubian articles, but in the early 1930s, he was a stern critic of the policies in Austria:

> Under free competition a situation such as that [Austria is experiencing] is unlikely to develop. No productive agent can permanently receive more than what is technically called its "marginal net product"; any attempt to obtain more than this is punished with unemployment, a restriction of supply, and such a rise in prices as permits the establishment of a new equilibrium.[3]

Kaldor came through as a strictly orthodox economist.

Prescient note on welfare economics

In 1939, in a characteristic display of brilliance, Kaldor wrote a note on welfare economics, inventing "the compensation principle." He is given, along with Hicks, credit for establishing a large part of the theoretical foundations of cost-benefit analysis that today is one of the major policy applications of economic theory.[4] Hicks acknowledged Kaldor's contribution in this statement:

> They gave me a Nobel Prize (in 1972) for my work on general equilibrium and welfare economics. The former, I took it, referred to *Value and Capital* (1939), the latter to a number of papers between 1939 and 1946, which laid down main lines of what came to be called the "New welfare economics" or "Kaldor-Hicks welfare economics"—for it was from Kaldor's note on "Welfare propositions in economics" (EJ, 1939) that my work started.[5]

The development of the compensation principle provides a wonderful example of how economists communicated through economic journals during the 1930s. Roy F. Harrod in his presidential address before Section F (Economics) of the British Association for the Advancement of Science at Cambridge in August 1938 brought up the question of interpersonal comparisons of utility. Harrod's question was, in part, whether economists had any scientific basis for prescriptions of policy.[6]

In the first edition of *An Essay on the Nature and Significance of Economic Science,* Robbins had questioned whether there was any scientific foundation for economists making policy judgments on the basis of interpersonal comparisons of utility. He persisted in this view through later editions in spite of raising a storm of protest within the profession. Robbins argued that the law of diminishing marginal utility—which implies that the more one has of anything the less one values additional units of it—was "merely specious" when applied to real income. He felt it was illegitimate to extend the concept of diminishing marginal utility into the field of interpersonal relations. He further argued that the law of diminishing marginal utility makes assumptions that cannot be verified by either observation or introspection. He thought the whole process begged the "great metaphysical question of the scientific comparability of different individual experiences."[7]

Harrod took this to mean that all the economist could do was to give the real policymaker an outline of the consequences of various actions and never say what ought to be actual practice. But in Harrod's view economists could give advice on the basis of their understanding of "preference maps," which are drawn with reference to facts of the situation such as unequal distribution of wealth and the kinds of banking institutions in existence. From preference maps the economist has a "view of the economic field as a whole."[8]

Harrod also denied Robbins's thesis that in arguing for a more equal distribution of income an economist was going outside his proper scientific role. Harrod was convinced that "the marginal utility of two pence is greater in the case of a poorer man than in that of a richer." He noted that the repeal of the Corn Laws, recommended by David Ricardo in 1819, had provided economic gains to the community as a whole, although at a loss to the landlords. Harrod argued that the gain to the community exceeded the loss to the landlords but only on the assumption that individuals are in some sense equal. Without this assumption how could one compare individual losses with general gains?[9]

Robbins replied that his objection was indeed to "this assumption of equal capacity for satisfaction." To illustrate, he told the story of the Brahmin who claimed to be ten times more capable of happiness than the untouchable. Robbins conceded that an economist could prescribe, but insisted that he not call it science. Economists must keep "philosophy in its proper place."[10]

At this point of the argument, Kaldor wrote a four-page note. Without questioning Robbins's view of interpersonal comparisons, Kaldor demonstrated that the classical argument for free trade involved "no such arbitrary element."

Siding with Harrod, Kaldor pointed out that in the case of the Corn Laws, the point was that *total income* was not diminished when they were repealed. Only *distribution* was affected. Introducing his compensation principle, Kaldor said

It is always possible for the Government to ensure that the previous income distribution should be maintained intact: by compensating the "landlords" for any loss of income and by providing the funds for such compensation by an extra tax on those whose incomes have been augmented. In this way, everybody is left as well off as before in his capacity as an income recipient; while everybody is better off than before in his capacity as a consumer. For there still remains the benefit of lower corn prices as a result of the repeal of the duty.

Kaldor concluded that whenever a policy leads to an increase in physical productivity and thus aggregate real income, the economist's case for the policy is unaffected by the question of the comparability of individual satisfactions. In any case all the economist must prove is that it is *possible* to make everybody better off. That is, after establishing that all those who suffer losses might be compensated, the *community itself* will be better off. Whether the losers should be compensated is a political and not an economic question.

Kaldor's piece moved the question of whether there was a place for economic policy prescriptions away from interpersonal comparisons toward a different rule. In a footnote he added that there is no necessity for interpersonal comparisons of satisfaction in judging a policy designed to increase the sum total of wealth. Money value increases "of course" would not meet the test, as there could be losses of the nonpecuniary kind. The rule proposed was "only if the increase in the total real income is sufficient to compensate those adversely affected and still leaves something over for the rest of the community is the prescription justified without resort to interpersonal comparisons." Kaldor made it plain that he did not argue that "welfare is necessarily greatest when there is complete equality." He was "not thinking so much of differences in the capacity for satisfactions between different individuals, but of the satisfactions that are derived from the prospect of improving one's income by one's own efforts—a prospect which is necessarily excluded when a regime of complete equality prevails."[11]

Kaldor's rule freed economists to make policy statements with assurance. He wrote one other article during this early period, which, in effect, applied his rule in the case of tariffs. Using what he called "community indifference curves," that is, treating countries as individuals, he demonstrated that between two countries the introduction of import duties could reproduce the same effects as the introduction of monopoly. Thus it would be theoretically possible to exploit the foreigner to the extent of the elasticity of the foreign demand for the protected country's products, limited by the extent to which the foreign power desired or was able to retaliate. Although retaliation might leave both countries worse off than they were originally, assuming that the elasticity of demand were less than infinite, "there is always *some* rate of duty which it is advantageous to introduce in the absence of retaliation."[12]

Not everyone was satisfied with the compensation principle. Tibor Scitovsky criticized Kaldor's test, suggesting a more complex double test would be valid in some cases, while in others, he argued, no test at all is possible.[13]

Hicks saw the value of the compensation principle and carried on. It is characteristic of Kaldor that he dashed off these articles of fundamental importance and then, having had his say, dropped the subject. And it is characteristic of J.R. Hicks (as he was known at the time) that he recognized an important point and hammered away at it.

Independent version of the *General Theory*

Kaldor was in the United States on a Rockefeller Research Fellowship when Keynes's *General Theory* was published in 1936. He was never a member of the inner circle of Keynesians and thus not party to what Warren Young cites as the burgeoning split within the original General Theory group.[14] Nevertheless, Kaldor, like Keynes, was interested in getting across Keynes's basic ideas.[15] To this end he wrote a paper that allowed Pigou to accept Keynesianism where he had initially rejected it, using an argument based on some of Hicks's work. Hicks proposed a relationship between a family of savings functions (S), a conventional investment demand curve (I), liquidity preference functions (L), and a curve representing the quantity of money (M). In what may seem an irony, the IS-LM diagram, hated by such Cambridge Keynesians as Joan Robinson and Richard Kahn, was used to provide a bridge to the acceptance of the Keynesian General Theory. We are indebted to Warren Young for a detailed account of how this came about.

In September 1936, Hicks presented a paper that came to be known as the origin of the IS-LM diagram. The diagram implies that Keynes's case was not general but was a limited one. The paper was read before the Econometric Society meetings where both Roy Harrod and James Meade had ideas similar to Hicks's on how to extend the Keynesian analysis. But it was Hicks's diagram that prevailed and became influential within the profession.

Upon Kaldor's return from abroad, Hicks showed the diagram to him. Kaldor "thought it was rather clever." He did not see it as a Walrasian concept as was later claimed and did not think Hicks had presented it in that way.[16]

Nor did Kaldor have the suspicions of Kahn and Robinson who thought that IS-LM would and did do more harm than good to Keynesianism.[17] Actually Kaldor attached little importance to the diagram. He thought of it as useful in "illuminating" the problem that Keynes had in mind and in simplifying Keynes for students. In 1982, in a letter to Kaldor, Hicks confirmed that he had regarded this system as "an exercise."[18]

Pigou had written an article attacking Keynes, passing it to Dennis H. Robertson, who cheered him on. At the time, both Pigou and Keynes had recently had heart problems, and Keynes, when he read Pigou's paper was horrified that it had been recommended for publication because he thought it was full of error. Keynes wrote to Kahn that he considered the publication of Pigou's article "an unforgivable crime," that Pigou should have had the mistakes pointed out to him before acceptance.[19]

However, Pigou's article was printed and represented a full-scale attack on the General Theory. Keynes wrote an article answering Pigou and sent it to Robertson, insisting that Pigou's article was "outrageous rubbish beyond all possibility of redemption."[20]

Kaldor also wrote a criticism of Pigou's article, sending it to Keynes. Kaldor said, "I am sure there must be several people in Cambridge who could point out the same thing, yet I am sending it along in the hope I get in first!"[21]

In a later version of this article, Kaldor made use of IS-LM which Young calls "one of the earliest examples of the application of the IS-LM approach."[22]

Pigou had, thought Kaldor, ignored the importance of savings being a function of income as well as interest rates, a point Kaldor saw as crucial to the General Theory.[23]

Keynes replied that he had also written a reply to Pigou. He would send it to Kaldor, and it had "one editorial merit over yours, that it is immensely briefer!" He agreed with Kaldor that Pigou was "tacitly denying, as you point out, that saving is a function of real income."[24]

Kaldor was surprised that Keynes had himself written a reply to Pigou and offered to shorten his own paper and to read Keynes's with great interest. Kaldor thought "it really is the assumption that savings vary with real income which constitutes the main difference between the classical economics and the Keynesian." He differed with Keynes on a couple of points and won a concession from Keynes, who said, "You are, of course, quite right. I meant 'neutral' and not 'unstable.' "[25] In further correspondence they continued to disagree on certain points of criticism and emphasis, Kaldor meeting Keynes on his own ground.[26] Keynes sent both his and Kaldor's comments to Pigou.[27]

Pigou promised, though still ill, to try to concentrate on the subject within the next week.[28] Then Keynes decided to publish both his own and Kaldor's articles in the next issue of the *Economic Journal*, but suggested a correction, which Kaldor made.[29]

Keynes also corresponded on this subject with R. F. Kahn, who replied that Robertson, Kaldor, and Pigou "all fail to see the fundamental fallacy—which is the determination of the rate of interest by the rate of discount of the future." Though he had not seen Kaldor's article, Kahn opposed publishing it, commenting with some suspicion, that publication of it "will darken counsel." He said, "all of us," meaning members of the Circus, could write replies to Pigou if Keynes wanted them.[30] Keynes replied that, clearly, he had to print Kaldor's article, and, anyway, no one else had sent him any comment on Pigou.[31]

Pigou's answer to the two criticisms was scheduled for publication in the March 1938 *Economic Journal*. Keynes told Kahn that he considered Pigou's answer "a complete and frank withdrawal of the whole of his previous argument." Keynes added that one of the remaining differences between him and Pigou was over Pigou's alleged "conviction that the theory of the relation between money wages and employment, via the rate of interest was invented by Kaldor."[32]

Keynes accepted Kaldor's paper as a restatement of his General Theory with certain assumptions, but he thought those assumptions used by Kaldor limited the general case in which he was interested. Young points out that those assumptions allowed the Hicks type of analysis to be applicable as Kaldor had shown.[33] Thus through letters and journal articles Kaldor was instrumental in making the General Theory acceptable to other leaders in the profession in England. This occurred before what Young calls the "IS-LMization of Keynes's General Theory."[34] And before, if we believe Samuelson, anyone in Cambridge, Massachusetts "really knew what it was about."[35]

Ludwig Lachmann has characterized this era in economic thought as one of an open world without economic orthodoxy. He thought it ironic that a "natural dissident" such as Hicks "should unwittingly have spun the thread of a new orthodoxy he has long since come to disdain."[36] It was only in later years and even after Hicks's recant that Kaldor, in an interview with Young, disowned his own use of IS-LM in that early article answering Pigou. He said, "I see now that by writing an IS diagram, we presuppose that the investment demand function is a single valued function of income and the rate of interest. Well, that is nonsensical . . . ."[37] Be that as it may, Kaldor's success in interpreting and spreading the General Theory stands as a monument to his early, precocious work.

By these three examples of the evolution of Kaldor's thinking, I do not mean to slight other contributions during this pre-war period. His survey of capital theory will come up later; his "Speculation and Economic Stability," discussed in the next chapter, marks the beginning of his post Keynesian contributions. In the year Kaldor died, Hicks wrote him, "Here is a piece of fanmail for you. I hope you won't tear it up." Hicks thought his "Speculation" paper was "the culmination of the Keynesian revolution in theory," adding, "I ought to have been reading it every year since it appeared!"[38]

Upon Kaldor's death, Samuelson wrote to Clarissa:

> While still a veritable lad, I met Nicky at Harvard (I believe during the course of your 1935–6 honeymoon?) Schumpeter gave an elaborate party at the Harvard Faculty Club and Nicky was brilliant on capital theory. (Until he outgrew that phase, Kaldor was the best neoclassist of us all!). . . . I grew up on his great *RES, Economica, EJ*, and *Econometrica* papers.[39]

Kaldor's ideas continued to evolve throughout his career. From laissez-faire and neoclassicism he moved boldly beyond Keynes into new problems and paradigms.

NK

CHAPTER FOUR

World War II and Cambridge University

When World War II engulfed England in 1939, Nicholas Kaldor was a married man with a growing family—Katherine was three years old and Frances on the way. Although Kaldor was a British subject with an established reputation in economics, he seemed to be ineligible for any important civil service position.

Evacuees to Cambridge

The Kaldors, along with the whole of LSE, were evacuated to Cambridge in autumn 1939. After Germany invaded the Low Countries and France in May 1940, the war went so badly that, with the fall of France, Kaldor feared that the war was lost.[1] At his insistence, the Kaldors considered sending Katherine to foster parents in the United States. Clarissa Kaldor's family, being English born and bred, were less pessimistic. As it turned out, Kaldor lost his resolve when he was to put Katherine aboard the ship bound for America. Instead, he brought her home to greet her new sister Frances. Thirlwall reports that Kaldor considered emigrating to Australia and struggled with his conscience over whether he should enlist to fight Hitler, but, at his friend Piero Sraffa's urging, he remained at Cambridge with the LSE, teaching and writing. After the bombing of London had begun, Kaldor's mother begged him to bring his family to Hungary, which was still neutral. Then Hungary declared war on the United States and the USSR in 1941 as an ally of Germany and Italy. Between 1938 and 1944 Hungary, with the help of the Axis powers, regained territories from Czechoslovakia, Rumania and Yugoslavia. But when Hungary tried to withdraw from the war early, Germany occupied the country in March

1944. From that date until the Soviets drove the Germans out in March 1945, Kaldor's relations were in grave danger. His brother-in-law, Aurel Varannai, was a reporter for the British Reuters news agency. The tale of their efforts to elude the Germans' deportation of Jews and subsequently the Stalinist Hungarian regime makes an awful chapter in the family history.[2]

Economists throughout Eastern Europe had migrated to the West either in the 1930s (especially after Jews were fired from the universities in 1934) or early in the war. These included Joseph Schumpeter, Wassily Leontief, Abba Lerner, and Oskar Lange,[3] as well as two other Hungarian economists, Thomas Balogh and Tibor Scitovsky. Scitovsky wrote to Kaldor from America of his problems. Scitovsky had arrived on a visitor's visa, which the United States Department of State refused to renew. Although actually a refugee, Scitovsky was threatened in 1940 with deportation from the United States and was told by the Department of State that he could not go to England. Scitovsky wrote, "I seem to be the only one, all other refugees and Hungarians seem to be immigrating gaily." He was allowed to join the army and gained citizenship through his service.[4] Scitovsky remained on friendly terms with Kaldor throughout Kaldor's life. Balogh stayed in England and was to be a rival influence on the Labour party during Kaldor's years as adviser to the chancellor of the exchequer.

Kaldor's immigration had occurred before he had completed his education, of course, and he was established as a citizen of the United Kingdom. But he was also fortunate in how well he fitted into the Cambridge scene both intellectually and politically, for Richard Kahn and Joan Robinson shared his politics as well as his Keynesian bent. At wartime Cambridge, Kaldor became a member of the "war circus" and the postwar "secret seminar" and went with Robinson and Kahn on their Sunday walks. In 1939, soon after his arrival, Keynes invited him to give a course of lectures. Robbins would not allow Cambridge to pay Kaldor directly. He insisted that Cambridge pay LSE, which could then pay its own staff member.[5]

Speculating beyond Keynes

War created paper shortages, and it was difficult to continue economic publications. As editor of the *Review of Economic Studies,* Ursula Hicks wrote Kaldor that certain advertisers had reneged on their promises, and she was afraid she might have to call on the "richer members" of those founding the journal. She urged Kaldor to sell some ads and to send her his article "Speculation and Economic Stability."[6] However, when paper was available, publication could be speedy in those days.

Her request was in September and the article was published in October. This article, mentioned previously, went beyond Keynes's General Theory in that Kaldor generalized Keynes's theory of money, interest, and employment on the basis of a general theory of speculation. In 1960 Kaldor described his as

> a theory of the inter-relationships between the *flow* demand and supply curves (as governed by consumption and production) and *stock* demand and supply curves (as governed by the expectations of future prices relatively to current prices).

His article had made the point that the model presented in the *General Theory* was a "special case" and that he had provided "a missing link—or rather, one of the missing links—between Keynes' ideas in the *Treatise* and in the *General Theory*." He thought Keynes had

> invented some short-cuts through the maze of complications of a multi-market analysis and thereby reduced the essential aspects of the problem to manageable dimensions. That it was a short-cut of a genius . . . does not relieve us of the need to show the specific assumptions required for a formal demonstration of its propositions.[7]

Kaldor's article stimulated much interest even though the war was soon in full swing. He followed up in a note with answers to R.G. Hawtrey and J.C.R. Dow [8] and with a paper, "Keynes' Theory of the Own-Rates of Interest,"[9] which further supported Keynes's argument that capital markets do not behave in such a way as to adjust the flow of capital expenditure (i.e., investment) to the current flow of savings as traditional theory held.

Kaldor was among those believing that the revolutionary issue in Keynesian economics was that the level of capital expenditure was determined by factors other than savings. The new view was that changes in incomes and employment are generated by changes in capital expenditure, and, in point of fact, govern the flow of savings. Cantabrigians came to call this the investment dog wagging his savings tail.[10] Kaldor showed that it is speculators who help to bring about the equality of savings with investment because of the dependence of the current rate of interest on the level of interest rates expected in the future.[11]

Keynes conceded to the young Kaldor that his argument might be right. John Hicks from the very beginning believed the article was one of Kaldor's best.[12] Kaldor was invited by Keynes to a tea party in the same month of the speculation paper's appearance and reported that

> Keynes came up and told me that he had read the article with very

great interest and he said that I may well be right on the reasons for the behaviour of the capital market being due to inelastic expectations and arbitrage rather than "liquidity preference" in a more fundamental sense. It is a pity that he never came to write on this subject again. He was then engaged in writing some articles on How to Pay for the War and then entered the Treasury, but he must have been an amazing man to read and grasp a paper by a comparatively unknown young man so soon after its appearance.[13]

Reviewing wartime White Papers

Kaldor may have fit in well at Cambridge, but he was still on the payroll of LSE, and there was some friction with his London School colleagues. He continued his lifelong practice of writing letters to the London *Times*, which he had begun in 1932, debating current economic topics and often disagreeing with Robbins and Hayek. In addition to a heavy teaching load and the writing of journal articles, he reviewed the wartime economic White Papers of the coalition government for the *Economic Journal*. It was at Keynes's request that Kaldor wrote the first of these reviews,[14] which became an annual feature of the journal and helped Kaldor to establish a worldwide reputation.

Helping Beveridge prepare the UK for peace

While the war was still going on, Kaldor also worked on and for the Beveridge proposals to reform social services in the United Kingdom. Barbara Wood claims the ideas that went into the final report were in fact E.F. Schumacher's who had some difficulty in convincing Beveridge of the program. Joan Robinson was supposed to have "helped knock the final book into shape."[15]

Lord Beveridge acknowledged "the cordial and helpful co-operation of many others" in *Full Employment in a Free Society* but did not single out anyone in particular. The subtitle of the report was "Misery generates hate." The proposal was for a complete social security and health system to supersede the programs inherited from the prewar past.[16] Because Beveridge anticipated that the British would fear they could not afford such a system, Kaldor was asked to write Appendix C, "Memorandum on the Quantitative Aspects of the Full Employment Problem in Britain" to allay their fears.[17]

Kaldor's was a Keynesian argument for the promotion of the growth of national income through public expenditures financed at least in part through public borrowing, but he offered other alternatives. He defended the plan in the *Manchester Guardian*, noting that, "The total burden of the plan by 1965 will amount to only a small fraction of the increase in real income that can be confidently expected."[18] In 1945, the European war having ended, LSE returned to London. Kaldor did not endear himself to his London colleagues by remaining in Cambridge and commuting to give his lectures and classes. He was unhappy in the general right-wing atmosphere of the London School, and was promoted to reader, not at Robbins's behest, but at the urging of Harold Laski.[19]

Perhaps even Kaldor did not realize that a new life was about to begin.

Part II

Applying Theory in the Real World

NK

CHAPTER FIVE

Analyzing and Planning for Recovery

Kaldor's analyses of the White Papers for the *Economic Journal* won him an international reputation and provided a guide for policy using Keynesian tools.[1] After World War II he was invited to join the worldwide effort to recover from the war.

American Strategic Bombing Survey

In 1945, Kaldor joined the economics section of the U.S. Strategic Bombing Survey under the direction of John Kenneth Galbraith.[2] The question investigated was what effect the Allied bombing raids had on German industry and productivity. Scitovsky suggested Kaldor not only because of his eminence, but also because there was a need for economists who were fluent in German.[3] The survey got going in London under some urgency, since the findings were supposed to aid Americans in the war against Japan, which was still going on. The survey was an American undertaking, although it had been discussed with the British government. There was a complement of 350 officers, 500 enlisted men, and 300 civilians to assist in research analysis. By May 1945, the teams were ready to undertake the European investigation. Before sites could be investigated, all potentially relevant intelligence information had to be gathered, and factories and high officials had to be selected for interviewing and for seizure of documents. There was discussion of the need for "speedy on the spot investigations and speedy entry into liberated territory." On the scene, the researchers were to have all of the new technology, which included the use of IBM Punch Cards.[4] Bad Nauheim, a West German spa twenty miles north of Frankfurt, was the most important forward headquarters, though the movable headquarters actually followed the advance of the Allies. One of the advantages of being there was that, as E.F. Schumacher wrote home, the American military provided "three excellent meals a day."[5]

Scitovsky says that initially the economists broke into small groups of one or two jeeploads of people and went around interviewing and detecting and looking for German generals and other important people. He says, "Kaldor and I enjoyed this detective work immensely." Kaldor and Scitovsky were lucky one day when they saw a train standing on an open track with a soldier walking up and down. Scitovsky recognized that the soldier was an officer, a colonel standing guard, and stopped. He and Kaldor found a large number of German generals and high-level civilian employees waiting to be discovered. They immediately began interrogating them. Later they heard on the radio that no personnel should question Germans until the Germans had been properly "captured" by the Allies.

Kaldor was especially keen to interrogate Albert Speer who was probably the most important person in the German war economy. Speer is given credit for the rationalization and recovery of production after the Allied air raids.[6] Initially Speer could not be found. Kaldor persuaded Galbraith to lend him a jeep and went from one of Speer's girlfriends dwellings to the next, always arriving too late. Once, he found that Speer had left a suitcase behind and seized it. Kaldor thought it must be important and brought it in. When the lock was broken, it was found to contain a hammer on a velvet cushion. Hitler had used this hammer to begin the building of the Siegfried Wall. Kaldor was disappointed when Galbraith claimed it as property of the Pentagon. Speer was later found by an army sergeant who walked up a street, saw Speer's visiting card thumbtacked under a doorbell, and rang it. Speer answered the door.[7]

The most important interviews for the economists were those with Speer, Goering, and Admiral Doenitz. Scitovsky said Kaldor was especially helpful in being able to ask the right questions, in evaluating the work of Speer, and in drawing conclusions from what they had learned. Kaldor also interviewed General Franz Halder, who had been Chief of the General Staff of the German army in 1938 before the surrender of Czechoslovakia and who continued in important roles until he was retired by Hitler in 1942.[8]

Twenty-five years later this interview was still fresh in Kaldor's mind. He wrote from the Kaldor summer home in La Garde-Freinet, Var, France, to agree with other correspondents in the *Times* who had claimed that Germany's military situation at the time of the Munich agreement (1938) was such that the Czechs could have denied Hitler a quick victory there. A flurry of letters filled the *Times'* s column, with two former Czechs confirming this view—that it was the civilian government under

Dr. Edouard Beneš that had wanted to capitulate rather than the army. The Czech generals had wanted to resist the invading Germans, and the British and French had wanted them to do so. One correspondent argued that Beneš had sidestepped the possibility of aid from Stalin for fear of being seen as a Bolshevik and that the Czechoslovakian capitulation was not the fault of the British and French. It was alleged that neither the British nor the French were at that time prepared to fight, but the Czechs were. On another issue, Dr. Otto John, one of the correspondents, took a dim view of General Halder's claim of a 1938 general's plot to incarcerate Hitler, thus preventing his blitzkrieg into Eastern Europe. But as Kaldor replied, surely someone must now know whether the German army was or was not strong enough to quickly defeat the Czechs in 1938. (The German-Soviet Union Pact was not signed until 1939.)[9]

In the field, Kaldor used his skills as a journalist in conducting extensive interviews. His fluent command of German and his analytical tools as an economist allowed him to put German wartime production into perspective. He also had a good time and made many friends among the stellar group that Galbraith had gathered for the task.[10]

The German war economy

After returning to England, Kaldor read a paper, "The German War Economy," before the Manchester Statistical Society. Giving his source of information as the "monster 'research project' " of the Strategic Bombing Survey, Kaldor argued that Germany did not fight a "total war" before 1944, that is, did not put the economy on a total war footing in the sense that the United States and the United Kingdom did. This meant that the German economy remained "elastic and resilient" and that it showed "high adaptability" in the face of the Allied air attacks and military defeats in Russia. The survey had found that the German war effort was never limited by bottlenecks, shortages of factory space, manpower, or raw materials (with the exception of oil and electric power) until very late in the war.[11]

In fact, Germany's "administrative and industrial inefficiency" constituted a vast reserve for the necessary efforts to absorb the shock of the bombing by calling this reserve into use. Because of its total war effort, British production of aircraft was "considerably in excess of German in 1940 and even more in the later years."[12]

Before the summer of 1943, air raids had no appreciable effect either on German munitions production or on national output, according to the survey.[13] Indeed, Hitler's optimism had far more effects. For example, in the late summer and fall of 1941, Hitler regarded the war against Russia as won and ordered discontinuance of all munitions production in Germany, shifting workers from the war sector into the civilian sector.[14]

But in the first four months of 1944, the Allies became capable for the first time of carrying out repeated attacks deep into Germany, concentrating on aircraft and ball-bearing targets. After the autumn of 1944, morale deteriorated among the Germans under nightly aerial attack, but they remained able to work efficiently even as "they lost faith in their leaders."[15] Kaldor said that when the Allied air force had knocked out 70 percent of the fighter assembly plants by February 1944, Goering was forced to hand production over to Speer. Through Speer's rationalization of production, the preraid level of production was exceeded by April 1944 and nearly doubled by July with only an increase of 15 percent in the labor force.[16]

From September 1944 onward, disorganization caused by air attacks on the railroad and loss of territories caused a decline in production followed by a complete industrial collapse in the early months of 1945. Kaldor did not see the German experience as evidence of the inefficiency of "planned" or "controlled" economies. Instead, "its failures were due to the absence of planning and co-ordinated control, and not to any abandonment of a *laisser faire* system." Kaldor called the German war economy a "monument to the inefficiency of a system of personal dictatorship."[17]

Hungarian Plan 1946

In 1946, Kaldor, still on the staff of LSE, was asked to advise the Hungarian government on postwar plans. The new government had adopted a republican constitution and probably hoped to retain the boundaries reestablished through the aid of Germany and Italy. Communist influence was very weak at the time, because the conquering Soviet and resisting German armies had devastated the country. However, the peace treaty signed in Paris in 1947 restored the Trianon boundaries instituted after World War I. The wing of the Communist party which was subservient to the USSR had gained power by 1949. Ruthless land reform and nationalization of industry went forward, and Kaldor's plan was forgotten. But he had a more promising experience in France.

Adviser to Commissariat-Général du Plan, France

Jean Monnet, in his *Memoirs*, says that in the aftermath of World War II, he feared that France would "content herself with frugal mediocrity behind a protectionist shield."[18] Monnet, who had had a distinguished career in industry,[19] turned to public service. In December 1945, he sent a five page note to General de Gaulle entitled "Proposals for a Modernization and Investment Plan." He argued that not only experts and French bureaucrats but also representatives of industry and trade unions should be drawn into making a plan to modernize France. The object was to set priorities and to make proposals for the essential industries. The French cabinet approved his proposal January 3, 1946. There were some thirty senior officials on the Planning Commissariat, and the whole staff, "including secretaries and doormen" was never more than a hundred or so, according to Monnet. Kaldor was invited by Robert Marjolin, whom he had known in London before the war, to act as an adviser. Monnet described Marjolin as looking "like a tall student in the grip of theoretical ideas." Marjolin was thirty-five years old and Kaldor thirty-nine. Monnet said that the war had confirmed Marjolin's conviction that "thought without action was not enough," and this view permeated the work of the plan. Marjolin had certain characteristics that attracted Monnet—his effectiveness in civil service circles and the trust in him shown by the Socialist trade unions, characteristics that were to distinguish Kaldor in his British career as well. Marjolin's title was deputy planning commissioner, and his job was to work out the general economics of the plan.[20]

Kaldor's work with the plan had him focus on the basic problem of how to ensure monetary stability without sacrificing the level of real investment. He, of course, had the Keynesian tools in hand and naturally turned to fiscal and monetary policy. But it is important to note that this work preceded developments in theoretical circles of an interest in growth theory.[21]

France was in a period of relative stability but had recently experienced inflation. The plan was to propose extensive reconstruction and investments, and Kaldor was to tell how this might be done in a climate of monetary stability. Kaldor concluded that it would be necessary to reduce potential consumption, particularly of luxury goods, and to reform the tax system. At the time, the total tax return to France was a meager 20 percent of Net National Product compared with 44 percent in Britain, even though tax rates in some instances were higher in France than in Britain. Profit and interest paid only 3 percent of the taxes collected compared with 38 percent in Britain. A problem inherited from the war years was that agricultural and industrial prices had become distorted relative to each other. In addition, the price of wheat was too low relative to the prices of other agricultural goods. Kaldor advised a continuation for the immediate future of the controlled prices accompanied by subsidies until other goals could be met, since other alternatives were inflationary. Accompanying this would be a tax reform program following, to a large extent, one put forward by the confederation of unions, Confederation Générale de Travaillers (CGT). Making the income tax more uniform would make it possible to replace various existing income taxes. Other suggestions were an annual tax on capital, a tax on capital gains, and a uniform value-added tax on business as a substitute for the current sales and turnover taxes. Kaldor proposed a merger of tax administrations and the strengthening of controls and penalties to meet France's serious problems of tax evasion and avoidance. He estimated that this program would increase French revenue by 50 to 60 percent within two years. In addition he thought it wise to put taxes on luxury spending in order to discourage it. Another proposal was to tax business in the form of compulsory loans bearing interest in order to create an investment fund for reconstruction and development. As Thirlwall notes, these were recommendations that Kaldor would make often, especially to developing countries calling for his advice.[22]

Working with the Commissariat appears to have given Kaldor his first introduction to the value-added tax (VAT), which was to come up in his career again and again, though he did not always support it.[23] Working with Marjolin gave Kaldor a firsthand view of what might be accomplished through economic planning that involved the cooperation of experts, civil servants, industry, and labor. He never doubted that such planning was essential to solving the postwar economic problems of Britain. But his European postwar experience was not at an end. Beginning as a theorist, Kaldor was now deep into applied economics, and his next assignment was to embrace all of Europe.

Economic Commission for Europe (ECE)

When Robert Marjolin declined the post of director of the Research and Planning Division for the Economic Commission for Europe (ECE), a subsidiary of the United Nations, Kaldor was suggested to Gunnar Myrdal, executive director, by Paul Rosenstein-Rodan. Kaldor preferred this post to one he had been offered with the International Monetary Fund and went to Geneva on leave from his academic post at the London School of Economics. Initially, ECE was to administer the Marshall Aid Program, but when the Soviet Union refused to participate, the Organization for European Economic Cooperation (OEEC) took over the Marshall funds. Instead, Kaldor's division, including fifteen or twenty economists and assistants he had chosen, prepared the *Economic Surveys of Europe.* Thirlwall says that Kaldor wrote the 1947 and 1948 *Surveys* singlehandedly.[24]

Kaldor recruited a staff of the highest calibre which, as in the case of Galbraith, is the mark of a man who does not fear to surround himself with bright people.[25] The original *Survey* report was brilliantly conceived, for, rather than separate studies of individual countries, "the guiding principle" was the presentation of an "analysis of the dominant features of the economic situation of Europe as a whole." There were problems, of course. Information from the Union of Soviet Socialist Republics was such that it could not be assimilated, so most of the estimates excluded the Soviet Union or confined it to the appendices. But otherwise it was thought that the *Survey* was able to account for 70 to 80 percent of the prewar industrial production of Europe and up to 90 percent of its agricultural production.

Actually, two analyses were made: one including Germany and the other excluding it. The object was to map the recovery of production, trade, and the balance of payments and to attend to the problems of inflation and production and of intra-European trade. By April of 1949, the *Survey* could note that, "Inflation, the shortages of basic materials and many of the other problems which dominated the immediate postwar period have largely been overcome, and Europe's production and trade are now close to their pre-war levels" in spite of the many underlying economic problems and political tensions that continued to threaten Europe. Without mentioning the Marshall Plan, it was conceded that "the progress of the past year would in many areas have been impossible without outside financial assistance."

In Geneva, as a United Nations official concerned with Europe as a whole, Kaldor appropriately took the international point of view rather than merely representing what were at the moment conceived to be British interests. When LSE, under government pressure to call him home, would not give him an unfettered leave of absence to remain in Geneva, he resigned his LSE readership. Meanwhile, Joan Robinson and Richard Kahn promoted Kaldor's return to Cambridge as a lecturer and don of King's College. He returned to England in 1949, having delayed Cambridge a bit so that he could complete some of the reports he had started at ECE.

Cambridge and beyond

Once more he found Cambridge an empathetic environment. But he was not to be allowed to climb quietly into the ivory tower. Hugh Gaitskell, who would in the future be the Labour party's chancellor of the exchequer, became instrumental in opening "unexpected doors in high places in Britain and overseas."[26]

Nicholas Kaldor was only forty-one years old when his future life at Cambridge and in government beckoned him. In his twenty-odd years as an economist, he had become an international figure, one known for his intelligence, candor, and commitment to a better world and for his contributions to pure economic theory.[27]

NK

CHAPTER SIX

The Expenditure Tax— An International Debate

Nicholas Kaldor is remembered for his ideas in many fields, but there is one issue in economics that cannot properly be discussed without mentioning his name: the expenditure tax. With his book of less than three hundred pages published when he was forty-seven years old, he initiated a debate on taxes that is not yet over. (See chapter note 6.1, American tax debates and the expenditure tax.) Before writing "The End" to his book, he stated his belief: "Taxation can be a powerful instrument of social progress but it cannot be made into an engine of social revolution. The noble experiment of gradually building a society that is both free and just through progressive taxation is bound to fail unless we recognize that fact."[1] While an adviser to Labour governments, Kaldor did not advocate an expenditure tax for the United Kingdom.[2] Yet Kaldor's tax proposals were by many English conservatives considered revolutionary, and Kaldor soon learned that proposals for progressive taxation can precipitate a riot in a developing country.

Expenditure taxes defined

Kaldor's book, *An Expenditure Tax,* is radical only in the sense that it represents a departure from using the now traditional income base for taxation. An initiate must take care to differentiate an expenditure tax from both income and consumption taxes. An expenditure tax is a tax on an individual's or a family unit's spending out of income. (See chapter note 6.2, Outline of the expenditure tax.) As such, it differs from the income tax, which is a tax on an individual's receipts of income. It also differs from certain consumption taxes—for example, from a value-added tax which is a tax on each addition of value to goods sold, and from a sales tax, which is a tax on purchases. The argument for using spending as a basis for taxation goes back at least to Thomas Hobbes who, three hundred years before Kaldor, argued that a person should be taxed according to the amount he took out of the common pool, and not on the basis of what he contributed to it.[3]

Short history of the expenditure tax idea

Historically, a stellar listing of economists supported the idea including John Stuart Mill, who objected to taxing savings as the income tax does, and Alfred Marshall, who thought an expenditure tax superior to all other forms of taxation and yet a "Utopian goal." A.C. Pigou had troubling questions regarding the administration of such a tax, however, and John Maynard Keynes thought that such a tax, while "perhaps theoretically sound is practically impossible."

As Kaldor noted, the expenditure tax was called up and dusted off by Irving Fisher, who spoke at the American Section of the Econometric Society in Colorado Springs in July 1936, a session Kaldor attended. Kaldor did not at the time agree with Fisher about the desirability of such a tax base. After all, Keynesians during the 1930s thought *oversaving* was a problem. It was only when Kaldor began to deal with tax problems as a member of the Royal Commission on the Taxation of Profits and Income after World War II, that he remembered Fisher's argument that a graduated tax on personal expenditure might well be administratively feasible. Hugh Gaitskell suggested to Kaldor that "the expenditure-tax-principle might be explored in specific relation to surtax."[4]

Kaldor had been appointed to the Royal Commission by the Labour government of Clement Attlee when Gaitskell was chancellor of the exchequer, but when the government changed hands, the new Conservative chancellor R.A. Butler, ruled that Kaldor's proposal fell "outside the Commission's terms of reference," so that it was not included in the commission's report. There is some question of whether Kaldor intended his book to explore the replacement of the income base with the expenditure base, which is how I read it, or whether his whole intention was related to the proposal (his chapter 8) to amend or replace the British surtax then in force with an expenditure tax. Brian Reddaway who, according to Kaldor, "cleared [his] mind on a number of intricate points,"[5] says that the book was written essentially to make a case for the expenditure tax as a replacement for the British surtax.[6] Thirlwall says the book must be regarded as complementary to the ideas on other tax matters contained in the Minority Report of the Commission.[7] Kaldor wrote that the Minority Report proposal, which he signed, and his own proposal are indeed complementary and not alternatives.[8] And yet, in arguing "the issue in principle" (chapters 1–6) in that book and elsewhere, Kaldor clearly thought the expenditure base superior to the income base for fair taxation. The question is which concept approximates the taxable capacity and/or the ability to pay.

In a talk in Washington at a Brookings Conference in 1978, Kaldor gave credit to Irving Fisher for the idea that the real meaning of income is not some number in dollars or pounds, but personal satisfaction derived through consumption or destruction of things having an exchange value.[9] Kaldor concluded that, looked at in this way, income over a period of time is really consumption. Savings or that part of funds set aside is, then, not current income but delayed income. In order to tax Fisher income fairly, an expenditure tax must be levied. Since savings are in fact the discounted value of the increment to the flow of future satisfactions, they will be taxed either when gifted to heirs or at a later date when the consumption and satisfaction occur. In the final analysis, death taxes would recover society's due. By definition it is not fair to tax savings before that time, for the accumulator is adding to society's wealth. Kaldor reiterated his belief that an expenditure tax also recognizes the philosophical condition proposed by Hobbes that a person should be taxed not on what he contributes to the common pool but rather on what he takes out of it. Kaldor pointed out that an expenditure tax could be graduated by taking account of the number of persons in an income unit and the wealth of the unit.

Traditionally juxtaposed against Fisher's definition of income is one associated with the names Robert Murray Haig and Henry C. Simons, who were writing, as Fisher was, before World War II. The Haig-Simons definition holds that the relevant point is command over scarce resources, and that money income, including savings, is the measure of a person's economic power. Haig-Simons income is, from this point of view, the proper yardstick for measuring capacity to contribute to the expenses of society.[10]

Kaldor explained that while he held the Haig-Simons conception "intellectually more appealing" than the Fisherian conception, except on the social ethics test for taxing people for their contribution, he thought it impossible to tax "net saving" fairly because of the existence of capital gains. One must distinguish between accrued and realized capital gains. If gains are taxed as they accrue, even though they are not "realized," you have an "administrative nightmare." If you tax gains only when they are realized, you do not treat all taxpayers the same.

More important still, inflation—that is, changes in the purchasing power of money—affect people differently: If two people made a net saving of $100 each (thus increasing their theoretical "economic power"), and the inflation rate was 10 percent annually, the taxpayer with $2,000 to begin with would actually experience a decline in actual economic power, while the person with $1,000 to begin with would not. Nor would he have increased his economic power. If inflation put him in a new tax bracket with a rise in the marginal rate, he would be poorer. Kaldor argued that the same kind of revaluation would result from a change in the rate of interest and even from uncertainty about future earnings. He considered the expenditure tax a "second best" tax, knowing that it would penalize spendthrifts and reward misers. But he argued that allowances for such factors as the number of dependents could easily be made in the case of the expenditure tax, while the effects of inflation destroy the equitability of the income tax. Consequently, thought Kaldor, in the real world as well as in theory, the expenditure tax base or "Fisher income," would better reflect taxable capacity than the Haig-Simons definition. Thus his argument for an expenditure tax was an equity argument more than anything else, expenditure being the better measure of ability to pay than income.[11] These statements encourage my belief that Kaldor always saw the expenditure base as a substitute for the income base for progressive taxation. After the Brookings report appeared, Kaldor wrote to Joseph Pechman complaining that the published reports did not cover all he said, including his statements that the income tax is unsatisfactory for those who derive income from capital and that for most people income and expenditure are closely geared, so that having expenditure taxed rather than income wouldn't matter to them.[12]

An Expenditure Tax in precis

Writing in the immediate postwar period when the British Empire was being dismantled and capital investment was in great need, Kaldor found two fundamental shortcomings in the concept of income as a basis for taxation: first was its failure to tax dissavings so that established wealth in England could simply mine the capital investments of the country; and second, individuals were allowed to manipulate their taxable income capacity and in so doing avoid taxation. Reddaway thought this was of special concern to Kaldor when writing his book.[13] However, Kaldor insisted that if Haig-Simons income is used as the basis of taxation, capital gains and property should be taxed for the sake of equity; otherwise, the rich might escape taxation altogether, because political pressure from the rich and powerful probably would result in income tax amendments that sheltered their income from taxation. In comparison, he felt the expenditure tax, progressively applied, was more equitable, did not discriminate against either saving or risk bearing, and would alleviate any disincentives of progressive taxation. Gift and inheritance taxes would retain equity in the system.

Kaldor was also writing in the context of Keynesianism where economic efficiency and progress depend on additions to capital investment. He said,

> There is no need to look upon the egalitarian or re-distributive objectives of progressive taxation as being necessarily in conflict with considerations of economic efficiency and progress. This conflict undoubtedly exists with the progressive income tax. But if progressive taxation were levied on an expenditure base instead of an income base it would be possible to advance towards an egalitarian society whilst improving the efficiency of operation and rate of progress of the economy.[14]

Kaldor thought that the income tax as then constituted in Great Britain aggravated the undesirable effects on the propensity to save, to dissave, and to assume risk just at the time the United Kingdom needed investment, not consumption.[15] He had accepted the Keynesian revolution, he said, which meant that taxation was no longer just a means of "finding the money" for government expenditures but was "one of the primary weapons in the Government's armoury for ensuring general economic and monetary stability." Where an objective of financial policy was to secure a stable and progressive economy, the "maintenance of a stable level of prices, and an adequate rate of capital accumulation for steadily rising standards of living," the "primary purpose" of taxation would then be "to ensure that the total of public and private spending is adequate, and no more than adequate, to secure the full utilization of economic resources."[16]

Kaldor would apply the tax on expenditure per head, as the French did on income tax, adding all expenditures and then dividing by the number of members of the household. He recognized that the household unit might be of unrelated individuals, and that children, for example, might count as one-half or more, depending on their ages.[17] He visualized the tax as one of self-assessment, as in the United States income tax system, and thought that the risk of cheaters being found out was much greater with grossly understated spendings than with grossly understated earnings.[18]

Thus his argument was complex. The income tax stimulated the wrong economic behavior in the private sector—consumption over investment when it was investment that was needed—and created political pressures to break down the progressivity of the tax.[19] His concession was to recognize the problems of transition to a new system. He advised "a cautious beginning by introducing an expenditure tax side by side with the existing income tax, so framed as to apply to a limited number of taxpayers only in the top brackets."[20]

Kaldor's views on corporate income taxes followed from his analysis of the superiority of the expenditure base. He said flatly:

> The justification for company taxation would disappear if the principle

of taxing income were abandoned in favour of taxing expenditure. For under an expenditure tax, all capital gains would automatically be brought into charge in so far as they were spent, while in so far as they were saved, they would be no more liable to tax than any other form of saving.[21]

Since Kaldor's expenditure tax would be accompanied by large gift and inheritance taxes, society would reap its earnings from capital gains at the incidence of expenditure, gifts (treated as expenditures), or inheritance. This would avoid both the unfairness of taxing realized as compared with accrued capital gains in the case of a capital gains tax, and the difficulties of estimating corporate profits, depreciation, and so on.

Kaldor saw the expenditure tax as favoring the entrepreneurial class over the *rentiers*. He said:

> The accumulation of individual fortunes is an inevitable bye-product of capitalist enterprise. It is the entrepreneurial classes, not the rentiers, who are hit by the taxation of savings; the millionaire-rentiers like the landed aristocracy, *possess* large fortunes but they do not *accumulate* them.[22]

There is a social function in accumulation, not in inheritance. Kaldor would treat all gifts (including inheritance) the same, taxing them progressively.

As for the taxation of undistributed profits, he argued that companies had succeeded in passing the increased burden of taxation on to their consumers, and that, in fact, higher taxation of business profits—for example, wartime undistributed profits—had not had any direct influence on profit margins because dividends had been cut.[23] He pointed out that while real savings had actually risen during the period of high taxation, capital investment had not followed suit. He concluded that, "Whatever factors may have been responsible for the limitation on the rate of capital investment, financial stringency caused by heavy taxation could not have been an important cause." In the postwar United Kingdom at least until 1952, scarcity of resources other than financial, was the important factor.[24] In the then current system, the burden of increased company taxes fell on consumers and shareholders, the one in higher prices, the other in smaller dividends. Kaldor conceded that this made the corporate profits taxes in a sense a capital gains tax on shareholders. But he thought it a "crude and clumsy" method of going about that. He found evidence that the higher postwar taxes on company profits, while keeping down shareholders' personal consumption, also had lowered the market valuation of companies' assets, reducing the importance of the stock market in the process of capital formation. Many companies, instead, turned to their own internal financing. He concluded that, "There is nothing in company taxes as such which could not be more justly and appropriately 'got at' by taxes levied directly on individuals instead of indirectly through the undistributed profits of companies."[25]

British response

British reception of the ideas in *An Expenditure Tax* varied. Thirlwall reports that Ursula Hicks's anonymous, hostile review for *The Economist* surprised and annoyed Kaldor. Her review suggested that the taxpayer avoiding the British surtax with some success would "have a lot of fun with an expenditure tax." Others would find that "tax bankruptcy would be the only way out of an impasse."

The *Times* praised Kaldor's argument but expressed skepticism as to the practicality of the expenditure tax. I.M.D. Little, however, felt that it would "be foolish to dismiss the expenditure surtax," that the British needed either a capital gains tax or "Mr. Kaldor's tax" or even both. He thought that the expenditure tax could be "a more effective instrument for restraining the consumption of the rich, and it would be more equitable as between individuals, and more beneficial economically, than a capital-gains tax."[26] R.F. Kahn and Thomas Balogh differed in an exchange of letters, Kahn defending the expenditure tax and Balogh insisting that it would cause further inequality in the distribution of wealth.[27] *An Expenditure Tax* was translated into Spanish, Italian, and Japanese and sold 6000 copies within ten years.

American response

Although directed mainly at a British audience, *An Expenditure Tax* was favorably received in the United States. Richard A. Musgrave then at the University of Michigan gave credit to Kaldor for a "high idea-to-page ratio."[28] Musgrave thought that questions of the equity of income versus consumption tax bases were essentially "matters of taste," meaning there is no definitive way to choose between an accretion or income basis (Haig-Simons) which he preferred and a consumption basis a la Hobbes and Kaldor (Fisher income). He pointed out that Kaldor's argument that the income tax discriminated against risk taking did not hold in the United States (1957), because capital gains were treated separately and taxpayers were able to write off their losses on capital.[29] He thought Kaldor's most important point was that a lower level of consumption was needed to permit Britain to experience a higher rate of growth and thus maintain a competitive position. He agreed with Kaldor that any such changes should be along egalitarian and progressive principles. As a reviewer, Arnold C. Harberger of the University of Chicago lavished high praise on the book. He said,

This is surely one of the best books of the decade in public finance. In my view, it ranks with the works of Edgeworth, Pigou, Simons, and Vickrey on the all-too-small list of modern classics in the field.

Harberger agreed that an expenditure tax is more equitable than the "ideal" income tax, and thought that the case for an expenditure tax as compared with the "current setup is far stronger." However, he did question whether Kaldor was right in arguing that company taxes were ineffective in taxing the equity shareholder.[30]

Kaldor's book brought the issue of the expenditure base into international theoretical and policy discussion, which still goes on. The American Treasury, presidential candidates, and senators have considered it, during the 1970s and again in the 1990s. (See chapter note 6.1, American tax debates and the expenditure tax.) The president of the American Economic Association, Joseph A. Pechman, a friend of Kaldor's, addressed the issue of the expenditure tax in his 1989 presidential address, opposing it. The Meade Committee in the United Kingdom endorsed the expenditure base in 1977. While Kaldor's two "experiments" in the late 1950s— the expenditure taxes legislated in both India and Ceylon—were withdrawn, the issue of the fairest base for taxation remains unsettled. Perhaps the greatest irony occurred when the military regime of Chile attempted to introduce an expenditure tax in 1982 using Kaldor's name. As in many misapplications of economic ideas, the expenditure tax in Chile bore no resemblance to Kaldor's and sought instead to reduce the effective burden of direct taxes on higher-income groups.[31] One cannot but toy with the idea that the "Not Socialist, Not Capitalist" societies emerging in Eastern Europe[32] are in a position to benefit from this international debate. Instead of copying the Haig-Simons definition of income employed in the West, they could adopt a Fisher income base and Kaldor's expenditure tax. Because of state ownership and control, there are no entrenched propertied classes whose members might argue that they have already paid taxes on their savings and should not have to do so when the funds are spent. Some of the savings, investment, and risktaking so desperately needed in these countries might be fostered if Fisher-income concepts and the expenditure tax were legislated.

Kaldor did not live to see the dissolution of the Soviet Union, but in 1985 he wrote to Peter Mihály of the United Nations that he thought the expenditure tax more important for capitalist nations than socialist nations, "where individuals do not possess capital of any magnitude." In this letter Kaldor emphasized the effectiveness of the expenditure principle in a nation of small traders. Kaldor reminded Mihály that in Hungary before World War II the income tax "was sometimes levied on the basis of the *apparent* standard of living," an expenditure tax in effect.[33]

NK

Tax Advice, LDCs, and Riots

Between 1956 and 1977, Kaldor was called upon by eight countries to give advice on their tax systems. A ninth was Chile, where he offered an unwelcome opinion of the country's bourgeoisie. The countries were all "less developed," (LDCs), some newly independent, one still a Crown colony, none so stable that tax reforms could be simply imposed from the top, if that indeed, is ever the case.

Kaldor's previous experience had been with the countries of Europe, and his first concern with the less developed countries was signaled by a paper he read to the International Conference on Underdeveloped Areas in Milan in 1954. He made the statement that, "A true theory of economic growth—which is lacking at present—would . . . explain *why* some societies have experienced . . . enormously accelerated expansion . . . and why the movement has not spread to others." He felt that the rise of modern capitalism could "only be explained in terms of changing human attitudes to risk-taking and profit-making" and that "economic progress . . . necessarily entails a reduction in the *proportion* of manpower engaged in agriculture." He concluded that the "key to an accelerated growth of the underdeveloped areas of the world lies in bringing about fundamental changes in both the mental outlook and the technical knowledge and skill of their peasant populations." A precondition to success was the "growth of the food surpluses of the agricultural sector."[1] This was the framework from which Kaldor gave tax advice to the LDCs he visited. His proposals were broad but detailed and included reforms on administration. In no country did he advise the simple reliance on an expenditure base, including the first country, India, where the expenditure tax was adopted along with other taxes. His aims were always the same—a fair and progressive tax system that would help solve the economic problems facing the country. For Kaldor, it was a learning-by-doing experience.

After advising five of the countries, he remarked, "My experience as a tax adviser has thus brought me face to face with the realities of *power*, in a setting that is not normally within the province of an economist."[2]

In 1963, *Foreign Affairs* put to him the question, "Will underdeveloped countries learn to tax?" His answer in part was, "What can actually be accomplished does not depend merely on the individual good will of ministers or on the correct intellectual appreciation of the technical problems involved. It is predominantly a matter of political power."[3] He said he had found that analysis and advice were the easy parts. Gaining acceptance of a plan and implementing it provided the difficulties. In retrospect it is clear that the immediate results sometimes differed from the long-term value of his all-encompassing advice, and, as we shall see, Kaldor often had the pleasure of being reminded of this fact.

Advising the newly independent India

Under the auspices of the International Economic Association Kaldor had been one of the teachers at a "summer school" in Poona, India, in 1955. After the school was over, he was invited to give some lectures by Professor P.C. Mahalanobis, head of the Indian Statistical Institute, where Mahalanobis was working on the Second Five-Year Plan for India. Kaldor was on sabbatical leave, and his family accompanied him.[4] He worked in India from January to March 1956, the longest period spent in any country where he gave tax advice. Other Western economists visiting at that time included John Kenneth Galbraith, his friend from the Strategic Bombing Survey days, who would return to India in 1961 as American ambassador.

Indian independence and Commonwealth status were only six years old. The problems of inadequate revenue for the new aspirations of social welfare and economic development were pressing. Kaldor proposed a bold system of direct personal taxation based on the simultaneous application of yardsticks such as income, disposable wealth, capital gains, gifts and bequests received, as well as personal expenditure.[5] What happened was that although new taxes on capital gains, wealth, personal expenditure, and gifts were proposed, they were enacted only after the expenditure and gift taxes were "heavily riddled with loopholes and exemptions" during "turbulent" sessions in the Lok Sabha (Indian Parliament).[6]

Kaldor's suggested reforms in business and company taxation and in the administration of taxes were not even proposed, though the minister of finance, Mr. T.T. Krishnamachari, had made "a grandiose attempt." Even so, "the essential *props* of the system (the comprehensive return, the reporting system and the large reduction in the existing rate schedules) were missing" from the original governmental proposals.[7]

Ursula Hicks, reviewing Kaldor's recommendations for the *Economic Journal*, called it "an outstanding and remarkable achievement." She particularly admired the long-term value of the plan, the integration of the proposals, the self-checking features, and the administrative improvements proposed. She highlighted the problems of an economy that was able to collect only about 7 percent of the national income in taxes at a time of great need for revenue.[8] According to Thirlwall, some Indian economists thought the Kaldorian proposals a disaster,[9] but Sukhamoy Chakravarty of the Delhi School of Economics disagreed. Chakravarty said Kaldor's plan was put forward as a "healthy complement" to Mahalanobis's economic plans. Mahalanobis believed that "what is physically possible must be financially feasible." Unlike some of his later LDC tax reports, Kaldor did not specifically recommend a land tax for India. However, he pointed out that agriculture "and allied pursuits" accounted for more than half of the net domestic products in India.[10] Part of the problem of most of the LDCs Kaldor visited was that the main source of wealth was land. He was aware that the Japanese had to a large extent financed their economic development by taxing in such a way that land was forced to be either productive or sold, but it was not until he visited Turkey in 1962 that he proposed a land tax. Kaldor did propose an annual wealth tax, borrowed from Scandinavian countries, which would include real estate. According to Ursula Hicks, the Indian government rejected the inclusion of real estate and raised the exemption limit according to a "sacred tenet" of Indian politics that the tiller of the soil is too poor to pay taxes. Before World War II a land tax had been a major source of state revenue, but it became a minor source through inflation and the failure to revalue land.[11] Kaldor believed in considering many sources of wealth and income as bases for taxation. Twenty years later (1978), he reiterated his opinion that a country like India probably should base its taxes on a number of criteria—from income, expenditure, and capital gains, to net wealth and receipt of gifts and inheritances.[12]

Invitation to Ceylon

On Indian Prime Minister Nehru's suggestion, Kaldor was in 1958 invited to visit Ceylon, as Sri Lanka was called until 1972, to advise on tax reform. Ceylon, like India, had gained its independence in the postwar period (1948). The country was likewise dependent on agriculture and had an exploding population. Unrest unrelated to economic factors produced riots between the Sinhalese majority and large Tamil minority in the same year that Kaldor visited.[13]

Kaldor was asked to provide proposals "designed to create a system of progressive direct taxation suited to the needs of a democratic socialist community." The object was to provide incentives to progress and to bring about greater social and economic equality.[14] Again, within a broad array of taxes, Kaldor proposed an expenditure base. Thirlwall reports that while Prime Minister Bandaranaike was able to enact many of the Kaldorian reforms, subsequent governments, apparently including those of Bandaranaike's widow, were not strong enough to enforce them.[15]

In any case, the expenditure tax, which had become an issue in both countries, was withdrawn in India in 1962 and in Ceylon in the 1970s.[16] Kaldor reported that in neither country did the expenditure tax yield much revenue; he didn't know whether the true cause was corruption of tax officials or connivance of ministers. From these experiences, he learned "that passing laws aiming at income redistribution through taxation is not likely to succeed in its object unless there is a genuine will and ability to carry the laws into execution." To this end, Kaldor regularly advised countries to use the Chinese Maritime Customs as a model for establishing a *corps d'elite* of financial inspectors, as this had "effectively ended bribery in the administration of taxes in a country where corruption was as deeply ingrained as Imperial China." Although India had a career civil service, the enforcing officers were comparatively low-grade officials on low salaries. Mexico, where Kaldor made his next visit, had a "spoils system" where tax officials changed with every new administration.

"Secret" visit to Mexico

Kaldor's visit to Mexico in 1960 was on the invitation from the finance minister, Señor Antonio Ortiz-Mena. His mission was considered so controversial that it was at first a state secret. Kaldor "found it difficult to believe that Mexico was politically ready for a major change in the system of taxation in a progressive direction, but the Minister insisted that he was very keen" on Kaldor's doing the work.[17] Under the moderate president Adolfo Lopez-Mateos, Mexico seemed more stable and much farther along the path to development than either India or Ceylon. Nevertheless, his visit was considered so sensitive that he remained "incognito" for the first month he was there.

"On political grounds," an expenditure tax proposal was omitted.[18] Kaldor said in his Mexican report that while he was convinced that the expenditure tax was a "very important element in an integrated structure of progressive personal taxation," the experience in India and Ceylon had led him to believe "that the opposition of the property-owning classes to the idea of such a tax is so violent that it would be unwise to attempt to impose it alongside a reform of income tax and the introduction of a wealth tax, since it might jeopardise the success of the whole scheme."[19]

Otherwise, his proposals were similar to those made in India and Ceylon. But in Mexico, Kaldorian reforms were blocked long before they could be considered by the legislature, probably by the president and his cabinet.[20]

Nevertheless, when Kaldor returned to Mexico in the late 1970s, he was told by several economists working for the Mexican government "that quite a number of the recommendations concerning a simplified system of income tax had, in fact, been carried out and others were under consideration." The recommended changes had taken some time to be implemented.[21]

Having wet his feet in the giving of advice, Kaldor looked forward to more invitations.

Tax riots: Ghana and British Guiana

The most controversial visits were still to come: Ghana and British Guiana. Kaldor knew "with benefit of hindsight" that what could be done was limited by "the frailty of the existing power base for bringing into operation the requisite restraints and reforms." And there were other requirements, such as the avoidance of balance of payments crises and the enabling of sound development. Here were two more countries relying on agriculture and mining for economic production. Again, there were problems of mixed populations and unstable governments. Much of the economic and political power was in the hands of global companies, which were able to conceal their profits through "transfer pricing" between subsidiaries. Kaldor even came to suspect an "unholy alliance of capitalist interest and organised labour," which was used to generate popular disturbances opposing tax reform. John Toye notes that Kaldor's proposals of the 1960s differed from those given India and Ceylon, and even Mexico, and were more tailored to the economies in question.[22]

Proposals to British Guiana and Ghana

In neither Ghana nor Guiana was the expenditure tax an issue. The centerpieces instead were proposals for taxes on global companies to prevent their tax avoidance through transfer prices, and compulsory savings taxes on workers. Neither tax was well received by the people affected. The compulsory savings taxes were to be deducted from wages and salaries at 5 percent and from other income at 10 percent. Incomes under $1,000 were exempt. Contributors were to be given non-transferable government bonds registered in their names. The Ghanian bonds were repayable together with accrued interest at the end of ten years or any time afterward. In British Guiana bonds were redeemable in seven years. Kaldor thought "a scheme on these lines might provide very considerable internal resources for development."[23]

In Ghana, independent since 1957 as a British Commonwealth country, President Dr. Kwame Nkrumah had in the year before Kaldor's visit transformed the country into a "republic," naming himself president for life. Nkrumah introduced the rule suggested by Kaldor that profits of expatriate companies would be deemed to be no lower in relation to their local turnover than the ratio of their consolidated world profits to their consolidated world sales to third parties. Kaldor heard later from a Canadian who served in Ghana under United Nations technical assistance that Kaldorian reforms there, including the above, had raised revenues from nine million pounds in 1960–61 to nearly twenty-nine million in 1964. Kaldor reported that his scheme to deal with corruption among ministers and party bosses had, however, brought on a "minor revolt of ministers and their collaborators" in Ghana.[24]

British Guiana (Guyana since 1966), was still a Crown Colony with a British governor general when Kaldor arrived in 1961. The population was mixed, roughly 50 percent East Indian, 33 percent African freed slaves, 5 percent native Indian, and 13 percent mixed European and Chinese. The finance minister Charles Jacob, on behalf of Prime Minister Dr. Cheddi Jagan, asked for a comprehensive examination of the tax structure aimed toward changes that would increase revenue and distribute the tax burden more equitably. Kaldor had arrived on an urgent call only to find there had been a flight of capital over the previous eighteen months and that the civil service had been almost in a state of revolt from having had no pay increases during the past eight years of rising prices.[25]

An international incident

What Kaldor could not know was that he had walked into an international incident. The United States government under President John Kennedy was determined either to prevent the British from giving independence to British Guiana until Jagan could be removed from office or to precipitate an uprising to bring down Jagan's government. CIA operatives were already active in British Guiana to this purpose, and consultations with the British government had already taken place. Fresh from the Bay of Pigs fiasco, Kennedy was trying to prevent the establishment of another communist-type regime in the American hemisphere, particularly before the next election.[26]

Kaldor fulfilled his assignment in nineteen days, proposing exchange controls, an increase in import and excise duties, detailed changes in personal and company taxation, and new taxes on capital gains, property, and gifts. His daughter Frances, then reading economics at Oxford University, accompanied him and helped him to get out his report. Both the New York and London *Times* praised the proposed budget. The London *Times* observed that Jagan's proposals (which Kaldor had initiated) were "courageous and certainly not far from what Guiana must have."[27]

The aftermath and the reality

The aftermath became the international incident. Jagan, head of the left-wing People's Progressive Party, was a Chicago-trained dentist of East Indian origin married to an American. The opposition leaders were Forbes Burnham, an African-Guyanese who had earlier split with Jagan, and Peter d'Aguiar, a businessman of Portuguese descent. When mobs defied the pleas of both Jagan and the British governor, Sir Ralph Grey, to disband peacefully, a company of British Royal Hampshire troops were brought from Jamaica to quell the disturbances. But not in time to save the Jagan government.

Asked by a reporter of the London *Times* about his proposals, which were said to have caused the riots, Kaldor assured the reporter that they had been "moderate and reasonable" and that it was "absolute nonsense" to suggest that they were in any way communist. Kaldor thought the riots originated from a political conspiracy to get rid of Jagan and his government. The Commonwealth Commission of Enquiry into Disturbances in February 1962 thought so too.[28] Kaldor noted that the same hysteria had been experienced in Ghana, but that it had taken six weeks to work up to a general strike, whereas it took only three days in British Guiana. In both countries strikers had demanded the withdrawal of the whole budget "including anti-avoidance provisions, which could only be of eventual benefit to the workers."[29]

Apparently rethinking its initial praise of Jagan's program, the London *Times* accused Kaldor of proposing "very large increases in taxation" as a program for "forcing development." Kaldor replied that since British Guiana had a deficit of over $7 million and no foreign reserves and no banking and currency system of its own, he had suggested raising $10.5 million, of which $7 million was in higher customs and excise duties on a limited range of items (mostly nonessential goods); a further $1 million by a fairly modest reduction in personal allowances to income tax; $1 million by an annual tax on property; and another $1.5 million on all other proposals. He added, "Given the fact that the precarious state of the foreign balance made some reduction in imports essential, and that a rise in import duties was the best method to achieve this, I wonder whether any other responsible adviser could or would have tendered any very different advice, either as to the amount or the kind of taxes to be raised." The compulsory savings scheme, which was to raise $2.5 million from individuals and $3.5 million from companies, "would have gone only one-third of the way to cover the financial gap in the existing development plan, which as you yourself [the

Times] indicate is by no means an ambitious one." Kaldor agreed that requiring British Guianian citizens to declare their foreign security holdings and foreign bank balances did hit the "bourgeois" as the *Times* had said, but noted that the *Times* had failed to mention that the amount of money sent abroad by that same "bourgeois" during the past few years more than offset all the economic aid that the United Kingdom and other international organizations had offered to British Guiana.[30] Furthermore, what one letter writer to the *Times* had called "draconian" exchange control measures were instead identical with those in force in most of the independent members of the sterling area: India, Pakistan, Ceylon, and Australia, for example. All of those governments restricted capital transfers by residents to both sterling and nonsterling areas. The flight of capital that caused the crisis had started even before Jagan was elected— apparently in response to talks about a new constitution and the possibility of independence.[31]

What followed

In evaluating whether Kaldor's recommendations were timely or catastrophic, we must concern ourselves with what followed. The African party led by Forbes Burnham won the pre-Independence elections in 1964. As V.S. Naipaul says, this was done "with American help, and after serious racial disturbances." Kaldorian reforms had no place in the new government. According to Naipaul, "through a series of rigged elections," Cheddi Jagan and his Indian followers were kept out of power while Guyana had a kind of Marxist-African "cooperative republic" from 1971 to 1984.[32] One would like to know why the American government preferred Burnham's Marxism to that of Jagan. British Tory M.P. Iain Macleod could have warned the Americans. He said in a debate on British Guiana in June 1964 in the House of Commons that the American attitude seemed dangerous in that if you put off independence in order to avoid one left-wing government, "the most likely thing to happen is that you will get a government even further to the left."[33]

Naipaul says that under Burnham, every important industry, including bauxite and rice, was nationalized and the plantations run with nearly slave labor conditions. One-third of the Guyanese population emigrated to avoid the harsh conditions. The Guyanese deficit grew from 4.2 million Guyana dollars in 1965 to 1,309 million in 1988. Burnham died in 1985, but Cheddi Jagan was still waiting in 1991 to come to power.[34] Should we conclude that a nation would rather suffer anything but a progressive tax system?

For Guyana the pendulum is still swinging. The *Economist* in 1992 reported that British sugar companies had been invited back to run the Guyanan state-owned sugar firm.[35] Perhaps a progressive tax system is next

Brief encounters: Turkey, Iran, Venezuela, and Chile

Kaldor had still more junkets to make. In 1962, he was invited to prepare a memorandum on fiscal reform for the confidential use of the prime minister of Turkey, Ismet Inonu.[36]

A Turkish land tax

Turkey was also heavily dependent on agriculture but had benefited for more than ten years from Marshall Plan loans. There was some unrest, and the year before Kaldor wrote his report, the country had adopted a new constitution. Once again Kaldor argued that tax revenue should be increased in order to further economic development and increase productivity in agriculture. He found agriculture "hardly taxed at all."[37]

He based his proposed land tax on the average net product of agriculture for each particular type of land "as defined for purposes of national accounting" rather than on the market value of land. He suggested a progressive tax, according to the size of the landholdings of the individual farmer. Thus it would be a tax on "potential output." There would also be taxes on business profits and capital. Kaldor was highly critical of a report by the Turkish Tax Reform Commission that put more emphasis on incentives for investment than on the reallocation of real resources. Kaldor noted that investment allowances in the United States from which this incentive was copied, served an economy in which there "is no shortage of genuine savings and the rate of investment does appear to be limited by a lack of profitable investment opportunities." [38] He thought Turkey was a country where insufficient growth and investment was a consequence of a lack of resources and that it was necessary to increase "the taxation even at the cost of worsening it disincentive effects."[39]

Toye says that "Kaldor's skepticism" toward tax concessions that presumably provide incentives to investors in developing countries was heretical in the early 1960s, but that by 1989 this view was "very widely shared."[40]

Compulsory savings for Iran

Kaldor's 1966 visit to Iran was a short one, as he was at the time a tax adviser to James Callaghan. He submitted his report after only eight days of work and returned home with a splendid purchase of a venerable rug. The problem he was asked to work on in Iran was that of delaying consumption effects of increases in pay that had been granted to civil servants. Once more Kaldor suggested compulsory savings taxes, giving three alternatives.[41] He expressed other views as well, applauding Iran's land reform program as paving the way to economic development by freeing labor from agricultural employment. And he urged the extension of credit and the better organization of marketing and efficient agricultural services for farmers.[42]

On the other hand, he was highly critical of the income tax proposal that came from the Iranian Tax Commission. Rather than making the tax system fairer, the proposal made it less fair, for wage incomes were taxed at an effective rate of 16 percent, while the "effective rate of tax on incomes derived from property" and business was about 1.5 percent.[43] The government of Iran was, like Turkey, trying to copy the Western penchant for incentive taxation, when the need was to commit more resources to development.

Venezuela's "exonerations"

Kaldor's advice to Venezuela was actually a comment on the proposal by the minister of finance, "Mr. Hurtado." The problem in Venezuela was one of long-term adjustment to the eventual loss of oil revenues. Unlike the other countries Kaldor had visited, Venezuela had surpluses in its budget and balance of payments in 1962, but these were not expected to continue. Kaldor thought the proposed reforms neither furthered nor conflicted with the objectives of long-term adjustment. He did think the economic effects of proposed land taxes would be favorable, particularly those on unutilized land.[44]

Kaldor considered the marginal tax rate of 55 percent on company taxation too high. The law, as written, allowed too many avoidance schemes. He preferred instead a lower tax of, say 35 or 40 percent which would apply irrespective of the amount of income. He was particularly critical of what he called "exonerations," which allowed too much discretionary power to the tax administrator and therefore invited both tax avoidance and tax evasion.[45]

Chile's propertied class

One of Kaldor's most stirring and prescient pronouncements on taxation and development, but one of the least popular, was made in Chile during the same sabbatical year that he visited India. He was in Chile for three months as a consultant to the United Nations' Economic Commission for Latin America (ECLA), invited by Raul Prebisch to advise on ECLA's first studies on fiscal policies for developing countries. His views were so controversial that ECLA declined to publish his article in their *Bulletin*. He had concluded that Chile's low rate of accumulation was not the result of insufficient capacity to generate investible resources from abroad, but of "peculiar consumption, savings and investment behaviour of the local property-owning class." In short, the large share of profits in national income was not accompanied by high levels of savings. This view was unpopular not only in Chile but also with the United Nations staff members who regularly blamed slow development in South America on "external factors" such as the failure of the developed nations to provide investment. Even though his paper had not yet been published, some of Kaldor's policy recommendations were leaked during the 1958 Chilean presidential election campaign and used by right-wing parties as a scare tactic. His so-called "leftist propositions" included "a more effective system of taxation (including special tax measures designed to increase the proportion of profits retained by enterprises) in order to reduce the proportion of property income allocated to personal consumption to a figure nearer to that of Britain."[46]

J. Gabriel Palma and Mario Marcel note that the experience of Chile in the last thirty years has "clearly tended to confirm [Kaldor's] hypothesis . . . that economic backwardness in Chile is not the result of lack of investible resources (both domestic and foreign), but simply and directly the result of the tendency of the upper income groups to squander, in luxury and wasteful consumption, a large proportion of the investible resources available to the country." Palma and Marcel find it depressing that after thirty years "most of [Kaldor's] policy proposals are still on the agenda."[47]

Looking back on tax advice

When, in 1980, Kaldor wrote the introduction to a reprint of his tax studies, he confessed skepticism of the possibilities of improving the distribution of income and wealth through taxation "or of introducing effective reforms when these are perceived, in anticipation, as affecting adversely the interests of the property-owning classes." This limitation on tax reform was present not only in developing countries, but in Britain as well.[48] In the less developed countries, Kaldor's first priority was economic development aided by a *fairer* tax system, as there was not enough income in such countries. His advocacy of taxes other than those on "taxable income" came from his experience with the Royal Commission when he signed the minority report that said "neither the public nor the legislature, nor the Courts, are conscious of the extent to which the tax system, behind a facade of formal equity, metes out unequal treatment to different classes of the taxpaying community."[49] His penchant for compulsory savings taxes and land taxes was from a recognition of the imperative need for investment and for rising agricultural productivity in developing countries.

Clearly Kaldor's tax advice was out of kilter with local politics nearly everywhere he went, but because it was good economics, it could be, as in Mexico, of long-term influence. Kaldor became concerned when invitations from Latin and South America declined. He wrote to P. N. Rosenstein-Rodan, inquiring:

> What is happening in Latin America and the Alliance for Progress? The O.A.S. people, after being extremely keen on my helping them on tax reform, now seem to have got cold feet, though I am not sure whether the cooling of the feet comes from the Mexicans, etc. or the [American] State Department and I should love to find out.[50]

For whatever reason, there was a lapse of fifteen years after his visit to British Guyana before Kaldor was invited back to advise another South American country (Venezuela).

In evaluating his tax work in LDCs, Toye says that Kaldor departed from what Albert Hirschman has called "the visiting economist syndrome," for Kaldor did not give the "standard remedy, deduced from and validated by universal economic principles and claimed to be appropriate to all." Toye rejects both the "hostile caricature" of the British conservative newspapers that Kaldor's advice "was responsible for, or the cause of, revolution, inflation and toppling governments" and the milder caricature that he advocated a large public sector and disregarded the impact of taxes on personal and business incentives. Toye concludes that Kaldor's brilliance in tax reform was in his "superb ability—superb both in terms of speed and approximate accuracy—to manipulate the complex interdependencies in a scheme of tax reform." While admitting that Kaldor may have lacked some "sensitivity to administrative issues," Toye argues that Hirschman's "hiding hand" by which project planners underestimate the problems and difficulties that will arise in a project, may be a necessity in tax reform:

> It is not clear that any tax reform would ever occur in developing countries *unless* tax reformers consistently overestimated the political acceptability of their proposals. Tax reform (like development policy more generally) seems to contain irreducible elements of opportunism and optimism.[51]

While his experiences made him skeptical of what can be accomplished, Kaldor never lost his belief that a better tax system can make a better world and that economic advisers can discern what a better tax system is.

Part III

Practicing Political Economics

NK

CHAPTER EIGHT

Joining the Government

After World War II, along with the dismantling of the British Empire, the United Kingdom had periodic crises in its balance of payments position. By the time Labour came again to power in 1964, the problem of the balance of payments was at the crisis level. The most fundamental economic question was whether this was a temporary problem that could be papered over with loans or a continuing condition requiring emphatic adjustment in the exchange rates. It was at this time that Kaldor was invited to join the government as adviser to the chancellor of the exchequer James Callaghan.

Slow growth, world markets, and the Labour party

Already it was apparent that the UK economy was growing more slowly than the economies of some of the members of the Common Market and of Japan, and that Britain and the United States were losing market shares even as world markets expanded. For Britain, this had raised the question of whether she should attempt to join the thriving European Economic Community (EEC), which was scheduled to become a custom union first and a political and monetary union soon. The economic question was whether Britain would, as a member, grow at the same pace as those countries within the Common Market, benefiting from the larger market. However, in joining, Britain would have to abandon not only the Commonwealth system but also the European Free Trade Association. The British government was obligated to seek reasonable terms of trade for both.

The wild card in the balance of payments and growth issues became North Sea oil. (See chapter note 8.1, Politics and North Sea oil.) But in 1964 no one could know this, nor was it clearly apparent during the later negotiations for joining the EEC.

The Labour party Kaldor was to join was a coalition of interests having a left, right, and center. Historians have made the following points: Labour, although initially committed to socialism, never challenged the English political system; that is, there was never any question but that when Labour lost an election, the party would step down. Labour in power acted like any other political party guided by, but not subservient to, its constituents. What is most interesting is that aside from the nationalization of the Bank of England and several major industries such as coal, railways and canals, gas, and steel, the economics of the Labour party *when in power* turned out to be very close to that of the Conservatives when they were in power. This was true throughout the period from 1945 to 1979. Faced with the same economic problems, usually a balance of payments crisis, the Labour party applied many of the same domestic economic constraints that the Conservatives did in their turn. Given a challenge to the pound, Labour would defend it; given inflation, Labour would deflate; given wage pressures, Labour would attempt an incomes policy to moderate wage and price increases, as did the Conservatives. There were differences, but they were more in degree than in kind. All this, of course, was before Margaret Thatcher became prime minister in 1979. Thatcher's monetarism and excursions into laissez-faire came after Kaldor was in the House of Lords and were the subjects of many of his speeches there.

Kaldor's recommendations when he was an adviser or consultant to chancellors James Callaghan, Roy Jenkins, and Denis Healey were not always followed. Callaghan's and Prime Minister Wilson's determined views against devaluation were, in 1964, little affected by Kaldor's arguments—when he was allowed to make them. The other Hungarian immigrant, Thomas Balogh, was at Wilson's elbow giving opposite advice.

Kaldor's stints in public office raise the question once raised by Robbins: Is the economist's role only one of general education, even when in supposed positions of power? If you counsel devaluation and the chancellor and prime minister balk because they have listened to others, or decide too late, or agree to only a little when a lot is needed, are you to be blamed? I would say no. Kaldor is especially admirable in that he continued to slog away as an economist, never as a wily politician, always giving advice based on information, statistics, and economic theory that was consistent with his insights and values as a person with world experience. In this he provides a model for economists who dare to try to influence policy directly. The fact that his views seldom prevailed at the time is of little moment. When economists aspire to influence policy, they necessarily have to become well informed about real world conditions, as economists of Kaldor's generation tended to be. Then like Keynes and Kaldor, they are in a position to refocus economic theory. That is not to say that economics is the only important consideration of governing parties, but failure of the economic program undermines any other goals a government might have. Experience has much to teach theorists. Kaldor never lost sight of this truth.

From his study of economics, his analysis of White Papers during the war, and his postwar experiences in Europe and developing countries, Kaldor came to a view which he pursued fairly consistently for the rest of his life. He believed that a fair system of taxation was fundamental to achieving economic goals. That was his long suit in influencing the policy of the Labour party and the issue about which he drew the most fire from the London financial community (often referred to as the City). Taxes never stood alone in his mind. He saw them not only as revenue, but as tools for influencing economic growth and the balance of payments, hence his compulsory savings tax for Ghana and British Guiana and his selective employment tax for the United Kingdom, which penalized services in favor of subsidizing manufactures.

Early alerts to the public

The contextual British "real world" in which Kaldor gave advice was a complex, ever-changing one, one that called for different policies at different times in different circumstances. Some problems, however, seemed to him to be long standing. He saw the United Kingdom as an economy squandering its opportunities to raise standards of living. He knew that this was so, because from the early 1950s it was plain that Japan and Germany and even France were growing more rapidly than the United Kingdom and that standards of living were rising in those countries at a pace the UK could not match. Kaldor saw it this way: the UK was losing world markets because of its failure to keep up in manufacturing industries, its tendency to export new technology rather than add to its own capital, and its failure to develop an industrial relations system in which labor and management pull together—in short, its failure to have a credible social contract and agreed upon economic policy.

To alert the public, Kaldor carried on a campaign in the Letters column of the *Times*. As early as April 28, 1950, he urged some restraint on the imports of petrol that were at the time used for lorries in the service industry, which the British call road transport. He supported a road transport tax, favoring the moving of coal, which was domestically produced, by train. He argued that the growing German and Japanese competition and the inevitable decline in British price advantages would make it even more difficult later on to expand British exports if Britain continued to rely on imported oil. He was thinking in terms of real commodities and the substitution of a local product for an imported one, seeing a need for some diversion of supplies, at least temporarily, to foster exports.[1]

The Conservative Government under Winston Churchill, 1951–55, was continuing a policy of rearmament, while the Germans and Japanese invested in exportable goods. Sir Anthony Eden's Conservative government followed Churchill's, with no major change in economic policy. By 1957, the Germans were running a major export surplus, and Kaldor was moved to point out to readers of the *Times* that under Bretton Woods, the surplus country was to take appropriate remedial measures, and that British devaluation would not correct the problem of an undervalued German mark.[2] But the pound continued to be under siege. Inflation aggravated the problems of the pound, and Kaldor reminded *Times* readers that raising taxes was as good a way to fight inflation as cutting government expenditures.[3] More Conservative governments followed—that of Harold Macmillan, 1957–63, and Sir Alec Douglas-Home, 1963–64. By 1963, Kaldor had stepped up his letter writing, complaining of what he called the Conservatives' policies of obstacles to growth. He called for a floating exchange rate and for following France in the stimulation of exports.[4]

Kaldor found the situation pressingly serious. Between 1950 and 1962, world trade in manufactures had increased 7 percent a year, which was unprecedented, while Britain's exports had increased only 2.7 percent a year; "and the ominous feature" was that the rate had dropped from 3 percent in the first half of the period to 2.3 percent in the second half of the period. In comparison, exports from other countries were increasing rapidly—France by a rate of 8.5 percent per annum, Japan by 8.9 percent, Germany by 10 percent, and Italy by 18.3 percent, in all cases except Japan at substantially higher rates than the growth of their gross domestic product.[5] Kaldor attributed Britain's slow growth partly to the deflationary policies pursued by successive Conservative governments. He now advised using a floating exchange rate to make British products dramatically cheaper in order to regain markets. France had devalued several times, and Britain must also.[6]

The Conservatives continued to meet the pressure on the pound by foreign borrowing, apparently on the assumptions that the pressure was a temporary strain and the imbalance between imports and exports an aberration.[7] There was also a political presumption shared by Conservatives and Labour that devaluation was a disgrace. Kaldor strenuously objected: "It cannot be emphasized too strongly that recourse to foreign borrowing for the purpose of financing a current account deficit is of an entirely different character from borrowing to counter a speculative attack on the currency . . . ."[8]

Public image

Twenty-two days after that stern admonition was printed, the October 1964 election returned Labour to power with Harold Wilson as prime minister.

Kaldor was appointed as adviser to Chancellor James Callaghan, and Oxford University's Thomas Balogh was made adviser to Wilson. "Observer" of the *Financial Times* characterized them both: Kaldor "is small, round, genial and immensely popular; Balogh is tall, acid and sometimes seems to enjoy making enemies." The article quoted another Oxford don as saying, "There are three kinds of conversation, dialogue, monologue and Balogh," and noted that Balogh was a strong anti-devaluation man and "Wilson's closest confidant." "Observer" saw other differences in the two: Balogh was often "shaky on theory and wooly on statistics" with worldly and political interests. Kaldor was essentially unworldly—"he is happiest in the remoter reaches of theoretical abstraction."[9]

Kaldor accepted the appointment on a part-time basis, continuing to lecture at Cambridge University, rather in the tradition of Keynes, who, after World War I, had divided his time between the City and Cambridge. Kaldor resigned from the boards of Investing in Success Equities, Investing in Foreign Growth Stocks, Anglo-Midland Trust, and Acorn Securities, enterprises he had pursued with great success.[10] From the beginning, the City understood that Kaldor favored a capital gains tax and a single corporation tax,[11] and that he had been "coaching" James Callaghan for his role in the Treasury.[12] A xenophobic campaign began immediately after his and Balogh's appointments, long before Callaghan had even proposed his spring budget. They were labeled the "Hungarian Mafia," the "Terrible Twins," and "B and K" (after Bulgarin and Khrushchev). Parliament discussed "security rules" apparently because of the appointment of Kaldor and Balogh.[13]

In December Harold Wincott wrote an open letter in the *Times* to Callaghan saying of the Kaldorian tax proposals for capital gains and corporate profits taxes, "There really hasn't been anything like it since Hitler wrote *Mein Kampf* . . . ."[14] Afterward the *Times* reported that it had received fifty-nine letters on the subject of which fifty-seven supported Wincott. The editor decided a letter supporting Kaldor was the way to close the discussion, and published a letter from nine of his Cambridge colleagues, two of whom were later to become Nobel Prize winners. One of the points made by the economists was that corporation and capital gains taxes were in force in a large number of other countries and that it was "quite misleading" to represent them as radical novelties.[15]

J. F. Child, in another letter, objected to the "scurrilous personal attack in a newspaper from which I have been accustomed to expect sober financial comment rather than third-rate political pamphleteering." Since civil servants could not defend themselves against public attack, he thought it improper to single Kaldor out for "personal vilification."[16] Wincott responded that Kaldor had spent a decade converting Harold Wilson.[17] This was a reference to the fact that Kaldor had been influential in the Labour aims expressed in the 1964 "Party Manifesto" that proposed an annual growth rate of 3.8 percent through "socialist planning." Wincott asked, if Kaldor works for the government on three days a week why can't he be attacked on the other two?

In February an article in the *Times* reviewed Kaldor's controversial experience in tax reform in Guyana, noting his unrepentant stand. "In retrospect I do not think that the advice I gave was wrong," Kaldor was quoted as saying.[18] "Observer" had raised the question of whether Kaldor were "somewhat naive" about the real world, adding that that was "no doubt why governments, after taking his advice on taxation, have had to call out the riot squads."[19] But what counted was Kaldor's credibility within the government. Thirlwall reports that Sir Alexander Johnston, head of the revenue, initially had not wanted to propose capital gains and corporation taxes at the same time, but took the risk anyway in the budget of April 1965. Kaldor had argued that the corporation tax would stimulate domestic investment, while the capital gains tax was mainly a campaign pledge toward fairness in taxation.[20]

Labour party policy 1964–70

The Labour party's economic goals were typically set out in advance in election "manifestos." All too often these had to be soft-pedaled or even abandoned while the Labour government struggled with short-term responses to overwhelming economic problems. British economic policy of both parties came to be known as "stop-go." Admirably ambitious goals were proposed by Harold Wilson in the 1964 campaign. He began bravely enough, with George Brown as head of a new Department of Economic Affairs and James Callaghan as chancellor. But he inherited a balance of payments that was running 800 million pounds in deficit, and his parliamentary majority at the outset was four, soon reduced to three.[21] In spite of these constraints, Labour offered a tax program that owed much to Kaldor's advice, for Callaghan's spring budget introduced the capital gains and corporation taxes. The policy exception was that devaluation was considered a dirty word, and advisers were restrained from even mentioning it.[22] The inherited balance of payments crisis was to be overcome in the traditional way—through seeking loans from foreign banks and raising of the bank rate. In "defending sterling" by these means, Wilson was more attuned to the City than to some of the party's economic advisers. Wilson made the decision not to devalue because he feared Labour's being labeled the "devaluation party."[23] Labour made Europe uneasy by levying surcharges on imports and by deciding to review the joint British-French project to build the Concorde.[24]

Domestically, with devaluation ruled out, Labour's long-term solutions were to be in the form of plans for economic growth and the securing of an agreement from industry and labor for a prices and incomes policy. Unfortunately, the long-term plans were generally to take a back seat to policies of periodic deflation that only aggravated the balance of payments problems. Finally, in November 1967, one devaluation of from 2.80 to 2.40 was initiated. In pursuing these policies, Labour was fending off pressures, not only from the City and from Europe, but also internationally from the Johnson administration in Washington, which urged heavy cuts in consumer demand as a condition of support for loans to meet the inherited crisis in the balance of payments. Paul Whiteley claims that by the end of the Wilson years, 1964–70, the goal of "full employment had been abandoned, growth and productivity forgotten in a rapid series of deflationary cuts." The stage was set for "stagflation," that pernicious phenomenon of recurring inflation accompanied by unemployment.[25] Certainly, Kaldor's opinion was not the only internal opposition to the government's policy. George Brown, who had become convinced that devaluation was the only way to save his economic program, resigned after devaluation was passed over in 1966. Robert Neild left the post of chief economic adviser to the Government, and Kaldor refused to accept the post in his stead, all because of disenchantment.[26]

When devaluation finally came in 1967, Kaldor saw it as "too little and too late." However, the balance of payments did have a substantial surplus by 1969 and 1970. The surplus was due, Kaldor thought, not only to the devaluation "but to Mr. Jenkins's budgetary measures, which for the first time since the war secured an overall public sector surplus." Not long afterward, Kaldor adopted the view that devaluation was no more than a minor part of the needed response to what ailed the British economy.[27] According to David Steel, Wilson's was the first government to rely, on a significant scale, on the practice of providing ministers with their own advisers instead of relying on civil servants. The advisers were like temporary civil servants and pretty much bound by convention. Kaldor worked more directly with civil servants in the Treasury than with Callaghan, but this widened rather than limited his experience and his influence.[28] There was a certain amount of rivalry between fellow Hungarian Balogh and Kaldor in spite of their being friends, for their economic views and advice often differed, not only regarding devaluation, but in general policy as well. Kaldor sometimes accused Balogh of believing that "grow, grow, grow" would take care of everything including the balance of payments deficit. In the 1960s Kaldor thought that devaluation and promotion of exports was the proper policy.

In an immediate sense, Kaldor's influence was probably limited to his recommendations on tax policy, and this mainly in the period 1964–67. His detractors were correct when they accused him of having been "educating" Labour shadow ministers for years. When it came to taxes, he was accepted as an undeniable expert, one who shared Labour's aims for a fair and growth-promoting tax system.

First service: success in SET

Besides the capital gains and corporate taxes proposed in 1965, Kaldor is given almost complete credit for the Selective Employment Tax (SET) proposed by Callaghan as chancellor and passed in 1966. Kaldor was by this time convinced of three things: (1) that Cambridge economists were correct in arguing that budget deficits and balance of payments deficits were related; (2) that devaluation was an appropriate policy for balance of payments problems, especially when accompanied by suitable taxes; and (3) that the means to grow was through the export of manufactured goods, as distinguished from fostering the expansion of domestic consumption. Since devaluation was off limits of Labour party policy early on and taxes were already high, the means of growth was to promote the manufacturing industries and thereby exports. SET attempted to do this by taxing service industries and transferring funds to manufacturing employers. Kaldor argued that this would promote rising productivity in both sectors.

The Department of Applied Economics under the directorship of Brian Reddaway began a study of the effects of the SET, publishing reports in 1970 and 1973.[29] In spite of the formidable problems of such a study, Reddaway et al. concluded that Kaldor's expectations of SET's effects on productivity, margins, and profits were vindicated. Reddaway also concluded that Kaldor was "decidedly unfair to himself and to SET" when in 1980 he deemed SET to have been a failure because of the general economic situation at the time. Labour went along with Kaldor's tax proposals in spite of the ingrained hostility to Kaldor in the City. And, according to Reddaway, "SET produced a real gain in productivity, and what was a failure was the general management of the economy."[30] The difference between their assessments was that Kaldor wanted gains in exports and in economic growth rates, while Reddaway saw success in rising productivity.

A new perspective

The Labour government of Harold Wilson was succeeded by Edward Heath's Conservative government in 1970. Kaldor did not watch the Heath government in silence. He commented in newspaper and magazine articles on every move. Finally, anticipating the Conservatives' faltering in the midst of yet another balance of payments crisis, Kaldor wrote two articles for the *New Statesman* spelling out his views of what had happened. "Mr. Heath's Road to Ruin" was portrayed as Heath's insistence on a "go-go" policy—his cutting of taxes as he increased expenditures, making consumption run ahead of production; his abolition of the Selective Employment Tax that had helped export manufacturers; his imposition of wage controls, which created social unrest; his failure to adjust internal policies after the pound was forced off parity when it was floated in June 1972. By trying to create prosperity with a faster rate of growth, Heath had brought on the biggest balance of payments deficit in history.[31] The change in Kaldor is evident. He now said that new policy was needed. Neither go-go nor stop-go policies had worked. Something was wrong with the techniques of economic management applied by successive governments. He derided the technique that had consisted of making short-term forecasts of the level of output and employment and responding in taxes and expenditures to that picture. He questioned the assumption that the balance of payments would take care of itself. He asked whether mass unemployment in Britain had *ever* been caused by excessive domestic saving. If not, then it could not be cured by budgetary stimuli. Indeed, Kaldor thought this question had "never been properly examined!"[32] He insisted that go-go could not and did not work. This was an unusual point to be raised by a Keynesian and an interventionist. Kaldor had already recognized that it was politically impossible for governments in power to introduce heavy new taxation before a general election, eliminating stop-go-stop as an accessible policy for a government that wanted to remain in power. Some new policies were needed.

For many years Kaldor had been interested in the topic of his inaugural address as professor delivered at the University of Cambridge in 1966: "Causes of the Slow Rate of Economic Growth in the United Kingdom." And by 1974 he was convinced that the problem had been insufficient exports in relation to the imports at what would be full employment, that is, the foreign trade multiplier.[34]

Kaldor recognized that after the war, all British governments had assumed responsibility for seeking full employment. "But it took a very long time—in fact until 1967—before it was realized (and then only in certain circles) that the true effect of the new system was simply to transmute the chronic pre-war unemployment problem into the chronic post-war balance of payments problem."[35] Kaldor was not arguing for a cessation of intervention but for intervention to promote exports in competition with the successful countries that had been *led* by the fast growth of exports. This could be done only through long-term planning and not through responses to short-term forecasts. Whether socialist or egalitarian like Sweden, or capitalist like France or Japan, exports were the key, he argued. Manufactures were subject to increasing returns, agriculture to diminishing returns. Britain should budget for a surplus rather than a deficit balance of payments, using fiscal instruments to stimulate exports rather than domestic consumption, which mainly raised imports. He feared that membership in the Common Market, which Britain had joined in 1973, might hamper the government in doing this, except, he noted, that Denmark, also a new member, had just passed such legislation.

Discovering the enemies of enlightenment

In those articles in the *New Statesman* Kaldor showed himself to be at odds not only with Conservative government policy, but also with Labour government policy over the years. Still, he thought that a Heath government could not do what needed to be done, so it was time for Labour to try.

Labour took office again in 1974 as the largest party in the House of Commons, but it formed the government thirty seats short of an overall majority. Steel reminds us that the election took place during a state of emergency due to the Conservative government's confrontation with the miners over its pay policy and the Arab embargo on Western oil supplies.[36] Kaldor was invited once more to advise the chancellor of the exchequer.

Labour had issued a manifesto calling for a reindustrialization policy, but events moved against its implementation. Perhaps if the wild card— the inflow of funds for the sale of oil abroad—had come into play, Labour might have been able to hold to something closer to its proclaimed course. The economic situation was much worse than that inherited in 1964, and there was a battle within Whitehall over the industrial policy proposals of Anthony Benn, the minister for industry and a left-winger. Wilson opposed the plans, and all of the proposals were watered down. Whiteley reminds us that Labour was faced with a dilemma, since the interventionist strategy of its manifesto was "an anathema to industrialists and bankers." Putting it into effect would have invited conflict with both industry and the City. Confronting the multinationals in Britain would have put many jobs at risk.[37] Over the years of government service, Kaldor had seen two enemies to enlightenment: first, the City, which had insisted on the protection of the pound against devaluation, especially in the 1960s when it would have done some good; and second, the belief in free trade. He said, "The nemesis of the belief in Free Trade and in free markets, after a century of failures, haunts us still." Historically, Britain had benefited from free trade, but it had meant that new industries could not be established in Britain as they were in protected economies like Germany, France, the United States, and Japan. Instead, British manufacturers had increasingly met tariffs abroad. Arriving at those conclusions, Kaldor, through experiences in the real world, had come a long way from the young man who thought Austria could use a good dose of free trade and laissez-faire.[38]

Beyond Keynesianism

In an important sense, Kaldor had moved beyond the Keynesian concern with full employment. He was calling for fundamental changes in the management of British industry, the British system of education, and the payment of workers in the nationalized industries. He conceded,

> A floating pound may well be an essential prerequisite to maintain an adequate rate of growth of export for Britain. But recent experience has shown that to switch over from a consumption-led growth economy to an export-led growth is not easy, and may require an intermediate stage of relatively high unemployment.[39]

There his argument stood in the 1970s before the onslaught of monetarism and Thatcherism.

NK

CHAPTER NINE

Opposing British Entry into the Common Market

The British take some credit for the idea of a union in Europe, relying on Winston Churchill's address in Zurich in 1946, which urged France and Germany to form something like a United States of Europe.[1] France sought a closer economic integration with the United Kingdom based on Monnet's five-year plan in January 1947, but this was overtaken by the Marshall Plan.[2] U.S. Secretary of State George C. Marshall proposed the Marshall Plan in a speech at Harvard University on June 5, 1947, and it was quickly passed through Congress. The legislation established the Economic Cooperation Administration to administer funds for the reconstruction and recovery of Europe. (Kaldor had expected to help administer the Marshall Plan in Geneva when he accepted the position with the Economic Commission for Europe in 1947.) Through a series of conventions and organizations, six European countries (France, Belgium, The Netherlands, Luxembourg, Italy, and Germany) plus the United Kingdom took steps toward organizing an economic and political union of Western Europe. Then on June 24, 1948, the USSR closed all the road and rail links from East to West Germany. The British Labour party's response was Ernest Bevin's statement, "We are in Berlin as of right. It is our intention to stay there." President Harry Truman sent United States B–29s to maintain the link between Berlin and the West. But the result was that these events shifted attitudes in the West so that West Germany became fully integrated in the European recovery efforts.[3] Finally, the Rome Treaties setting up the Common Market and Euratom were fully realized in 1958, with the Six ratifying the Rome Treaties.

Early negotiations

The Conservative party was in power in England through these early negotiations, and the UK did not sign. Only the Liberal party was in favor of joining during the 1950s. In response to the first internal European tariff reductions, which began to be enforced in 1959, establishing the Common Market with a wall around the Six, the British tried to promote a free trade area among the European countries that were not members of the Six. By the end of 1959 several nations (Austria, Denmark, Norway, Portugal, Sweden, and Switzerland) had joined the UK in setting up the European Free Trade Association. United States President John F. Kennedy proposed a design for an Atlantic Partnership in December 1961, just after Britain under Conservative Prime Minister Harold Macmillan had applied for membership in the market in August. But the United States did support Britain's application, probably in the hope that the UK would be a moderating influence in the customs union. Chancellor Adenauer of West Germany challenged the British entry, saying, "Britain's interests are different from those of Europe." De Gaulle was determined that France should have its own nuclear deterrent, and held that there could be no other possible Europe than a Europe of states no longer dependent on the United States. Kennedy countered, saying, a "coherent policy cannot call for both our military presence and our diplomatic absence" in Europe.[4] Meanwhile, the Six decided as early as 1961 that they would aim for political union, including a common currency.

At this time, while out of power, the Labour party was divided on the issue of the Common Market. At the 1962 party conference, however, Hugh Gaitskell, the current leader of the party, announced his opposition and received a tremendous ovation. Gaitskell worried that Britain might be relegated to the "status of a Texas or a California" within the unified market.[5] Many of the British unions were opposed to entry, as was the left wing of the Labour party. Gaitskell appealed for the continuation of the multiracial Commonwealth and thought a political union with Europe would be "the end of a thousand years of history."[6]

Economists speak out

Kaldor stood with colleagues R.F. Harrod, R.F. Kahn, and H.D. Dickinson in October 1962, in questioning the view that there is "some plain economic advantage in the United Kingdom joining on the terms now proposed by the Government." As economists, they did not want to express an opinion of the political arguments for joining, but they argued that the final choice should not be made on a belief in favorable economic advantages. Kaldor wrote to E.J. Mishan, approving of a radio talk on the subject that Mishan had given. Mishan replied that he was glad to know that Kaldor's opinion concurred with his. Kaldor said, "There are so many muddle headed enthusiasts on this subject, both right and left." He was glad to know that he wasn't alone in "holding out against the current."[7]

Kaldor, Kahn, and Harrod were mainly concerned with the loss of free and unrestricted importation of food and raw materials from the Commonwealth countries. They were responding to the fact that the previous January, EEC had determined the basic features of a common agricultural policy (CAP), with regulations for grains, pig meat, eggs and poultry, fruit, vegetables, and wine. This included setting prices for these commodities that were to be effective throughout the community and that were substantially above world prices.[8]

Kaldor had plenty of company in his appeal for caution. Oxford economist Thomas Balogh also advised the readers of the *Times* that it was "illegitimate" to assume that entering the market would necessarily improve British efficiency. The notion that what is lost by some industries will be gained by others, he called a fallacy. Kaldor added an argument that was to surface academically in his inaugural address at Cambridge four years later: "Economic integration invariably favours the most go-ahead industrial regions which are in any case likely to have the highest rates of expansion. It tends to retard the progress of the less favoured, more slowly expanding areas." He challenged "those who believe that industrial dynamism is just a matter of applying the healthy breeze of competition," reminding them of the 1920s when the opposite happened—the British economy had suffered from world competition. Kaldor did not hold that retarded growth was "bound to happen," only that it might happen. He was impressed with the reserves of manpower available to the Six as compared to Britain, an idea he made use of in his inaugural address, in which the major constraint to growth was alleged to be a shortage of labor. He found "plenty of room for doubt" about the salutary effects of joining and was questioning "the massive, confident, unquestioning optimism" of market advocates.[9]

Nevertheless, the Danes and the British applied, only to have their applications effectively vetoed when, on January 14, 1963, President de Gaulle objected to any enlargement of the community at that time. Negotiations were broken off, and Labour came to power the next year.[10]

Now Labour applies

During the 1964–70 tenure of Wilson's Labour government, in which Kaldor served, there were many external problems that made the venerable old Commonwealth seem less stable than it had been in Gaitskell's day, and that divided the Labour party. The party was split on the Vietnam War; there was a civil war in Nigeria; Rhodesia (now Zambia) became independent and under Ian Smith refused to return to constitutional rule. Obviously, British influence in the Third World was declining, a fact evident since the end of World War II. Harold Wilson and George Brown became determined to consider entering the Common Market, and in 1967 Labour sponsored the UK's second application to become a member of the EEC in spite of some in-party opposition even at the level of the cabinet. This time Britain was joined in its application by Denmark, Norway, and Ireland. Again their entry was opposed by de Gaulle, but their application was only tabled. Two years later, when de Gaulle resigned his presidency in April 1969, the prospects for enlarging the Community improved.[11]

By 1968, three years prior to the UK's final negotiations, the EEC customs union was complete and a common agricultural policy for price levels of agricultural commodities throughout the Common Market agreed upon. No part of the negotiations was as sensitive as that over agriculture. There were riots in France previous to the agreement on CAP and periodic renegotiations.[12] In 1968 the Six had a much larger proportion of their labor force employed in farming than did Great Britain—16 percent compared to Britain's 3 or 4 percent. This created serious political as well as economic problems among the Six and between the Six and Britain.[13]

Before forming the Community, the Six had been the world's largest importer of edible and nonedible farm produce, and CAP decisions inevitably were to affect all of the world. The early attempts at stabilization under the CAP agreement had produced large transfers of cash from one country to another through the Farm Fund. By 1968, when Britain was considering entry, there were massive surpluses in butter and sugar, and the cost of subsidies were many times what had been projected in 1962–63.[14]

Economists would, of course, be aware of relative efficiencies and surpluses; the public, mainly interested in the political opportunities in the market, might not. Nor need industry care particularly about the surpluses and fund transfers, since what industry sought were larger markets for manufactures. By 1967, all British political parties had officially decided that joining might be advantageous to the UK, but the nation and the parties themselves were split.

There were two main issues—the political one and the economic one. In the end, the political one, which offered a new arena for British influence, was overriding. Harry G. Johnson, who, like Kaldor, opposed entry on the terms offered, said flatly that the 1971 vote in Parliament ratifying entry was successful mainly because entry promised the British a position of international political leadership "by substituting the peoples and markets of Europe for her lost colonial empire."[15]

Kaldor and some of his colleagues within both Labour and academe opposed entry on economic grounds or, finally, on the economic terms that were offered. Kaldor's arguments rested in part on his view of the "real world": his knowledge of Europe and the operation of its CAP, of the problems of the international economic and monetary systems, and of Britain's situation domestically. Indeed, Kaldor knew Europe and the international economy better than most, and he took seriously the determination of the Six to persist in the common agricultural policy, to dump any surpluses on world markets, and to form a political and monetary union, including the creation of a single currency.

The further development of the EEC was along a rocky path. Britain was not alone in having exchange rate problems, for both the franc and the mark were adjusted in 1969. It is no wonder that there was a division of opinion in the UK over the wisdom of joining. Kaldor was not convinced that the UK could bend the Common Market to its will, as so many British politicians argued even up to Margaret Thatcher, who in 1991 thought that she could stop the creation of a single currency by shouting "no!" but succeeded only in ending her career as prime minister.[16] Between 1948 and 1972 and even beyond entry, the pot boiled in the UK on whether to enter the EEC and, if so, on what terms. Thirlwall says Kaldor was always skeptical of the political and economic benefits of joining the market.[17]

The public debate by economists of Kaldor's persuasion stuck to economics. Johnson, commenting on the White Paper of 1970, that discussed coming British membership, doubted that the "freeing of trade" would succeed in raising the growth rate as much as predicted. Kaldor chimed in to say that both Johnson and the White Paper had ignored the fact that "the economic argument for integration cuts both ways: we could gain a great deal through faster growth; we could also lose a great deal if integration leads to slower growth."[18]

The CAP issue

Throughout the spring of 1970, Kaldor continued to oppose entering the market. A paper he read to the International Press Institute in Paris in January was published in the *New Statesman* in April alerting the British people to "Europe's agricultural disarray." The cost of maintaining CAP had risen from one to six billion dollars in just ten years. Kaldor found CAP misconceived in seeking self-sufficiency and uniform pricing and insisted that Britain would pay two ways—in higher prices and in net transfers to the Farm Fund. Furthermore, he argued, CAP denies the less developed countries markets for their goods and limits growth of their purchasing power and consequently their demand for the industrial products of Europe. Finally, CAP makes the distribution of real incomes more regressive, since poor people spend a larger proportion of their income on food. In fact, said Kaldor, the Common Market's CAP was identical to the British Corn Laws adopted after Waterloo and abandoned in 1846 only after a "tremendous amount of intellectual agitation" generated by British economist David Ricardo. Kaldor concluded that CAP does not serve the object of European integration, that it maintains inefficient agriculture artificially through high prices, that it wastes resources, and that it raises the price of food unnecessarily to the urban consumer. Since the British population is mainly urban, this was a telling argument. He concluded that CAP limits export earnings of overseas countries and the rate of development of the rest of the world and ultimately of Europe itself; and that it imposes a growing and increasingly intolerable burden on both consumers and taxpayers. He thought CAP as constituted made it difficult if not impossible for Britain to join the market.[19]

CAP is enormously more complex today, but its essential outlines remain: prices are allowed to fluctuate within narrow limits and *intervention* (buying and storing arrangements) comes into play when EC prices are too low; commodities not sold within the market are sold on the world market through subsidies called *export restitutions*. Thus farmers are subsidized on a per unit rather than an income basis. The economic problems that arise include continuing surpluses that are expensive to store; tensions between the Common Market and producers that are now excluded (the Third World, the United States, and some Commonwealth countries). Some of the social problems generated are that the benefits help rich more than poor farmers and declining agricultural labor opportunities create special problems. Finally, within the market, the common policy is not "common" in that special "green rates" for individual countries are made through special monetary arrangements. These special arrangements were initiated mainly because of fluctuating exchange rates within the market during the 1970s and 1980s.[20]

Economic growth rates of the Common Market countries slowed down appreciably after 1970. Kaldor's argument that EEC had put a block on economic growth for the whole world with its CAP has some explanatory value. As for the future, the 1990 negotiations for the General Agreement on Trade and Tariffs (GATT) foundered on the demands by the United States and other primary producing countries for a lowering of tariffs, including EEC's tariffs and subsidies on agricultural products. Negotiations continued into 1992 with something close to a trade war being initiated by a frustrated United States in November 1992.[21]

Conservatives follow through

The Conservatives won the June 18, 1970, election, replacing Labour but continuing the effort to join the EEC. Kaldor, in turn, continued to berate those who believed that entering EEC would solve Britain's economic problems. He challenged Christopher Mayhew's claim that since real wages had been rising faster in the Six than in Britain, joining would cause British real wages to rise faster, too. Kaldor considered it an unsettled question whether productivity, employment levels, real wages, and profits might shrink after joining. He reiterated the argument that there was no guarantee that they would rise.[22]

Apparently Kaldor won his point that CAP would be costly, but he had not defeated the optimism of those who thought there were long-term advantages in joining, especially for industry. The Conservative White Paper in March 1971 claimed that there would be dynamic effects to joining and participating in the much larger "home market." Kaldor did not rule this possibility out but said that the key was the growth of exports of manufacturing and that this could be easily offset by growth of imports from other countries within the market. In another article in the *New Statesman,* Kaldor reminded readers that, in the 1960s, Britain might have equalled the growth rates of Germany, for example, by adjusting exchange rates and promoting export industries. But that was no longer possible. Analyzing costs and benefits, Kaldor concluded that, because EEC industrial protection was low while agricultural protection was high, Britain by joining would find that British manufacturing goods would purchase 20 to 30 percent less in foodstuffs. Furthermore, once within the market, Britain could not count on regaining competitiveness through devaluation. He added that if the terms of entry could be those for entering EFTA, these objections would not stand. His arguments in 1971 focused mainly on the terms of entry that were under negotiation.[23] But his and some fellow economists' warnings were lost in the wilderness of optimism.

On monetary union

There was another matter worrying Kaldor in the spring of 1971. He was convinced that monetary union could not occur without political union and political union would mean that individual governments would not be free to use economic policies such as devaluation to improve the status of their economies or to solve problems of unemployment. Parliament under both Labour and Conservative governments had struggled with the fact that parts of the United Kingdom had become deindustrialized. Kaldor pleaded that the UK might be the North Ireland of the European community. As he had argued in his inaugural address at Cambridge in 1966, growth was cumulative. Investment occurred where there was success rather than where there were unemployed resources.[24] The *Economist* editors ridiculed Kaldor's analysis which had been republished within a book entitled *Destiny or Delusion.* The *Economist* termed Kaldor's reservations, "Dr. Kaldor's cure for a cold: why, just stay outside." This exchange came in March 1971 at a time when negotiations had nearly broken down over what the British should pay to the community fund during the transition.[25]

Economist editors were particularly derogatory about Kaldor's fears of monetary union, calling the Werner report, the latest attempt at a plan for a union, a "museum piece." Kaldor answered the Economist's review, saying, "I fear you are misleading your readers in suggesting that the idea of a monetary union is now dead...." Kaldor referred to the recently issued White Paper, which made it clear that the UK had accepted the "general commitment of the community progressing towards full economic and monetary union."[26] He responded to the "stay outside" accusation, saying that there would be no economic objection to reviving de Gaulle's suggestion that Britain be "inside" for industry and "outside for agriculture."[27]

New monetary developments

Early in May, 1971, West Germany and the Netherlands decided to allow their currencies to float against the dollar. The Times reported Kaldor as being able to believe that these changes in Europe might be the means either of getting better terms for entry or for a unity of the EEC and EFTA under British leadership. Kaldor's main objection was now to Heath's "timetable," which he considered hurried. Immediately after the European adoption of the float, Kaldor was reported in the Times as having counseled that Britain should wait and see what happened, since the ability to float rates within the Community would remove most of his objections to CAP and also allay his fears of Britain's becoming the North Ireland of the Community.[28]

Kaldor demurred, saying that the Times report was not quite correct: while the floating of the mark opened up possibilities, it did not remove all of his objections.[29] Kaldor again questioned the apparent haste with which Heath was proceeding toward accepting the onerous, it seemed to Kaldor, terms offered. More than anything else, Kaldor was arguing for time, against capitulation. His view was that France was mainly responsible for the objectionable terms, an opinion shared by Harry G. Johnson. Johnson wrote that the EEC, led by France, took advantage of the "obligation not to rock the boat of European trade policy imposed on the British by their desire to win Common Market entry"; France proceeded to conclude other separate arrangements with Mediterranean countries.[30]

Should the populace be consulted?

Besides the issue of the monetary union, which the Economist had thought so silly, the question arose of whether it was appropriate for the Heath government to act on behalf of the UK without consulting the voters. On May 17, 1971, Labour MP Anthony Wedgwood Benn said that he thought not, since, "the European decision is a massive and historic one that will bind future parliaments in perpetuity."[31] It was argued that the ordinary way to get such a mandate was to dissolve the government and to have an election on the issue but since this was not to be done, a hue and cry arose for a referendum.

Nevertheless, the Heath government went full speed ahead. In July it issued a White Paper on the Common Market which Kaldor attacked as a vague, misleading document.[32] The question then arose as to whether the terms accepted by the Conservatives would have been accepted by Labour in 1967. The *Economist* reported that the Labour parliamentary party voted against entry on the present terms,[33] though the party was split. Michael Foot and Harold Wilson had opposed the terms. Denis Healey was for them. But Lord George Brown said in the House of Lords that Labour would have accepted the terms negotiated by Geoffrey Rippon. Kaldor thought the terms would not have been acceptable.[34]

The end of Bretton Woods?

The next major development of 1971 was the stunning decision in August by Richard Nixon, President of the United States to float the dollar. The *Times* commissioned several articles on the international monetary crisis, among them Kaldor's three entitled "Bretton Woods and After," in which he brought his historical and theoretical knowledge to bear on the problems. Essentially, he argued that given the unwillingness of the Japanese to revalue the yen and the tendency of the Germans to drag their feet in revaluing the mark, Nixon had had no choice other than floating the dollar. Actually, a new basis for international liquidity was needed to replace the role the dollar had assumed after World War II. Kaldor suggested that thirty commodities, of which gold could be one, could serve the purpose formerly served by gold and the dollar's fixed relation to it.[35]

EEC in spite of all

The movement toward entry into the Common Market was unphased by these domestic debates and world events. Kaldor and Johnson sent a questionnaire to six hundred members of the University Association of Teachers in Economics. The *Times* reported that a narrow majority of the 296 economists who were willing to sign their names to pro- or anti-market letters challenged the idea that the market would bring economic benefits, including a majority of professors at Cambridge and LSE. Kaldor fought on, challenging those writers to the *Times* who thought the mere joining of the market would bring full employment to Britain.[36]

On February 17, 1972, Parliament, under Heath's guidance, voted on the issue of joining the Common Market. The vote was an affirmative majority of eight, support having declined from a majority of 112 in October of 1971. Kaldor noted that public opinion had been consistently in favor of joining in 1967 and perhaps through 1969, but that support had been dwindling. He laid this not to public ignorance but to growing public understanding and awareness. He considered the terms imposed on Britain "humiliating."[37]

With such a division of opinion, the issue of having a referendum gathered strength even though the crucial decision had been made. Kaldor noted that referendums had been advocated before by two Conservatives—Earl Balfour and Stanley Baldwin when they were in opposition. One could not consider the suggestion of a referendum "alien to British traditions" as Sir John Foster claimed.[38]

The French were having a referendum in April on the issue of British entry, and Kaldor wrote two more letters of support for a British referendum.[39] Within the Labour party the division of opinion continued. In his anti-market stance Kaldor had, since 1967, been at odds with official party policy. At the most recent Brighton Conference, the party had supported the joining of EEC by a vote of five to one. It was only the parliamentary Labour party that was split on the issue.[40]

Kaldor defended the openness of the Labour party's internal disagreement, noting that the promarketeers included "at least 70 percent of the party's intellectuals and 80 percent of my personal friends." In challenging the Labour MPs who were promarket, he was merely reminding them that the basis of Labour support comes not from intellectuals but from organized workers who are *still* overwhelmingly against the Market, as the recent Harris poll has shown."[41] However, Kaldor acted as a peacemaker within Labour, defending both Benn who was pro-referendum and Dick Taverne who was promarket.[42]

The year 1972 brought other developments as well. In June, the decision was made to float the pound and to engage in an incomes policy. After two years of trying a traditional, laissez-faire approach to the domestic economy, Edward Heath's government dramatically changed direction in the face of rising inflation, unemployment, and balance of payments deficits. The incomes policy was a voluntary pay and prices policy. Kaldor expressed support and was quoted as saying that Heath "could usher in a period of social and economic progress exceeding in scale and duration that of any previous era of British history."[43]

Meanwhile, the movement toward the Common Market rolled along. In Paris, the Heath government agreed to "an economic and monetary union to be completed in all its states 'not later than December 31, 1990.'" Kaldor continued to believe that a monetary union required the creation of a central European government, for presumably the national governments would be deprived of the power to pursue policies of full employment individually. He feared a return to "*laisser faire* capitalism of the mid-nineteenth century, with governments reduced to the role of passive onlookers of market forces, offering rewards of wealth and prosperity to some and the misery of mass unemployment to others—with the sure prospect of revolution in the countries at the losing end of this game." He admitted that the official answer to this was that the Community would use its Regional Fund to finance special expenditures in lagging areas. But he believed that "Whereas the successful management of a national economy requires the simultaneous use of both the fiscal instrument (deficit budgeting) and the exchange rate instrument (floating rates or devaluation), monetary and economic union denies the use of either."[44]

The British Representatives signed the Treaty of Accession for joining in 1972, and British membership in the Common Market became effective in 1973. According to Geoffrey Parker, Britain obtained some concessions, including a five-year transition period and temporary trading arrangements for certain products of the Commonwealth, but otherwise, "This country accepted the Treaty of Rome as it stood, something which had appeared quite out of the question only a decade previously." Parker views the 1970s as a period during which Britain was transforming itself from a world power into a European power.[45]

Labour returned to Number 10 Downing Street in 1974, and in keeping with its pledge, held the referendum on British membership in the EEC. The 1975 referendum vote which settled the issue was two to one in favor.

Was it right to join?

The economic merits of entry have continued to be debated, especially if one takes into account Thatcher's attitude in 1991 toward the issue of a common currency. She called for a referendum on that issue, naming her critics "headless chickens" and Prime Minister Major "arrogant and wrong" for refusing to grant a referendum.[46] Indeed a poll had indicated that 55 percent of the British opposed the common currency.[47] When the EC held the Maastricht summit in December 1991, John Major won the right to give Britain, alone among the EC members, the right to refuse to join in the single currency.[48] January 1, 1999, is to be the deadline for "bringing in the ecu," with or without Britain. Ironically, in the period after British entry into the Common Market, slow growth, not only for Britain, but also for the community followed recurring international monetary crises.[49] However, as Harry G. Johnson said, from the beginning, the political advantages of being a part of EEC were widely accepted.

Although many economists have tried, it is probably impossible to assess the value or costs of Britain's entry into the Community. Kaldor did not take an active part in this, but the Cambridge Economic Policy Group did, calling into question in the 1980s the relationship of the UK to the EEC and the rationale for continued participation of the UK in the Common Market given the then current conditions.[50]

Ali M. El-Agraa of the University of Leeds asked the question in 1984 "Has membership of the European Communities been a disaster for Britain?" because he thought many economists and politicians thought so. His answer was that Britain's economic problems, which were severe during the ten-year period of membership, were "deep-seated." He thought that membership had helped ease the situation.[51] Richard Pomfret of the Johns Hopkins University Bologna Center is critical of El-Agraa's attempts to make counterfactual comparisons. His conclusion is that British membership is an "emotional issue," but that, in regard to the economic aspects of the problem, El-Agraa had failed to shed any light. What had actually happened was that after the British entry, real income growth rates of both the UK and the EEC Six had fallen, so that El-Agraa was arguing that UK growth rates would have fallen even more if Britain had not joined the community. Pomfret says flatly that El-Agraa's method and assumptions make his argument "totally unconvincing." The decade of the seventies was turbulent for all but, during the seventies, Britain had developed a major new resource, North Sea oil, which should have placed the economy in a more favorable position.[52]

The still burning issue is that of proposed monetary integration. While there is some disagreement on the economic meaning of this, let us take El-Agraa's prescription that monetary integration means: (1) an explicit harmonization of monetary policies, (2) a common pool of foreign exchange reserves, and (3) a single central bank.[53] Because of these requirements, Kaldor thought political union was a necessary prerequisite of monetary integration, but he was not for it. Thirlwall confirms this.[54]

The 1970s had provided a nightmarish sequence of international monetary crises. Harry Johnson, who had long supported the floating of exchange rates, said: "My personal view is that the pound should have been floated in 1964, or at latest 1966, and I have no quarrel with the June 1972 decision to float as such...." He accused the British of choosing ''independence of and not interdependence with Europe'' in her insistence on continuing to float the pound after her entry.[55]

The question of whether to go along with the seeming inevitable movement toward monetary integration was still plaguing the British. In October 1992, drastic measures were called for by Prime Minister Major to support the pound. Both Italy and the UK were forced to withdraw, at least temporarily, from the European exchange mechanism. Julian Barnes likened Thatcher's position in 1991 to St. Augustine's cry ''Give me chastity and continency but not yet," accusing her of desiring economic and monetary union "but not yet."[56] Like many issues that Kaldor raised, the economic controversy over British entry into the EEC and into the European Monetary Union still hangs fire long after his death.

NK

CHAPTER TEN

Exposing Monetarism

Before it was called monetarism, the quantity theory of money was a favored doctrine of pre-Keynesian and Austrian economics. (See chapter note 10.1, Political economics of the quantity theory of money.) By monetarism I mean the doctrine of the quantity theory of money that says: *Because of* the stable velocity of circulation, increasing supplies of money *cause* prices to rise. Early monetarists were assuming that full employment was a natural condition, or at least that a tendency toward full employment was a natural condition, or, as later monetarists argued, that there is a natural rate of unemployment that cannot successfully, i.e., in the long term be changed by fiscal policy.[1]

The Treasury view and the Keynesian perspective

In the United Kingdom monetarism is tied to what is called the "Treasury view."[2] Historically, monetarism was also related to the gold standard and the gold exchange standard, a system of fixing exchange rates to a stable gold price. Monetarism is both a theory or explanation of working relationships in monetary aspects of the economy and a prescription for policy. In the twentieth century Britain has long debated the efficacy of monetarism through its system of blue ribbon committees that took evidence from economists and representatives of banking and other affected groups. In the 1920s the Cunliffe Committee recommended the return to the gold standard, a policy subsequently pursued by Conservatives and Labour alike with disastrous results. As late as June 1931, the Macmillan Committee of Inquiry, of which Keynes was a member, favored remaining on the gold standard. Nevertheless, Britain was forced off the gold standard later that year on September 21. When on the gold standard, the internal supply of a country's money is dictated by the balance of payments, which is what binds the gold standard to monetarism and to the quantity theory of money. At an earlier date, Keynes had branded the gold standard as "a policy which the country would never permit if it knew what was being done."[3]

Keynes's *General Theory* had provided an alternative to the Treasury view and thus to monetarism both in the theoretical explanation and in the prescriptions for policy. But monetarism still had powerful friends, especially in the City and among the Conservative parliamentary party. In 1957, while Macmillan was prime minister, another grand inquiry was called to review monetary policies. Kaldor testified that while monetarist policies had seemingly worked during the Korean War boom year, they had not worked after the balance of payments crisis in February 1955. He added, "Opinion was fairly general that there was something wrong with the way monetary controls operate."[4]

Lord Radcliffe was chairman of the 1957 inquiry. He was a man Kaldor admired and one with whom he had worked amicably on the Royal Commission on Taxation and Profits and Income in the early 1950s. Radcliffe's Committee on the Working of the Monetary System had only eight members, including two economists, Professors Richard Sayers and Alec Cairncross, and six distinguished public figures. Though Kaldor was not a member, he was invited to submit evidence to the committee.[5] Kaldor had said that he would not give evidence unless requested.[6] He was sent a list of questions, but instead of answering them he presented his views in what he considered a more organized sequence. He apologized for putting forth "a paper devoted to elementary propositions" but argued that it was necessary for a basic understanding and thus an evaluation of methods. His first proposition was that there is no direct relationship between the amount of money in circulation, regardless of how one defines "money supply," and the amount of money spent on goods and services per unit of time. This is because there are no valid grounds for believing that the velocity of circulation is unaffected by changes in the amount of money.[7]

Instead, one must look to the interest rate to effect changes in the demand for goods and services when there are changes in the money supply.[8] That is, the changes in the demand for goods and services are related to the changes in the interest rate, which may have been affected by changes in the money supply. This was, of course, the Keynesian view.

Kaldor thought frequent changes in interest rates were thoroughly undesirable, and that seeking stable prices had its own dangers, since stable prices are "only consistent with low rates of profit which may be insufficient to maintain the inducement to invest."[9] Indeed, he thought both monetary and credit policy "at best, a crude and blunt instrument for controlling inflationary and deflationary tendencies in the economy."[10] Kaldor analyzed the possible sources of instability other than changes in the supply of money, targeting excessive pressure from resources, including a shortage of labor such as the UK was then experiencing; unbalanced development between different sectors of the economy; wage inflation that outran growth in productivity and total production; and fluctuations in investment, particularly in stocks (inventories).[11] This again was the Keynesian rather than the monetarist approach to comprehending instability, including inflation. When the Radcliffe Committee reported in 1959, their report was unanimous and said simply that while the supply of money is not an unimportant quantity, it is only part of a wider structure of liquidity in the economy.[12] Roy Harrod noted "a certain family resemblance on critical issues" between Kaldor's memorandum and the Radcliffe report.[13]

While praising the Radcliffe Committee's rejection of the orthodox view of the relation between the money supply and the level of demand, Kaldor wished that the report had made "more explicit" reference to economic theory. Still, the report had denied that there was some normal velocity of money and that changes in the supply of money had any causal significance.[14]

Monetarist counter-revolution

Though the Treasury view was never considered quite dead in Britain, Kaldor was probably surprised when monetarism became once more, in the campaign of Milton Friedman's "counter-revolution," a serious challenge to Keynesianism. (See chapter note 10.1, Political economics of the quantity theory of money.) Kaldor had, along with other Keynesians, opposed monetarism and the Treasury view at least since embracing the General Theory. To this end in March 1970 he lectured at the University College in London on "the new monetarism," debating the arguments that Friedman had so far put forward.[15] Kaldor cited the "'monetary' counter-revolution" as one which claimed that Keynesianism "had been shunted on to the wrong track." He said, "this new doctrine is assiduously propagated from across the Atlantic by a growing band of enthusiasts, combining the fervour of early Christians with the suavity and selling power of a Madison Avenue executive." And that it was "very largely the product of one economist with exceptional powers of persuasion and propagation: Professor Milton Friedman of Chicago."[16] Kaldor challenged the theory so propagated and the statistical studies offered to support it. He didn't think the time-lag argument, that prices change after some lapsed period of changes in money supply, was proof of any causal relationship; he questioned the idea that changes in the money supply were exogenous in a credit system, that is, outside the functioning of the economy itself; he showed that a stable velocity of circulation could be compatible with other explanations than the one proffered by the monetarists. Kaldor did not object to Friedman's prescription that the best thing to do is to secure a steady expansion of x percent a year in the money supply. He just doubted that the object was attainable by the monetary authorities. If it were, it would mean: (1) that all of the other economic problems had already been solved, such as stop-go cycles emanating from abroad or from the private sector; and (2) that successful fiscal policy or income policies guaranteed a reasonable relationship to the rate of growth of productivity.[17]

Thus Kaldor gave his answers even before Friedman made his famous October sortie that same year to London to announce the counter-revolution. In an article appearing in March, which Kaldor had not seen prior to his address, Friedman had denied the alleged tautological aspects of the quantity theory, seeking to escape from tautology by differentiating the nominal and real aspects of the supply of money. However, Friedman had not altered his general view. He reiterated that "substantial changes in prices or nominal income" are "almost invariably" the result of changes in the nominal supply of money.[18]

Debating with Friedman

The debate continued in *Lloyds Bank Review.* Kaldor thought Friedman's way of argument when challenged, was to fail to answer the challenge and instead fall back to some other kind of "evidence."[19] Kaldor wrote to Henry C. Wallich at Yale University that the trouble with Friedman was that "he simply ignores any point of criticism which he is not able to answer. ... He really should not be taken seriously."[20] Another American, Rudolph L. Weissman of W. E. Hutton and Company, wrote to Kaldor that he thought Friedman had so misread the history of the 1920s in the United States as to cast doubt on Friedman's interpretation of the money supply.[21]

In answer to Kaldor's arguments in London, Friedman merely said that he had always known that there were factors other than money that contributed to business fluctuations, and he had always recognized that in the case of a scientific problem, "the final verdict is never in," but he [Friedman] was relying on "qualitative historical circumstances" to prove his point. He stood on his "evidence."[22]

Since Friedman had not attempted to refute any of Kaldor's contentions and had virtually agreed to Kaldor's point that the issue turns on whether money is exogenous or endogenous in character and had rested his case on "empirical evidence," Kaldor spoke to that evidence. He noted that the time-lag argument had been relegated by Friedman to a "suggestive but by no means decisive" status (1964) and then "expunged" in the *Quarterly Journal of Economics* in May 1970 without altering Friedman's confidence in his conclusion that "money exerts an independent influence on income." As to Friedman's alleged evidence that there was essentially the same relation between money and income for the UK before and after World War II and for such various countries as the United States, Yugoslavia, Chile, Japan, and others,[23] Kaldor thought this was nonsense.

Instead, Kaldor pointed out contrary evidence as between Canada and the United States. Indeed, Kaldor found that international comparisons challenged rather than supported the Friedman postulate of a "stable demand function."[24]

John Hicks joined the fray in *Lloyds Bank Review* in an article on monetarism in October, 1975, which prompted Harry G. Johnson to jump in, not so much in support of monetarism but to vent his rage against Hicks's article, which he called "a woeful and unworthy disappointment" supporting "the amateurish views of the Cambridge economic policy group."[25]

Monetarism gathers political strength

Nevertheless, with all the problems in the British and world economies of the 1970s, the monetarist view continued to gather strength in both economic and political circles. Margaret Thatcher was elected in 1979 partly on a monetarist platform, and her government assembled still another committee of inquiry on monetary policy. Kaldor gave evidence before it in July 1980.[26] Kaldor first called attention to the possible conflict among the objectives of full employment, a satisfactory balance of payments, absence of inflation, and a high rate of economic growth, noting his opposition to the Thatcher Government's "over-riding priority to reducing inflation."[27] This policy, which he thought mistaken, was often claimed to be justified by the tenets of monetarism, so he centered his attack there. He argued that the monetarist model is essentially the Walrasian one, which assumes a finite number of products and services that are traded in perfect markets under conditions of perfect competition where one of the commodities serves as money—for example, gold. While all other commodities trade at the "market-clearing" price, the price of the commodity money is related to its quantity. Thus an increase in commodity money lowers its price, and that is the same as raising the prices of all other commodities. Modern monetarists, said Kaldor, follow Walras in three assumptions: of the self-regulating functions of markets; of the essential identity or no important differences between the commodity-money and the credit-money economy; and of the belief that a successful control of the growth of money supply will *in itself* moderate inflation. In this context a modern monetarist would deny that wage changes can cause absolute price changes.

Kaldor attacked these assumptions. He argued that the assumption of the self-regulating nature of economies failed to recognize the differences between demand and cost inflation. In the Walrasian model, inflation can occur only as a result of excess demand, whereas in the real world many instances of rising prices of goods and services are the consequences of rising costs, including wage costs. The second assumption implies that money has an exogenous origin so that the quantity available is independent of the demand for it, which can be true only of commodity money. However, in the real world of credit money, the increase in money is prompted by a demand for it. The third assumption, which assumes that control of the money supply can control inflation, implies a stable relation between the supply of money and the velocity of its circulation. This requires a degree of control over the money supply that the banking system does not have in the credit economy, because liquidity demands must be met. It also implies a stable velocity of circulation that does not exist.[28] The rest of Kaldor's argument had to do with the direct and indirect banking operations and the effects of the government's strategy of monetarism on the demand for labor, workers' bargaining power, and its negative effects on industrial capacity in Britain.[29]

On the basis of statistical evidence, Kaldor said, you could not establish whether changes in the value of national income were caused by changes in the money supply or vice versa.[30] Examining both the Keynesian and non-Keynesian definitions of the supply of money, he concluded that the "supply side of money" was represented by non-Keynesians as a quantity and by Keynesians as the bank interest rate which determines the cost of credit.[31] Clearly, interest rates are the best representation because they indicate some measure of liquidity. Then he attacked "the myth of the time-lag" by which monetarists claim that changes in the money supply require some time to affect inflation.[32] The intricacy of his argument, which was woven into the fabric of statistics—he had help here from the Department of Applied Economics, Cambridge—cannot be easily summarized, but there is little doubt that it influenced any uncommitted British economist who read it, though not Margaret Thatcher.[33]

For thirty years, Kaldor had argued consistently that the quantity theory of money was bankrupt as economic theory and policy. He consistently insisted that the demand for money had always been "a *reflection* of the demand for commodities, and not the source of that demand," and that monetarism was based on two fallacies: (1) that the money supply of each economy is exogenously determined by the monetary authority, and (2) that the "public's *demand* for money, as a proportion of income, is a stable one, not much influenced by changes of interest rates and other factors." On such fallacious propositions, the monetarists had concluded that inflation could be cured by the monetary authority's restricting the money supply.[34] The Treasury view, propped up by the monetarists, became a popular idea within newspaper and political circles. With Thatcher in office, restrictive monetary policy became the economic policy of the UK for a time. Kaldor claimed that monetarism caused Britain's economy to perform far worse in 1979–81 than in 1929–32. The next sections follow these events.

Prelude to monetarist policy

Before 1970, British postwar governments were essentially Keynesian, but with conservative, "City" overtones when it came to facing negative balances of payments. When Edward Heath came to Number 10 Downing Street in 1970, he inherited a surplus in the balance of payments from Harold Wilson's retiring Labour government, but all the other problems of slow growth and lagging exports were still there and the North Sea oil had not yet changed the picture. Heath adopted a less regulated approach and cut taxes, including the elimination of the Selective Employment Tax. He canceled Labour's efforts to control prices through wage restraint and curtailed social welfare costs on the assumption that these policies would create a climate for increased investment, greater efficiency, and higher levels of employment. His strategy included hastening entry into the Common Market to insure markets for industry and thus to foster investment. Instead, within the first two years of his government, the balance of payments surplus was wiped out, inflation accelerated, labor unrest grew, and deficits both nationally and in the balance of payments exploded. In 1972, Heath made an about-face; he floated the pound and introduced an incomes policy. As we have seen, Kaldor applauded this new approach, which limited wage increases *and* price increases through a voluntary agreement among the government, the Trades Union Congress (TUC), and the Confederation of British Industry (CBI). Kaldor was quoted as saying, "It is far superior to anything ever thought out during the whole administration of Harold Wilson and far more radically socialist in character." However, he added that it must be perceived as fair to all in order to be successful.[35] In November of 1972, Kaldor emphasized that the people of Britain would respond only if they "could be satisfied that the necessary sacrifices were equitably shared."[36] By March of 1973, he was completely disillusioned when the government

proposed to rein in consumption by increasing taxes paid by wage earners and reducing taxes on companies. Kaldor suggested an excess profits
tax as a counter-inflation policy in order to achieve a balanced budget
and a fair incomes and price policy[37] and presented his ideas at a hearing
before a House of Commons panel. Joe Rogaly of the *Times* called it an
"angry paper flamboyantly presented." Kaldor was opposing the
government's "tax credit system" as a "monstrosity."[38] All this occurred
after the monetarist counter-revolution had been declared by Friedman,
but before monetarism had become government policy in either the
United States or in Britain.

In February of 1974, when an election was called for by Heath, the
Times in an editorial accused the left-wing members of the National
Union of Mineworkers (NUM) of purposely breaking the incomes policy
of the Heath government and indeed of breaking the government itself.
The floating of the pound had failed to cure the balance of payments
problem, and a new crisis was in the offing. Inflation was rampant. The
Coal Board had placed the miners on a three-day week in December, and
pay negotiations had been unsuccessful, so that the miners had struck.
There were various proposals for settling the strike, such as paying the
miners extra wages through the CBI rather than having the governmental
Coal Board pay.[39]

The *Times* asked, "Where did the idea of the industrialists' scheme to
buy off the miners originate?" and concluded that it might have been
from a letter written by the "prolific Professor Nicholas Kaldor," though
Kaldor demurred.[40] In an editorial entitled "Britain's Credit in the
World," the *Times* said the election was the first in British history to be
forced by an industrial dispute. The angry editorial called for a vote for
Conservatives, since, inevitably, foreign borrowing would be necessary
to the next government and because "bankers do not trust Labour Governments" since Labour is pro-Israel and pro-trade union and causes "the
world" to believe that "there is a British national commitment to inflation."[41]

Kaldor answered in kind: "You totally ignore the fact that it has been
successive Tory Governments, not Labour Governments, which have reduced this country to this miserable state of dependence on foreign borrowing and which has caused our international prestige to sink to the
point where we are habitually compared with the Turks in the nineteenth
century as the sick man of Europe." The cause was the "financial profli-
gacy" of Tory governments that brought on the balance of payments
crises of 1956 (Eden), 1961 (Macmillan), 1964 (Douglas-Home), and 1973–74
(Heath), all because of "the Tories' habitual dislike of taxation and their
addiction to deficit finance." He pointed out that Labour under Wilson
had handed the present government a balance of payments surplus of

1,000 million pounds. This had been squandered, and now the Tory government was running a deficit of 3,000 million pounds in the last quarter of 1973 and even higher at his writing—4,500 million pounds perhaps? Kaldor argued that Labour's Roy Jenkins could correct this, as he had in 1968–70.[42] Frank Hahn, also of Cambridge University, chimed in, saying, "If the extreme left has gained influence in Labour affairs, so has the extreme right." He claimed, correctly as it turned out, that if Labour were elected, Denis Healey "would be under strong pressure to produce a large budget surplus and reduction in the money supply . . . ," adding, "The conversion of some of the most influential of Labour economists to the doctrines of Professor Friedman is almost complete."[43] Kaldor answered his colleague: "If Professor Hahn were in the least familiar with my writings he could not possibly attribute to me the 'extreme right wing' view of wishing to discipline the unions by means of more unemployment and by using the tax weapon to bring this unemployment about." The problem, as Kaldor saw it, was that Tory governments attempted to compensate for unemployment by consumption-led booms engineered through tax reductions, when what was needed was greater exports.[44]

Though the election was for a time in doubt, Labour formed the government in 1974, still thirty seats short of a majority in Parliament. Kaldor was asked to act as an adviser to Chancellor Denis Healey. Lord Balogh was a working peer in the House of Lords and minister of state in the Energy Department, so that the famed B and K of the earlier Labour government were back. Anthony Shrimsley of the *Times* remarked on Kaldor's appointment that Healey had found the man "to help him soak the rich—and maybe some other people as well." Shrimsley claimed that Kaldor had "become more left-wing since he left Whitehall," four years earlier (1970).[45] Apparently Kaldor was paid 14,000 pounds annually for his advice.[46]

One wag was quoted as saying, "The only benefit of the change of Government is that we have been spared [Balogh's and Kaldor's] contributions" to letters to the *Times*.[47]

The Cambridge debate

Besides the issue of monetarism, there was a public argument over policy dubbed by the *Economist* as the "Cambridge debate," a debate between a new Cambridge school led by Kaldor and Robert Neild and the old Cambridge school led by Richard Kahn and Michael Posner. The *Economist* claimed that the new chancellor of the exchequer, Healey, had been told by Kaldor and Neild that the balance of payments was a reflection of the budget deficit, and that he should tax away "the idle savings of the

rich."[48] (See chapter note 10.2, Cambridge Economic Policy Group [CEPG].)
What emerged was truly a post-Keynesian debate. The issue was not whether but how to manage an economy. Kaldor was recognized as a pioneer of the New School, but Kahn and Posner confined themselves to a discussion of the views of Robert Neild, Wynne Godley, and Francis Cripps who became identified as members the Cambridge Economic Policy Group (CEPG). While welcoming the effort of reappraisal of policy, Kahn and Posner challenged the assumptions of the CEPG, fearing that increasing taxes would lead to a greater recession than necessary. They said, "Our complaint is that the New School often seem indifferent about the proportions in which personal consumption and company investment are reduced in the deflationary process . . . ." They added that where there was any bias, it seemed to them that the New School was in favor of personal consumption more than investment. The Old School said that Keynesian orthodoxy was not at fault, but that too high a proportion of national output was in consumption and too low an amount in investment. On the other hand, the Old School was less pessimistic than the new and believed that if the investment climate were right that business would respond with more investment.[49]

The *Economist* thought that the two views could be reconciled if it were noticed that the New School pointed to "the longer-term trend position" of the economy, while the Old School drew attention "to the detours on the way, in which we are in fact always stuck." They reminded readers of Keynes's saying that in the long run we are all dead. However, the *Economist* thought both schools were wrong, the solution instead being to index incomes with no rise in real income, to cut public spending "by a lot" and taxation "by much more," and then to go for economic growth; there should also be tighter controls on the money supply.[50]

Refuge in the House of Lords

Although allegedly and initially influential in selling the Labour ministers on export-led growth, Kaldor asked to be relieved of his post as of August 2, 1976. He was sixty-eight and the current president of the Royal Economic Society.[51] (That was also the year Harold Wilson resigned as head of the Labour party and passed the wand to James Callaghan.) Kaldor left "because he was very disillusioned with the orthodox policymaking at the time."[52] His retirement from active government service allowed him to rejoin the board of Investing in Success Equities, to enter the House of Lords, for which he had been eligible since 1974, and to resume letter writing a year before Labour Chancellor Healey was to resort to monetarism.[53] In October 1976, Kaldor wrote that he thought the trade and budget deficits were surely related, and that years of devaluation had failed to prevent a continual shrinkage of net exports of manufactures, thus publicly aligning himself with the New School of Cambridge.[54]

In November 1976, Kaldor delivered his maiden speech in the House of Lords. (See chapter note 10.3, House of Lords.) Another international credit crisis was at hand. The petrodollar surplus associated since 1974 with the quadrupling of the price of oil by the Middle Eastern producers (OPEC) continued to plague the international credit system. Country after country was being forced into borrowing, and the International Monetary Fund was counseling deflationary measures, which, Kaldor argued, merely passed the buck to another country by diminishing trade.[55]

After further difficulties, Healey in 1977 proposed income tax cuts to stimulate the economy and increase employment levels. This was, of course,ilar to the earlier policies of the Heath government and signaled the fact that Healey preferred income tax cuts to cuts in value-added taxes. The Labour government under Callaghan then abandoned its policy of keeping the pound steady against the dollar and allowed it to rise. Ironically, this was the year the wild card of North Sea oil came into play and the British balance of payments made an "astonishing turnaround." (See chapter note 8.1, Politics and North Sea oil.) In December 1977 Kaldor was quoted as thinking that the Labour government had "fallen prey to monetarist hawks." Allowing the pound to appreciate in order to avoid an inflow of foreign currency had hurt British manufacturing exporters. Kaldor is quoted as asking, "Why worry about the money supply when the economy is stagnant?"[56] He was branded a "protectionist" because he wanted to protect British manufactures from West German and Japanese imports. He countered, "Free trade is fine if you are on the winning side. But if your industry is suffering from lower productivity there is little chance it will catch up by being exposed to foreign competition." For Britain's lower productivity he blamed British management for failing to establish an employer-labor consensus, which he thought characterized the West German, Japanese, and United States industries. He is quoted as calling it "crazy" that the Labour government had followed monetarist policies that trade off expansion of the economy "for the alleged benefits of pleasing the International Monetary Fund."[57] However, in a picture accompanying an article entitled "Kaldor attacks Healey strategy on sterling" the two men are together, smiling. Kaldor, still critical of Healey's dropping the policy of export-led growth in favor of an appreciating pound, said, "There will be a flood of imports into this country, and there will be nothing to stop them. British industry—instead of being stagnant—will just go down."[58] The Labour government lasted until 1979, with Kaldor continuing his public pressure to restore the policy of export-led growth as an alternative to deflationary policies. Healey was not listening.

In retrospect, Kaldor always reminded his audience that post-World War II monetarism was first adopted in Britain under a Labour government, sometime in 1977. He did not think that made it any more palatable.[59]

Incomes policy as an alternative to monetarism

As early as the summer of 1950, Kaldor was arguing the case for a permanent incomes policy. In a memorandum to Sir Stafford Cripps, he pointed out that, "The need for income restraint in a full employment economy is a permanent need and not a temporary one," requiring a system of flexible and continuing restraints on both wages and dividends, which he outlined.[60] (See chapter note 10.4, Incomes policy.) In 1978, Kaldor was still talking incomes policies as a means of avoiding inflation and as an alternative to the deflationary policies so desired by the monetarists. He thought social stability might be at stake. In an exchange that also involved Hayek and George Fink, Kaldor reminded *Times* readers that it was not the influx of Jews into Germany that had been responsible for the rise of Hitler, but the increase in unemployment from one million in 1928 to seven million in 1932. This extraordinary rise in unemployment was due, said Kaldor, to the monetarist policies of the German chancellor, Dr. Bruning.[61]

Arguments to the contrary notwithstanding, monetarism was gaining not only attention but also support in the *Times*. Tim Congdon, author of a booklet *Chile: the Rule of the Chicago Boys*, defended the record of the monetarists in Chile.[62] Dudley Seers, a fellow of the Institute of Development Studies, while admitting that in the five years of the Pinochet regime inflation had been slowed and foreign payments had been balanced, noted that there were costs. Foreign capital had not been attracted even though wages were low, and the economy was so weak in Chile that Friedman was "now disclaiming responsibility."[63] Congdon replied that at least Chile's credit worthiness had been restored.[64] Kaldor reminded them both that Chile was a dictatorship employing secret police and detention camps; strikes were illegal and free trade unions forbidden. He asked, should we regard a fascist dictatorship of some kind as "a necessary precondition along with monetarism?"[65]

Politically, the argument emerged as one between the monetarists, who desired deflation and the New Cambridge group, which desired a new social contract including an enforceable incomes policy. The *Times* announced in a leading article that, "In the debate between the value of incomes policy and monetary policy . . . *The Times* is unequivocally on the side of the monetarists. We believe that changes in the money supply do in fact emerge as changes in prices and that direct controls on wages do not control wages and prices but do distort them."[66] Kaldor replied that this argument rested on a fallacy that assumes that monetary authorities are in fact capable of regulating the money supply in a credit economy, and he quoted the governor of the Bank of England, who said, "Given the level of national income . . . we work on the theory that interest rates are the main determinants of the demand for money." Kaldor thought it wrong-headed to argue that regulating money supply is more effective than direct control of incomes.[67] Anyway, argued Kaldor, there is no way in which monetary authorities can "regulate M1"—money supply—so as to control the volume of spending except through influencing monetary liabilities as a whole. Admittedly, a rise in interest rates, if large enough, may powerfully reduce investment and thus demand, level of production, and employment. Kaldor thought British inflation was due not to excessive demand, but to a continuing rise in costs of production.[68]

Britain had set foot on the slippery slope of monetarism under Denis Healey. What was ahead was more monetarism and then Thatcherism. Kaldor's public work was cut out for him.

Thatcher embraces monetarism

From the first administration of Margaret Thatcher beginning in 1979, Kaldor saw her as an ideologue, a major departure from the pragmatic Tories of the past.[69] Still, Kaldor saw in her election "a rare opportunity to test the validity of certain basic theorems or propositions about the working of a capitalist economy." The House of Lords had seating by party as did the Commons; Kaldor promised that if the "Noble Lords opposite" are proved "fundamentally right," he would have the intellectual honesty to admit it. This did not become necessary.

The two main tenets of the new right-wing government's philosophy were, according to Kaldor: (1) that the inefficiency and low productivity of British industry was due to "lack of material incentives of business leaders and of the main decision makers, and [could] therefore be remedied by both higher pay and lower taxes for those who occupy the top responsible positions"; and (2) "that inflation can be avoided simply by regulating the money supply and that this makes intervention in any other form unnecessary."[70] Kaldor claimed that those tenets were accompanied by the "apotheosis of inequality," an attitude that had not been pervasive in former Tory administrations. To illustrate the attitude toward inequality, he quoted the *Sunday Telegraph* which said in reference to the high prices of petrol, "There is wisdom and even a kind of justice in allowing scarce and inessential commodities to become the preserve of the rich."

The government proceeded to lower income taxes and raise VAT, which, Kaldor argued, "is highly regressive and not a progressive way of taxing spending." He declared that it was the first time in history that a British government "—indeed any government I know of—has published an official forecast showing the expectation of a negative rate of economic growth." He strongly objected to the "two main contentions of the Chancellor, that the economy must be 'squeezed' in order to get rid of inflation, and that top people must be made better off in order to induce them to work harder and become richer . . . ." What about the poor and unemployed?[71]

The second oil crisis in the summer of 1979 created balance of payments problems for Thatcher in spite of the burgeoning North Sea oil sales. Unfortunately, those sales had been made at world prices prior to the OPEC action and prior to her election. Kaldor greatly feared that her government would rely on monetary means for raising interest rates, worsening the woes of British industry while attracting funds and imports from abroad because of the stronger pound, and consequently worsening inflation.[72] And that is what was done.

Faith in monetary solutions was indeed fundamental to the new government. In the fall of 1979, Thatcher's government issued a statement that incited Kaldor to address the Lords again. He said that the government held that, "Public expenditure is at the heart of Britain's present economic difficulties . . . , [that] increases in taxes have made inflationary pressures worse and reduced incentives . . . , [and that] it is essential to contain and reduce progressively the growth of the money supply. This means that Government borrowing must in turn be firmly controlled. It is the main determinant of monetary growth."

To Kaldor, this was nonsense and he quoted statistics from the International Monetary Fund to refute it: Money supply growth in the last five years in Germany, Switzerland , Belgium, and the UK had been 10 percent, but the average rate of inflation had been respectively 4.75 percent, 4.5 percent, 9 percent, and 15 percent. He said, "The growth of money supply no more explains the high rate of inflation in the United Kingdom than it explains the exceptionally low inflation rates of Switzerland and Germany."[73] At another time and in a lighter vein, noting that the money supply surged in November and December only to decline in January, he declared, "At last, I have discovered the cause of Christmas."[74]

Class struggle through taxation

Kaldor compared the government's "neo-Conservative manifesto" with Karl Marx's Communist Manifesto, which alleged that the history of mankind is a history of class struggles, and concluded, "I cannot say that

I ever believed in this, but the present White Paper makes me feel that there must be more to it than I had once thought."[75] One of the frequent claims of Conservatives was that the trade unionists were responsible for the noncompetitive costs of British industry in comparison with others, the Germans and Japanese particularly. This came to the forefront during the Thatcher administration in defense of lowering taxes on firms and management and raising VAT. Kaldor responded in debates in the House of Lords, arguing that it is the poor quality of business leadership and how leaders are selected in comparison with those countries that explains British inferiority: Germany has a tradition that a professor of chemical engineering may become the head of the biggest chemical concern. "In Britain the expert ends up as the best backroom boy. He is not in the administrative class, but only in the executive class, which is a rank below it." Kaldor denied that the British worker is inherently inferior to either the German or the Japanese worker. He quoted *Der Spiegel* which offered the German opinion that "it is the poor quality of business management that is mainly responsible for the weakness of British industry." The Germans claim that they could get the same kind of work out of British workers as out of their own, and the Japanese subsidiaries in Britain actually do that, added Kaldor.[76]

Thatcher catches the Dutch disease

By February 1980, Kaldor could report that in the previous year alone manufacturing imports had increased by 16 percent, while manufactured exports rose only a tenth of that, or 1.6 percent. He predicted that 1980 would be the year when for the first time Britain would become a net importer of manufactured goods, due to the combination of the overvaluation of the pound through monetarism and the North Sea oil sales.[77]

His plea was that interest rates be lowered and monetarism abandoned. He noted that there was more than one way to respond to the bonanza of oil sales. He compared how differently Holland and Norway had responded to the discovery of gas under the sea near Groningen. Holland, by selling its gas in other countries, had experienced a rise in the value of the guilder, which made it possible for other countries to pay for their gas through increased exports to Holland and reduced imports from Holland. This, said Kaldor, was an example of how market forces can produce undesirable results. What followed was "rapid deindustrialisation" of Holland and a slowdown in the growth of national income. He called it the Dutch disease,[78] and said Britain had caught it.

In comparison, Norway, "which is governed on Keynesian principles and not on Thatcherite principles" devalued the krone, even though the value of oil was a much greater proportion of its Gross Domestic Product than in Holland and Britain. With help from the Norwegian Central

Bank, the krone was prevented from appreciating, and Norway's manufacturing output and employment were maintained, with unemployment kept as low as 2 percent. Furthermore, Norway's gas reserves will probably last for a hundred years, while Britain expects exhaustion of its reserves in the early decades of the twenty-first century. Kaldor concluded, "You cannot rely on market forces to generate sufficient demand which alone can ensure the optimal use of resources . . . nor can you rely on the foreign exchange market to secure a satisfactory balance of payments." Both require appropriate government policies.[79]

Kaldor fought monetarism as long as it was a stated government policy. He decried those who "believe that the money supply is the main factor which causes inflation."[80] When the government's "Medium Term Economic Strategy" in April 1980 called for "a progressive reduction in the growth of money stock" in order to reduce inflation, Kaldor ridiculed this as an unachievable goal.[81] Lord Lever (Roy Jenkins) also rose to oppose monetarism. Kaldor found this "instructive," as he had not known, he said, what position Lord Lever took in 1977 when the Labour party opted for monetarism by setting a monetary target range of 8 to 12 percent. In turn, Thatcher's chancellor, Sir Geoffrey Howe, had merely to change the range, as he did, from 7 to 11 percent.[82] At least, added Kaldor, Healey had continued to support incomes policies, while any mention of wages to Conservatives tends to "elicit a hollow laugh." In fact:

> Professor Friedman assured his viewers in his evangelical programme on BBC 2 . . . that trade unions are 'a toothless lion'; they could do absolutely nothing; they could, if they wished, price themselves out of the market, but they could not, repeat could not, cause the price level to rise, because the price level was firmly tied to the money supply.[83]

Inflation survives monetarism

Because inflation had accelerated by the fall of 1981, Kaldor could say of Lord Cockfield who sat with the Conservatives on the Front Bench, that he could not envy his "having to eat quietly so many of his past words." Lord Cockfield had promised "a completely new world," but what had happened was that the Gross Domestic Product had shrunk in two years by 7.5 percent and "a fifth of manufacturing output disappeared"; money supply had increased at an annual compound rate of 18 percent as compared with 11.2 percent in the years 1974–79. Kaldor chortled, "What was missing from the noble Lord's excellent and wide-ranging account today was any reference to the money supply, whereas, by Jove, two years ago the money supply was the centrepiece of everything."[84] Inflation during the period 1979–81 had risen from 10 percent to 22 percent. Kaldor thought that because of the unanticipated explosion of prices and wages in 1980–81 and the impossibility of preventing the money supply from rising in line with prices, "strict monetarism—meaning Friedmanism— was quietly dropped because it did not work." Kaldor called the policy replacing monetarism "inverted Keynesianism," meaning that with growing unemployment the budget was tightened, interest rates and the value of the pound were allowed to rise, and a rigid pay policy in the public sector was initiated.[85] In fact, interest rates had been raised deliberately, first to 14 percent in 1979 and then to 17 percent in November 1981. Meanwhile, two million persons were unemployed, the 1981 unemployment rate having topped 10 percent.[86]

Friedman, in various speeches, Kaldor pointed out, had modified his insistence that money supply was the sole? major? source of inflation.[87] Even as the emphasis on, and lack of success in, controlling the money supply was being played out in the United Kingdom, Friedman, in a letter to the *Times*, recalled fondly a speech he had made in India in 1963 attributing inflation to the effort to promote full employment.[88] Kaldor added that Thatcher took up the theme that budget deficits associated with high spending were the source of inflation. The reader will notice that policies of full employment had become the enemy, and that is what Kaldor was talking about when he argued that the Conservative party under Thatcher was radically right-wing—ideology accounted for its having dropped the bipartisan policy of full employment that had prevailed through all British governments since World War II.

Even after Thatcher softpeddled monetarism, Kaldor's opposition to her continued to the end of his life. (Her administrations outlived him by four years.) Her ideology, he saw as the "apotheosis of inequality" and her economic policies and programs as disastrous.

The point has been made that Kaldor no more approved of Healey's monetarism than Thatcher's. In his July 20, 1977 address to the House of Lords he said, "We are here today to note, mourn or celebrate—as the case may be—the end of the present incomes policy." His alternative to monetarism being an incomes policy, while Labour was still in office he dared to hope and to believe that a consensus on relative earnings and thus an incomes policy "based on principles which are regarded as just and fair by the great majority of citizens" might emerge, but his hopes were dashed.[89]

Kaldor said that Friedman's Nobel Memorial Lecture also had given him hope, for Friedman argued in that address that the current trade-off between wage inflation and unemployment was not what the Phillips curve had predicted. (See chapter note 10.5, Phillips curve.) Rather, in stagflation, "the more unemployment there is, the faster will be the rate of increase of money wages. For once, [Friedman] reached this conclusion not from the first principles of basic economic theory, but, with commendable honesty, by studying the evidence."[90]

Lord Kaldor's "Nation"

Since 1976, Kaldor's major public platform had been the House of Lords. He believed the debates there had an important function; and he thought that much expert knowledge was shown on both sides of the aisle, and that it was too bad that the Commons need pay no attention to what was said, for the House of Lords can only delay but cannot amend legislation.[91] His enjoyment in attacking Thatcher from this public platform was evident. He called her a Marxist when she was quoted as saying, "Consensus seems to be the process of abandoning all beliefs, principles, values and policies . . . ." Kaldor added, "I can almost hear Lenin speaking those words when in October 1917 he bullied seventeen 'wet' members of his politburo in order to take risks and seize power which they were most reluctant to do."[92] He saw the Conservative party's use of American election specialists and advertising experts and the spending of large amounts of money in the 1983 election campaign as ominous: "To me it was all George Orwell coming true—except that it happened one year earlier, not in 1984. And for 'Big Brother' one must read 'Big Sister.' "[93] When Thatcher was reelected, it was not, one presumes, because of the success of her economic policies. Indeed, the Falklands war had more effect on her popularity than her failed economic policies.

Kaldor yearned aloud for the pragmatic Keynesian Tories of old. When Lord Stockton (Harold Macmillan) made his maiden speech in 1984, Kaldor said of him, "The noble Earl is in that grand tradition of the British Tory Party. The Governments led by the noble Earl will be long remembered for continuous full employment and for a remarkable period of industrial and social advance."[94] In another address, Kaldor called the Lord Stockton "one of our great national assets, although thankfully, he is not for sale." (Thatcher was selling off national industries in her privatization campaign.)[95]

In what was probably his only statement of approval of Thatcher, Kaldor enjoyed the "happy thought" she had in elevating another ex-Hungarian, Lord Bauer "to your Lordships' House, thereby laying once and for all the slur that all ex-Hungarians are Left-wing intellectuals . . . ." Then he launched into a stinging rebuke calling Thatcher's "the worst Government that we have had in this century . . . "[96]

There were moments of tension and excitement in the House of Lords. As is the custom, Kaldor was often interrupted, especially by those of the opposite bench who wanted to point out, for example, that the Labour government as well as their own had cut expenditures.[97] When Kaldor was arguing for bringing down the exchange rate in order to "reflate," the Earl of Gowrie rose to ask:

> "My Lords, did the noble Lord try to persuade the previous Prime Minister of the same point?"
> Lord Kaldor: "Well . . . "
> Noble Lords: "Answer!"
> Lord Kaldor: "The previous Prime Minister would never have said that he was against reflation. I do not think for a moment that he would have said that, but I agree that the previous Chancellor of the Exchequer, who was my chief at one stage, fell a victim to seductive influences coming from Threadneedle Street, and was persuaded to decap the pound. There is no doubt about that and that is the source of a lot of present evil."[98]

Confrontations aside, what was Kaldor's image of the economy of the United Kingdom and how it might prosper? In answer to Lord Thorneycroft's analogy that the nation was like a family that must cut its spending to match its income, Kaldor replied:

> The nation is like a very large family, whose members are engaged in rendering services to each other. In hard times there is no point in cutting down on such services; it is as if a family, being hard-up, decided not to do their own mending, their own house-cleaning or their own washing-up; whereas the sensible thing to do in the face of hardship is to do more of those things and not less; to do more of your own "make do and mend." Collectively, as a nation, we all take in each other's washing. So if I buy less from my neighbour and he buys less from me, and we both buy less from the shop around the corner, none of us will benefit and none of us will be in a better position to balance the books than we were before.[99]

Kaldor was speaking of real income, as he nearly always did. The last incomes policy under Labour had failed in consequence of Healey's dose of monetarism, he argued, because real income had fallen as prices had risen, and the workers had refused to continue to cooperate. In fact, many people thought that the first election of Thatcher was due in no small part to the strikes of the dustmen, garbagemen and other disenchanted workers who infuriated the public.[100]

When it came to an issue like plant closings because of losses, Kaldor thought closing plants was of social benefit only if the resources released were put to more profitable use elsewhere. He questioned the idea that profitability was "the true criterion of social benefit" under all circumstances.[101] In the case of the coal industry during a recession, he asked, why does not the government subsidize the production of coal "in the same way as our partners in the European Community."[102]

Still, Kaldor did not claim that either industrial peace or an incomes policy could be had in a democratic country without a rise in real income. Or at least not a decline![103]

How, then, was real income to rise? For Kaldor the appropriate policy, in the face of the North Sea oil receipts, would have been to follow the Norwegian example rather than to have caught the Dutch disease. Instead of monetarism and restrictive policies, he advised protecting export manufacturers to the point that the value of imports was balanced with the value of exports. Kaldor would opt for growth of the industrial sector rather than allowing it to decline under a pricey pound.[104] This might be stated as Kaldor's Rule:

> To get rid of unemployment, all you have to do is to restrict imports to the percentage which would be compatible with an equality of imports and exports at the full employment level.[105]

As Kaldor said, there are hundreds of ways of restricting imports—by duties, by licenses, by embargoes, but he warned:

> This is the sort of remedy which is incompatible with our membership of the Common Market. . . . I think the Common Market has been an absolute disaster. One cannot say that the Tories or Labour were responsible for it: the whole nation is responsible. . . . But whereas before we joined the Market we had an annual surplus in manufactured trade with the six countries of Europe, including Germany, of 400 million pounds at 1970 prices, which is equal to nearly 1,800 million pounds at present prices, last year [1984] we had a deficit in our manufactured trade with the countries of the European Community of 7,900 million pounds . . . ."[106]

Kaldor also offered less drastic remedies, such as the restoration of some of the policies he had put together for Labour, like the employment subsidies. These could take the form even of abolishing employers' social insurance contribution and surcharge, which amounted to a 10 percent tax on payrolls, a policy that was allowable to members of the Common Market.[107] He believed in encouraging home investment rather than foreign investment.[108] He insisted that the government again admit that wealth can be created by the public as well as the private sector.[109] He firmly argued for engaging in planning policies as Japan did, and to a lesser extent France and Germany.[110] He wanted to lessen alienation and avoid class war by fostering a social partnership between workers and management like that in Germany, for example, which might make an incomes policy possible and improve productivity.[111]

As for Thatcherism, Kaldor felt "it was a national misfortune that Mrs. Thatcher and North Sea oil came on stream more or less at the same time." He quoted a recent publication of the OECD, which stated, "The near coincidental timing in the United Kindgom, of North Sea oil development and severe disinflation was unfortunate." He did not hold Thatcher to account for all of Britain's difficulties: "She is responsible only for telescoping into a few years what otherwise might have taken some decades."[112] Monetarism was easily shown to have failed, but Thatcherism lasted until 1990, four years beyond Kaldor's power to protest.

Part IV

Constructing Post Keynesian Theory

Visiting Watertown, Connecticut, 1935. *Left to right* Eugene Rostow Gayer, Arthur Burns, Mrs. Rostow, Kaldor.

Leaving the John von Neuman's after a visit to Princeton University, 1935. *Left to right* Marietta von Neuman, Clarissa and Nicholas Kaldor, in front of the Kaldor's new car.

Outdoor Conference of Overall effects Division, United States Strategic Bombing Survey, Bad Nauheim, Germany, 1945. John Kenneth Galbraith, facing out, Kaldor second from his right. United States National Archives.

Tabulating Section, U. S. Strategic Bombing Survey, Bad Nauheim, Germany, 1945. United States National Archives.

Farewell Party for Visiting Professors, Indian Statistical Institute, 1956. *Left to Right* John Strachey, Catherine Atwater Galbraith, John Kenneth Galbraith, P. N. Banerjea, Clarissa Kaldor (speaking), Nicholas Kaldor, Katherine Kaldor, Frank Yates, Frances Kaldor, P. C. Mahalanobis, Head, Indian Statistical Institute.

*Nicky Kaldor following Maynard Keynes from Kings' College to
Whitehall* (Cartoon by Marc Boxer, 1964, Courtesy of Clarissa Kaldor)

Kaldor in Iceland, 1980

NK

CHAPTER ELEVEN

New Approaches to Growth and DistributionTheory

The years of Nicholas Kaldor's involvement with policy must not obscure from us his contributions to economic theory. While Targetti and
Thirlwall claim that "like Keynes," he was primarily interested in "policy
first and theory second,"[1] I would say that in his mature years, like
Keynes, he took his problems from the real world and tried to construct
theory that bore upon that world, but that policy and theory had equal
importance to these master economists, only different audiences.

Because of this interaction of theory and real world problems, Kaldor's
theory, like that of Keynes, must be seen in an evolutionary context.
Keynes had been confronted with the conflict between the real problem
of unemployment and traditional theory, which denied its existence.
Kaldor and his fellow Cantabrigians were confronted in the post-World
War II world with the need for development and economic growth,
which could not be understood in static theory, even that inherited from
Keynes. Each had to find his own way out of old patterns of thought into
more workable ones. Kaldor characterized the period after the war as one
in which:

> Some of us, Joan [Robinson] ... and I in another way, were struggling
> against what you call mainstream economics in America, which is neo-
> classical economics. This whole excessive emphasis on methodological
> individualism, the rationality of individuals and the maximization of
> profits ... and a tremendous emphasis, which was never openly admit-
> ted, on this principle of limited substitution, being the substitutability

at the margin . . . and the whole marginal economics, the marginal product, the marginal this, the marginal that. . . . Substitutability has a place, no doubt . . . but there is also complementarity, which is the opposite of substitutability . . . ."[2]

After the war Robinson and Kaldor and invited members met in what was jokingly called the Secret Seminar, meeting in houses or in R. F. Kahn's rooms at King's College. Attendees included Aubrey Silberston and Harry G. Johnson, who each remarked on the rivalry between Kaldor and Robinson over their theories of capitalist growth and the "near chaos" of the exchanges between them. Johnson departed for Manchester in 1956, considering Cambridge imbued with "ideological motivations for theoretical work."[3] But both Robinson and Kaldor found it necessary to escape the old modes of thought before they could introduce dynamics into Keynesian analysis, that is, into what is now known as post Keynesian economics.

These Secret Seminar exchanges must have been stimulating, for both Robinson and Kaldor were led to face up to the fact that neoclassical orthodoxy—that is, the Walrasization of Keynes—precluded the kind of dynamic growth theory that they thought was necessary. I am suggesting that these seminars, where theory was argued out, were a liberating force for our well-schooled master economist. In the atmosphere of the Cambridge Circus, Keynes had developed the General Theory. From the turbulent years in the Secret Seminar, both Robinson and Kaldor emerged with theories of distribution and growth that did not rely on all of the rigid assumptions of what both came to call "equilibrium theory." As Thirlwall has made clear, Kaldor was not a critic of the concept of equilibrium but of "equilibrium methodology," that is, starting with an *a priori* system that is tautological. He particularly objected to the assumptions of perfection competition and constant returns that seemed to be necessary to orthodox theory. And he agreed with Joan Robinson and Janos Kornai that the habits of thought engendered by "equilibrium methodology" became an impediment to the development of economics as a science.[4]

Breaking with the past

Kaldor set himself the task of developing a new approach and retrospectively divided his own postwar methodology into two periods, which overlapped each other in 1966. The last paper of the first period was his "Marginal Productivity and the Macroeconomic Theories of Distribution" in which he employed "deductive reasoning from macro-economic axioms of a rather general character." Thus he admitted to using traditional methodology, including assumptions of full employment, even as he sought to escape.[5]

Thereafter, Kaldor made a break from traditional method and "tried to find what kind of regularities can be detected in empirically observed phenomena and then tried to discover what particular testable hypotheses would be capable of explaining the association." He had become aware of this approach during World War II when he associated with scientists engaged in "operational research" and found it "in one sense more modest in scope (in not searching for explanations that derive from a comprehensive model of the system) and also more ambitious in that it directly aims at discovering solutions (or remedies) for real problems."[6] But he did not rely on the new method until mid-1966 and after. This change in method also inspired his striving in the last twenty of his fifty years as an economist to challenge other economists to follow him in abandoning equilibrium methodology and in trying to construct models built on verifiable assumptions.[7] Apparently, it is that effort that Blaug condemns as a failure, saying that nothing is more difficult than the task of turning a whole discipline around and that, "It is doubtful whether even so formidable a figure as Kaldor can expect to succeed in so daunting a task."[8]

As for Kaldor's most original contributions of the postwar period, Pasinetti cites the articles that preceded the change of method. For economists of all persuasions, then, the contemporary view is that Kaldor's best work was reformist rather than revolutionary as far as method is concerned. Pasinetti considers Kaldor's "Alternative Theories of Distribution" his "major original contribution," and this was developed prior to Kaldor's change in method.[9]

The most troubling part of Blaug's view of Kaldor is that, unlike Pasinetti, he considered only Kaldor's last work in evaluating his influence. On the other side, as Tony Lawson, J. Gabriel Palma, and John Sender remarked, "It is well known . . . that Kaldor's work—particularly, perhaps, his writing on growth—initiated numerous research programs."[10] Nevertheless, it was important to Kaldor that his change of method be noticed by one and all. One of the facts that he held responsible for changing his approach occurred after most of his famous growth models had been completed. It was during his advisory work in the Treasury, when he was searching for the reason growth rates differ among countries, that Kaldor noted "the extraordinarily close correlation between the rate of growth of manufacturing output and the rate of growth of the GDP."[11] But as we have seen, even before the Treasury years, which began in 1964, Kaldor saw himself as working toward freeing himself from the old methods.

On good authority, then, of the more than 100 articles written by

Kaldor after World War II, those on growth and distribution written within the ten-year period 1956 to 1966 are outstanding in their content, their method, their originality, and their lasting value. These papers, in particular, have been discussed in detail in books and journals and extensively by Anthony P. Thirlwall. The only way to do them justice is to read them. My task, rather than to repeat how Kaldor's thought developed, is to highlight the insights contained in those articles and the response of other economists to them.

Alternative distribution theory

Kaldor's first article of this series, and the one Luigi Pasinetti thinks stands above all others, was entitled "Alternative Theories of Distribution."[12] Characteristically, as he had in the case of capital theory in 1937,[13] Kaldor gave a valuable review of the various "theoretical attempts, since Ricardo, at solving this 'principal problem.' " He commented on the Ricardian, Marxian, neoclassical or marginalist, and finally the "Keynesian" approaches. Since the appearance of this article, the "Keynesian" has, ordinarily, been called Kaldorian.[14] Kaldor argued that Marx derived his theory from Ricardo's surplus principle, making profits a residual, while the neoclassical theories were split between the marginal productivity theory derived from Ricardo's marginal principle and a "degree of monopoly" theory of monopoly profit.

Kaldor found all earlier attempts wanting and offered the one he called "Keynesian" in spite of Keynes's lack of interest in theories of distribution. Kaldor relied on an idea gleaned from a footnote in *Treatise on Money* in which Keynes likened profits to the inexhaustible supply of a widow's cruse—"however much of their profits entrepreneurs spend on consumption, the increment of wealth belonging to entrepreneurs remains the same as before." Kaldor thought that Keynes's reference to consumption expenditures "should not blind us to the fact that here Keynes regards entrepreneurial incomes as being the resultant of their expenditure decisions, rather than the other way round."[15]

The other Keynesian part was the application of the multiplier theory to income distribution. Kaldor had first thought of doing this while writing his paper for the Royal Commission on Taxation in 1951, the same experience that gave rise to his book on the expenditure tax. He acknowledged the help he received from "discussions with Mrs. Robinson" and from a paper by Michal Kalecki in which he argued that "capitalists earn what they spend, and workers spend what they earn." Harry Johnson and Robin Marris helped him with the mathematics.[16] Richard Kahn accused Kaldor of "rushing into print with his distribution theory to deprive Joan Robinson of priority." Properly the theory could be called "Cantabrigian."

The essence of the Kaldorian theory, then, is that through investment expenditures, entrepreneurs generate profits. Wages are residual. This is the opposite of the Ricardian model in which profits, not wages, are residual. Kaldor had made the point earlier[18] that cyclical movements in the economy depended on something other than savings, savings being the traditional, pre-Keynesian, explanation. Even before his theory of distribution was published, he had begun arguing that trade cycles and dynamic growth were not inherently connected analytically, that is, he denied that the "cycle is a mere by-product of, and could not occur in the absence of, 'progress,' " i.e. growth.[19] But he insisted on a link between economic growth and long-term full employment, while admitting the possibility of periodic breakdowns in the investment process, due to the growth in output capacity outrunning the growth in effective demand. That would cause total output to be restricted so that full employment would not be ensured in the short run.[20]

Mark I

Three models of economic growth followed Kaldor's initial discussion of distribution, each employing and advancing the theory of distribution. In "A Model of Economic Growth," he demonstrated that in the "second stage of capitalist development," profits will be determined "in a 'Keynesian' manner, by the propensities to invest and to save."[21]

This model, which is sometimes called Mark I, stepped away from treating as constants savings propensities, the flow of invention or innovation, and the growth of population. Kaldor treated them, instead, as functional relationships. Initially, he insisted that growth, rather than being limited by effective demand, was limited by scarce resources, but he defended labeling that model "Keynesian" because he was using "the specifically Keynesian hypothesis that equilibrium between savings and investment is secured through a movement of prices and/or incomes rather than through changes in the rate of interest." Thereafter, Kaldor often debated with himself over the role of demand, which was crucial to growth of a single economy and the scarcity of resources that can limit world economic development.[22]

The major contribution of this article (and the source of much criticism) was the abandonment of the "production function" of neoclassical methodology in favor of a "technical progress function." This change brought technical progress into an interactive relation with capital, in which the growth in productivity was proportionate to the growth in capital. Rather than moving along a production function with a given state of knowledge and then shifting the whole function in response to a change in the state of knowledge, "*realised* technical progress" was made dependent on the rate of increase of capital per worker.[23] As Kaldor later explained:

> In a world in which technology is embodied in capital equipment and where both the improvement of knowledge and the production of new capital goods are continuous, it is impossible to isolate the productivity growth which is due to capital accumulation *as such* from the productivity growth which is due to improvements in technical knowledge. There is no such thing as a "set of blueprints" which reflect a "given state of knowledge"—the knowledge required for the making of, say, the Concorde is only evolved in the process of designing or developing the aeroplane; the costs of obtaining the necessary new knowledge is causally indistinguishable from the other elements of investment.[24]

Kaldor was also critical of the neoclassical belief in the importance for distribution of choosing between "labor-saving and capital-using" techniques, an analysis he associated with the acceptance of the marginal productivity theory.[25] However, he understood these choices along with the possibility of land-saving or natural resource-saving techniques as important to technical progress.[26] His other "new" function was the investment function, wherein investment takes place in response to an increase in output and/or change in the rate of profit in the previous period.[27]

A matter little remarked on but certainly of interest is Kaldor's insistence that his was a "long-run" model and not a predictor of short-run relationships—that is, he distinguished between what he called "trends" and "fluctuations." In a flourish, he had added a stage theory of capitalism to the debate on economic growth. Citing the most important characteristic of capitalist business enterprise as the continuous change and improvement in the methods of production, he noted that in the early stage of capitalist development growth in productivity was not accompanied by a rise in the standard of living of the working population, while in the later stage relative wage/profit shares tend to be stable and real wages rise as economic growth occurs.[28] John Hicks was to object to this introduction of stages and historical approaches, but not until after Kaldor's next model.[29] Kaldor judged Mark I as subject to a number of important limitations that he hoped to overcome in subsequent models.[30] This led to Mark II, "Capital Accumulation and Economic Growth," in which he lengthened his criticism of the production function and further developed both his own technical progress function as a continuous process in time and his investment function to include more past periods in the consideration of whether to invest. Frank Hahn and Luigi Pasinetti assisted him in the algebraic presentation of his ideas.[31]

Mark II

Kaldor gave the Mark II paper at the Corfu, Greece, meeting of the International Economic Association in August 1958. The meeting was attended by thirty invited participants from many countries and put Kaldor face to face with such notable Americans as Paul A. Samuelson, E.D. Domar, William Fellner, and Robert M. Solow, who were not likely to agree with his increasing attacks on the marginal productivity theory of capital and on their reliance on the production function.[32] Moving toward a new method, Kaldor suggested that the construction of theoretical growth models should take into account certain "stylised facts." These facts included continued growth in the volume of production and the productivity of labor; a continuing increase in the amount of capital per worker; a steady rate of profits on capital in developed capitalist societies; steady capital output ratios over long periods; a high correlation between the share of profits in income and the share of investment in output; and "appreciable" differences in the rate of growth of labor productivity and of total output among societies.[33]

In blending old and new methods, Kaldor sought to construct models that "explained" these "facts," arguing that neoclassical marginal productivity theory failed to explain them. Still, his method was traditional, setting out six assumptions in order to produce a minimum answer to the question of growth equilibrium and then removing the assumptions one by one to examine more complex situations. The only assumption he did not remove in this model was that of constant returns to scale and unlimited resources.[34]

As he removed the simplifying assumption of the absence of technical progress, he was aware that he lost the "precise meaning" of concepts such as "capital" and "income." The orthodox solution to these measurement problems at that time was to assume a linear and homogeneous production function, but he was determined to avoid that assumption in the interest of reality. His model as amended hypothesized that, "*Given* the technical progress function, the system tends towards that particular rate of accumulation where the conditions of 'neutral progress' are satisfied." He admitted that the only possible way to justify the hypothesis was on empirical grounds. Then he introduced the investment function, modifying his assumptions from Mark I to make the principle of increasing risk applicable.[35] The presentation of this paper led to what can be called the Corfu controversies.

Corfu controversies

The discussion of Kaldor's ideas at Corfu was extensive and heated. In his introduction to the published proceedings, editor Friedrich Lutz criticized the papers of David Champernowne, Nicholas Kaldor, and Robert Solow, saying:

> We can go on building theoretical models indefinitely. . . . Exercises in dynamic theory are admittedly intellectually fascinating, but they show a tendency to follow the principle "l'art pour l'art" which, in my view, is not a principle appropriate to economics. . . . It seems to me that if the theory of dynamic growth is not to lose contact with reality, empirical research is now more than ever necessary in order to allow us to distinguish the more fruitful hypotheses from the less-fruitful ones.

Lutz deplored the seeming inability for the attending economists to agree on the interpretation of the statistics offered by some of the econometricians. He also observed that the attacks on the marginal productivity theory were by a minority of participants, but that there was an apparent need for "a theory of distribution."[36] Individuals at the conference responded to Kaldor personally. Professor Domar said he was honored to be in the company of a heretic. Solow wondered if it were possible to "discover what precisely was the bee in Mr. Kaldor's bonnet."[37] J.R. Hicks found Kaldor's lecture "the highly original theory in which technical progress was brought in as a variable"; but, he did not consider it a proper model.[38]

Hicks later elaborated on the Corfu discussions in a journal article, weighing the arguments. He admitted that in the explanation of the process of capital accumulation, the neoclassicists or marginalists, "had been conspicuously unsuccessful," and he worried about the production function used by Samuelson, Solow, and Fellner, because they "lifted" the assumption of constant returns to scale from the micro level "where it does such good work" and applied it to macro problems. He commented, "In the days of marginal productivity we needed the constant returns to scale assumption in order to make it possible for factors to get their marginal products . . . but if one assumes a production function with increasing returns to scale, the marginal productivity theory of distribution goes by the board." He was not ready to embrace Kaldor, however, feeling that Kaldor had put "too much faith in automatic technical progress." His main criticism was that theorists should not try to explain growth, since each country's growth is "a single world story" and that the explanation of what happened is the historian's business, not the economist's.[39]

Kaldor answered Hicks by focusing on increasing returns as a part of the explanation of economic growth. He asked, "What do they mean by curves in Cambridge, Massachusetts, using assumptions which oblige one to treat seven-eighths of the empirically observed change as the result of shifts in the production function?" Is there so much difference between the assumption of increasing returns to capital and the assumption of continuous technical progress? Kaldor insisted that "the increasing returns associated with growth and capital accumulation is *not* a reversible relationship" and that the increase in productivity resulting from capital accumulation relative to labor depends on the speed of the accumulation, not only on the extent.[40]

Fourteen or so years later, Hicks, previously known as "J.R." redesignated himself John Hicks "a non-neo-classic who is quite disrespectful towards his uncle" J.R. By 1975, Hicks had "become very suspicious" of the production function, conceding that "by substitution something is learned."[41] Frank Hahn, in a reflective article about his debates with Kaldor, whom he characterized as "an economist of a remarkable mental agility and originality," agreed that there is "substance in the Kaldorian argument" that the technical progress function is non-linear, that there is always some learning in changing from one technique to another.[42]

In 1990, Mark Blaug argued that neoclassical growth theory is perfectly capable of accounting for Kaldor's stylized facts by employing appropriate assumptions: "Indeed, so elastic is the apparatus provided by neoclassical growth theory that it is capable of accounting *ex post* for any facts whatsoever." He saw no need for Kaldor's effort. Furthermore, said Blaug, since Kaldor sought to explain his stylized facts "in a genuine, causal sense," the validity of his theory "can be said to stand or fall on the occurrence of certain 'stylised facts.' " Blaug did not dispute the first three stylized facts: a steady rising trend in the growth of output and output per unit of labor; a steady rise in the amount of capital per worker; and a trendless rate of profit on capital that was in excess of the yield of gilt-edged bonds. But on the basis of Graham Hacche's analysis, Blaug challenged the fourth—a constant capital-output rate—saying, "There is actually little evidence in the data to suggest the notion that there is some 'steady trend' or 'normal' relationship between capital and output."[43]

However, as I read Hacche, he accepted this stylized fact, saying, "The international evidence thus appears to confirm that although there may be quite pronounced swings in the capital-output ratio in different periods, there is no well defined or generally applicable long-term trend, upwards or downwards; in this sense stylised fact (iv) may be accepted as valid."[44] Both Blaug and Hacche challenged the fifth stylized fact: a high correlation between the profit share and the investment income ratio and the constancy of wage and profit shares in the long run. Hacche challenged this on two counts—first on the stability of wage shares. Since his information preceded the 1980s, it would be interesting to learn whether the more recent corrective changes in wage shares in the United Kingdom and the United States might modify his views in terms of the long-run stability.

Hacche's second count challenged the positive correlation between the share of profits and the investment to output ratio. But he suggests one neat explanation for the concurrent rise in the investment ratio and fall in the profit share is that the post-war growth in the United Kingdom may have been "a purely temporary 'capital-deepening' phenomenon." Hacche had gone to enormous effort to define the problems of empirical testing. He thought that the important point was that such "stylised facts" were treacherous. Quoting Samuelson, he added "They do describe the facts, up until they cease to describe the facts. If these be laws, Mother Nature is a criminal by nature."[45]

Mark III

Mark III was an amended version of the preceding distribution and growth articles. Kaldor deemed "A New Model of Economic Growth," written with J. A. Mirrlees, a "considerable advance" over the earlier ones in that it "takes full account of the fact ... that technical progress is infused into the economic system through investment." Obsolescence was also treated.[46] Kaldor made a particular effort to reveal the limitations of the orthodox tool, that is, "the assumption of a linear and homogeneous production function, coupled with the assumption that with the changing state of knowledge this function is continually shifting upwards and outwards."[47]

But the timing of the model (1962) was such that interest among theorists was concentrated on the meaning of capital, a debate that had begun in the mid-fifties and in which Kaldor took no direct interest. Indeed, he was losing interest in mathematical modeling, himself, though he was quite pleased that when realistic values for the United States' economy were plugged into the parameters of Mark III, the model produced acceptable results.[48] Many years later, Kaldor was amazed to find that virtually the same model had been advanced in a doctoral dissertation in the University of Heidelberg in 1926 by H.J. Rüstow.[49]

For the next ten years growth theory declined in favor among mainstream theoretical economists, which, in turn, diminished the influence of Kaldor's insistence on an open discussion of method.[50] Hahn suggests that one of the reasons for this neglect of growth models "is actually Kaldorian: the formal models do not seem to capture the history of capitalist development as we know it." He thinks this fact accounts for Kaldor turning to "the more speculative and less formal mode of his later work."[51]

Last of the old methods

Kaldor used the old methods one last time, in his article "Marginal Productivity and the Macroeconomic Theories of Distribution." It was both a defense and an attack: a defense of the Keynesian argument that invest-

ment determines the share of profits in income and an attack on neoclassical methods used by Paul Samuelson and Franco Modigliani in their argument that the marginal product of capital determines the share of profits in income. Kaldor also objected to their treatment of externally provided finance as equivalent to internal finance ("ploughed-back profits"), claiming that 80 to 90 percent of business investment, including depreciation, is financed out of retained profits.[52]
He began boldly:

> Professors Samuelson and Modigliani have written a long critical essay on macro-economic theories of distribution which demonstrates not only the splendid analytical powers of the two authors, but also the intellectual sterility engendered by the methods of Neo-classical Economics.[53]

He launched a polemical attack on the assumptions and reasoning of orthodox economists, pleading for an economics "which starts from a non-perfect, non-profit-maximising economy." And more than that, in a much quoted statement, he condemned the orthodox method:

> It is the hallmark of the neo-classical economist to believe that, however severe the abstractions from which he is forced to start, he will "win through" by the end of the day—bit by bit, if he only carries the analysis far enough, the scaffolding can be removed, leaving the basic structure intact.[54]

Kaldor's complaint extended to the contrast between what Samuelson and Modigliani called "observed economic systems" and what he saw as the real world. He asked:

> Can't they see that it is *possible* for a market economy to be "competitive" without satisfying the neo-classical equations? Can't they imagine a world in which marginal productivities are *not* equal to factor prices, and are not in any definite relationship to factor prices—a world, for example, in which, with the approach of labour scarcity, the share of wages is falling, not rising, despite the fact that the marginal productivity of labour is constant or rising and Capital (in the relevant sense) is redundant in relation to Labour?

He concluded that, "Unless they make a more imaginative effort to reconcile their theoretical framework with the known facts of experience, their economic theory is bound to remain a barren exercise."[55]

Growth policy instead

Thereafter, Kaldor made no effort to please mainstream economists by constructing mathematical models. Instead, he set about blending his theoretical views with policy prescriptions. His arguments in "The Case for Regional Policies" (1970) is an early and outstanding example of this blend.[56] Abjuring resource endowment and location theory as adequate explanations of the difference in growth rates, he called instead on Myrdal's "principle of circular and cumulative causation," which he took to be nothing but the existence of increasing returns and on Hicks's "super-multiplier," which was applied to a region.

Soon, "A Model of Regional Growth Rate Differences on Kaldorian Lines" appeared, the work of R.J. Dixon and Anthony P. Thirlwall. Their objective was to formalize Kaldor's domestic regional model in order to clarify its structure. In doing so, they noted that "at the national level, a built-in balance of payments constraint would make the model more realistic." Recently, Thirlwall has produced a model that does include a balance of payments constraint, causing Paul Davidson to declare "Thirlwall's Law" to be "a post keynesian positive contribution to 'theory.' "[57] Indeed, a number of theoreticians have turned once more to a consideration of the theoretical aspects of economic growth. Both Hacche (1979) and Maurice Fitzgerald Scott (1989) have written large books on the subject.[58] In his *New View of Economic Growth*, Scott offers an analysis of recent growth models, including Kaldor's, and a new growth theory and model. Scott claims that his can be used to answer empirically the usual questions asked of any growth theory. This seems to be an adaptation of the method favored by Kaldor, for the questions Scott is trying to answer are: "why growth rates differ; why the shares of wages and profits are what they are, and have changed; why some alleged regularities . . . exist; how taxation affects growth; what is the optimum rate of growth and whether there is a case for government intervention to secure it; and why growth slowed down in many countries after 1973."[59]

Though Scott doesn't say so, this seems to be a wholly Kaldorian method of proceeding. He even starts with "stylized facts," though he notes that he has slightly changed and restated Kaldor's. This means that Scott, like Kaldor, started his growth theory with a steady state, and Scott refers to that similarity.[60] He also noted other points of "wholehearted" agreement with Kaldor, including Kaldor's:

> Side-swipes at orthodox growth theory, for example, the failure to take cognizance of imperfect markets, the futility of separating productivity growth which is due to capital accumulation from that which is due to improvements in technical knowledge, the robust statement that "there is no such thing as a 'set of blueprints' that reflect a 'given state of knowledge,' " and the scepticism regarding the production function.[61]

Scott also documented the undeserved hegemony of orthodox growth theory. In what he called the textbook test, he found that unorthodox growth theories were discussed in only three works up to 1973 and "not in any later works."[62] He thinks empiricists also neglected modern growth theory that was not orthodox. However, using a method that at least takes off from the Kaldorian platform, Scott arrived at different theoretical and policy conclusions. For example, he thought Kaldor's argument attributing faster growth in nonmanufacturing to faster growth in manufacturing, and the latter, in turn, to external demand was "hopelessly oversimplified." And he felt that Kaldor had offered "little more than assertion" to back up his later ideas.[63] Still, Kaldor might have drawn much pleasure from seeing Scott's take off, since Kaldor's major insistence was that it was the *method* for approaching growth theory that must be altered.

Whether Kaldor would be pleased to be cited as forming, along with Marx, Kalecki, and Keynes, the intellectual roots for a series of "structuralist macro models of developing countries" that are "Computable General Equilibrium Models," is more debatable, but this represents an interesting link suggested by Sherman Robinson.[64]

Accolades in the 1980s

In honor of Kaldor's seventy-fifth birthday, the *Journal of Post Keynesian Economics* published a symposium of Kaldor's growth laws in their latest form. Among the articles, Thirlwall offered "A Plain Man's Guide to Kaldor's Growth Laws." He guides us thusly: (1) there exists a strong relation between the growth of manufacturing output and the growth of GDP, which translates to mean that the faster the rate of growth of manufacturing, the faster the growth of total national output; (2) there is a strong relation between the growth of manufacturing and the growth of labor productivity in manufacturing, meaning the faster the growth of manufacturing, the faster the growth of productivity of manufacturing; (3) the faster the growth of manufacturing output, the faster the rate of labor transference from nonmanufacturing to manufacturing, so that overall productive growth is positively related to the growth of output and employment in manufacturing and negatively associated with the growth of employment outside manufacturing.[65]

Other celebratory articles discussed the evidence supporting or challenging Kaldor's theories of growth—just the kind of modeling and testing that Kaldor approved of. This represented a fine birthday celebration, but it is important to note that it appeared in the post-Keynesian journal where interest in economic growth had never been eclipsed. Meanwhile, Kaldor had spent the years since 1966 on other matters.

NK

CHAPTER TWELVE

Debating Kaldorian Distribution Theory

Not only the growth theory, but especially Kaldor's theory of income distribution drew immediate widespread attention. Again, the lines were drawn between orthodox economists and Kaldor who was aligned with others, notably Luigi Pasinetti.

Round one, 1960

In February 1960, The *Review of Economic Studies* published an exchange between Hiroshi Atsumi of Osaka, Japan; James Tobin of Yale University; and Nicholas Kaldor. Without denying the validity of Kaldor's theory, Atsumi insisted that it covered a special as opposed to a general case. In other words, while an increase in savings might be realized through redistribution of income, this was not the general case. Atsumi wanted to use both the principle of the multiplier and the marginal principle (production functions) to explain distribution.[1]

Tobin entitled his paper "Towards a General Kaldorian Theory of Distribution," complaining that, "For all the flaws that Kaldor detects in neoclassical distribution theory, it is general and his substitute should not do less." He argued that if labor and capitalists take Kaldor's theory seriously, "their maneouvres would destroy the relationship between wages and profits and the whole theory of distribution would then have to be surrendered to the game theorist."[2] Eleven years later (1971), Tobin admitted that his article had been "an irreverent spoof" of Kaldor's distribution theory and that it represented "a footnote to the running controversy between neoclassical growth theory and its opponents."[3]

Kaldor responded that Atsumi's criticism was essentially that his theory was incompatible with the marginal productivity theory. "Of course it is," said Kaldor. His aim was to offer an alternative, not a complement. "If the share of wages at full employment were uniquely determined by the marginal productivity of labour in relation to its average productivity, it could not at the same time be determined by the propensities to invest and to save." Kaldor noted that in the cases of economies of scale, technical progress, "or what-not," where an increase in both capital and labor is likely to involve more than a proportionate increase in the product, "marginal productivity can only provide a theoretical upper limit to factor rewards" and, furthermore, the marginal disutility of labor would provide only a theoretical "floor and need not play any role in the actual determination of wages." Or, Kaldor asked, is Mr. Atsumi prepared to argue the fact that in 1960, hourly wages were five times as high in America as in Japan, is a reflection of a fivefold difference in the disutility of labour in the two countries?[4]

Round two, 1966

After this first exchange, the *Review of Economic Studies* published in 1962 Pasinetti's version of the "Cambridge" theory of distribution, recognizing that Joan Robinson as well as Kaldor had put forward theories of distribution founded on Keynes's widow's cruse. However, Pasinetti attributed the theory to Kaldor,[5] arguing that the theory gave "a neat and modern content to the deep-rooted old Classical idea of a certain connection between distribution of income and capital accumulation." In his opinion this constituted a break with the "hundred-year-old tradition of marginal theory," and, he said, "It is no wonder that it has immediately become the target of attacks and eulogies of such strongly emotional character." He felt that "approval and rejection have almost invariably coincided with the commentators' marginalistic or non-marginalistic view."[6] He noted that the new theory represented a change from Kaldor's earlier views as expressed in his theory of capital article in 1937.

Kaldor had made this same point at Corfu: he had once defended Knut Wicksell but became "convinced that all he had written in defense of neo-classical theory was wrong and that Professor Knight was right." The difficulty was that the neoclassical school tried "to apply a generalized marginal productivity theory to the economy as a whole, a job he now felt simply could not be done."[7]

Pasinetti's article included what he considered "a more logical reconsideration of the whole theoretical framework regarded as a system of necessary relations to achieve full employment," an extension or clarification of the Kaldorian theory, stimulating some of the giants of the profession to join the debate on alternative theories of distribution. This led to Round two in the *Review of Economic Studies*.

Paul Samuelson and Franco Modigliani, while calling Pasinetti's paper "seminal," insisted that it did not have anything to do with Kaldor's "alternative theory of distribution" and that it furthermore "cannot help us to discriminate among alternative theories of distribution."[8] Throughout their article, they questioned Kaldor's theory and presented models that confirmed Pasinetti's for a limited range of cases. They then offered a model they termed "neoclassical and more general." Specifically, they denied that "marginalism is a modern irrelevancy," and insisted on their eclectic approach to methodology.[9]

Pasinetti replied that while their effort was excellent in many respects, "it has been written with the aim of defending a specific theory." He thought one of their preoccupations was with defending the theory of marginal productivity of capital, whereas this theory had become unnecessary for explaining the long-run rate of profit, a circumstance he thought they had actually admitted.[10] He argued that what they had done was to present other theories, such as Kaldor's and Kalecki's, and to frame them in such a way as to satisfy the assumptions required by the marginal productivity theory.[11]

Joan Robinson joined the fray, saying that it was a pity that Pasinetti's model had seemed "to encourage the tiresome neoclassical habit of confusing comparisons of equilibria with historical processes by talking about an ultimate equilibrium which the economy is approaching."[12]

Kaldor in turn objected that in Samuelson's and Modigliani's long essay, "There is no room . . . for increasing returns, learning by doing, oligopolistic competition, uncertainty, obsolescence and other such troublesome things which mar the world as we know it."[13] He labeled theirs an "anti-Pasinetti theorem," a name that stuck, and thought it a "barren exercise," having no connection to reality or "the known facts of experience."[14]

Samuelson and Modigliani replied to Pasinetti and Robinson, saying that Kaldor's paper had reached them too late for comment. They were dismayed that their paper had appeared to Pasinetti "as primarily apologetics for a specific theory." Indeed, their motivation had been to recognize Pasinetti's as one of two golden-age equilibria, being matched by what they called the dual equilibrium, arguing that these are two halves, one being as general as the other.[15]

Throughout his career Samuelson has argued consistently that he could use neoclassical or alternative models as he pleased, so it is not surprising to find that in 1991, twenty-five years after these exchanges, Samuelson commented:

Because Pasinetti (and Kaldor) are known to be trenchant critics of

neoclassical marginalism and because Meade, Samuelson and Modigliani have been known to explore the neoclassical models, there has
grown up the dubious tradition of dubbing the Pasinetti equilibrium a
macro-post-Keynesian distribution paradigm, while the dual equilibrium (non-optimally dubbed the anti-Pasinetti equilibrium) is sometimes thought to be peculiarly connected with the kind of neoclassical
marginalism paradigm that Piero Sraffa (1960) proposed to subject to a
careful critique. Speaking for no one but Samuelson, I wish to dissoci-
ate myself from such identifications. . . . Herring is good in its place.
Chocolate is good in its place. No need that I can see to provide a
"reconciliation" between them. That is also the proper attitude to take
toward so-called Pasinetti and anti-Pasinetti equilibria. Each obtains
under specifiable conditions.[16]

The core of the 1960s argument is that Kaldor wanted consistency
between theories and facts of the real world. Some other economists
thought this unnecessary.

Round three, 1968–70

Another exchange in the *Review of Economic Studies* which bore primarily
on the theory of distribution took place between Koichi Kubota, D. Mario
Nuti, Joan Robinson, and Nicholas Kaldor in 1968–70.

Kubota was critical of Kaldor's specification of his models.[17] Nuti
found the model inconsistent with Kalecki's assertion of the relation between monopoly and distribution and that the inconsistency might "un-
ravel the Cambridge theory of distribution."[18] Robinson suggested that
the missing link in the model was that "the level of employment is not
explained," but she thought this might not matter since "the speciality of
the Mirrlees-Kaldor [model] concerns the determination of the overall
rate of growth through the pay-off principle."[19]

Kaldor answered Kubota, Nuti, and Robinson. He suggested that
one of the problems of existing theories of imperfect competition was
that they were largely "micro" theories and were not readily applicable to a group of firms because they assumed all firms to be identical
in their cost and demand functions. He thought that "excess capacity"
was invariably linked to imperfect competition rather than to the state
of employment or "insufficiency of demand." He invoked Okun's law
in which "it is perfectly consistent to assume that, in long-term equilibrium both output and output capacity should grow at the same rate
without implying that the one is equal to the other." He reminded
them that Arthur Okun had found that the share of profit and level of
employment are positively correlated. Kaldor insisted that according
to Cambridge theory:

The labour market does *not* behave in accordance with the postulates of neo-classical theory: with a rise in the demand for labour, there is a rise in the share of profit, and a fall in the share of wages and not the other way round. . . . This is because a high demand for labour is associated with a high rate of investment and a high rate of profit on capital. Empirically, the evidence here supports Cambridge and not neo-classical theory: the share of profit and the level of employment are *positively* correlated, not negatively.[20]

Where do other theoreticians stand?

The Kaldorian, or Cambridge, theory has been neither accepted nor rejected by the profession in general. Tobin, in 1989, while not accepting the Kaldorian theory, argued that it deserved a wider audience. His concession, coming in a symposium devoted to the discussion of Kaldor's work, was that when societies are not characterized by competitive markets, the ordinary tools of neoclassical economics are much less useful, an admission that might have pleased Kaldor. But Tobin still thought differential savings propensities unnecessary to the determination of distributive shares. In a comradely way he presented a model in which the distribution of income between wages and profits cannot be explained by marginal productivities.[21]

In the 1990s, interest among theoreticians continues to focus on the post-Keynesian theory of distribution to which Kaldor made a major contribution.[22]

The structuralist view

Kaldor's theory of distribution had stimulated other responses besides the neoclassical response. K.W. Rothschild, in "Themes and Variations— Remarks on the Kaldorian Distribution Formula" sought to introduce the "sociological fact" of the reluctance of workers and trade unions to accept a deterioration of their acquired incomes in the face of rising investment. He concluded that in the relatively short run the Kaldorian mechanism of investment shares determining income distribution works within "certain narrow limits" that are themselves determined by "institutionally and sociologically circumscribed distributional behaviour." The Kaldorian mechanism he saw as continuing to operate in the long run, but not so restrictively. Rothschild argued that saving and consumption propensities are shaped by sociological and economic influences. Particularly, entrepreneurs are not independent of the conditions they meet in the labor market.[23] He likened his work to that of Jean Marchal of France and John Dunlop and Arthur Ross of the United States, who had argued that group pressure plays a prominent role in distribution. But Rothschild insisted that Kaldor's presentation of the new ideas had a greater influence on subsequent discussion than any of the other contributions.[24]

The predictability issue

Another of the effects of the debate over distribution theory was a rash of articles measuring relative wage and profits shares. Among these, Lowell E. Gallaway found in his study that the "predictive ability" of Kaldor's macro-theory was excellent. He was contradicting Melvin Reder who had taken a different view. Gallaway said that the discrepancy was due to the fact that Reder had used only those years when full employment was established, which were the war years.[25] Kaldor had produced, in collaboration with his Cambridge colleagues, a theory that yielded interesting and testable hypotheses as well as a theory that allowed for institutional and even sociological extensions. His theory of distribution remains a live issue in the 1990s. Now we turn to his theory contributions of 1966 and beyond.

NK

CHAPTER THIRTEEN

Emerging Policy Views

Even as Kaldor was developing his new method and his hypotheses on economic growth, he continued his interest in domestic economic policy. As the 1969–70 president of Section F of the British Association for the Advancement of Science, he arranged a program to analyze the conflicts in economic policy objectives. The assumption of the counter-revolution that Friedman called for in 1970 was that only a monetary policy was needed—a gradual increase in the supply of money. Kaldor's assumption was that there are and will be "economic policy objectives" and that governments will be judged by them. What he had to say is still true.

Conflicting national objectives

Kaldor cited the four major objectives of British postwar policy to be a full employment target, a balance of payments target, a growth target, and a wage-increase or incomes policy target. As Kaldor said, "the fact that these have come to be accepted as mandatory objectives of policy, i.e., as ends that the public can legitimately expect from its government, was the most important political result of the intellectual revolution engendered by the publication of Keynes' General Theory of Employment." He argued, however, that there was little understanding of the difficulties when government attempted to achieve all these objectives simultaneously. Some of the various objectives came into "open conflict" with one another.[1]

British Governments had tried to serve all objectives, but had done so without a formal plan. Kaldor was not referring to a rigid plan, but to a strategy such as Japan and Germany had used to obtain their national economic objectives. In 1970, his main criticism of British policy up to that time was that there was a tendency to treat the problem of full employment and growth as one of internal demand management, that is, as a problem of a closed economy. Instead, Britain is an "open economy," and exports and international competitiveness must be taken into account.[2] He was particularly critical of policies of "consumption-led" growth, which had been much relied on in Britain. However, he did not believe that the postwar attempt to manage the economy was a failure in the sense that Britain would have been better off without management:

> On the contrary I am convinced that in comparison to the restoration of the pre-war system of *non*-management—which would have meant operating under a system of fixed exchange rates combined with a "neutral" fiscal policy—we have achieved higher employment and also more stability of employment, a higher level of investment, a faster rate of economic growth and also a faster trend rate of growth of exports.

He concluded that consumption-led growth is "clearly preferable to economic stagnation."[3]

Public or private enterprise?

On a second topic, Kaldor proposed an International Economic Association conference on the role of public and private enterprise in mixed economies. Such a conference was finally held in 1980 in Mexico City.[4] Kaldor addressed the conference on "the issues," noting that the problems could not be analyzed without taking into account the framework of political and social institutions, traditions, and the history and stage of economic development of each country to be analyzed. He arranged countries into three groupings—socialist, developed capitalist, and developing countries. He thought there were many variations within these groupings, and he did not attempt to generalize what the "proper" mix might be.

Kaldor saw a role for both private and public enterprise in all three groupings. He found "the strongest argument in favor of private enterprise in the developing countries is that it is generally better managed and technically more efficient than public enterprise" in those economies. He thought that private enterprises have less bureaucracy and a better quality of management there, though this is not necessarily true in developed countries. Speaking ten years before the destruction of the Berlin Wall and all that was to follow, Kaldor noted that the socialist systems had not produced the results expected of them; however, he predicted that the more capitalism develops into a corporate state dominated by a small number of giant enterprises, the less likely its survival. He admonished, "As biological evolution shows, nature abhors giantism." He did not know what further development capitalism would take, except that it would not develop into "centralised socialism."[5]

The one advantage which public enterprise has over private enterprise Kaldor saw as the undertaking of risky ventures, "pilot enterprises."[6] He thought that since the major economic problem was more one of activating unused resources than of allocating scarce resources among competing uses, "we should not pay blind respect to profitability criteria."[7]

The French success after World War II he attributed to the use of planning and cooperation. He had proposed the same for the United Kingdom—"getting individual firms in different industries together to work out an optimal investment plan to their mutual advantage"—but he "was regarded as a 'madman' who wanted planning—by the bureaucracy in Whitehall. Events had now proved that France was right and Britain wrong." He agreed with Pierre Dreyfus, former president and director general of Renault, that private enterprise receiving instructions from the government was not the same as public enterprise. Kaldor thought that in both France and Germany there was a more cooperative spirit than in Britain. "The failure in Britain was due to the alienation of the working class from managers and capitalists."[8]

Kaldor denied that he ever meant to suggest that central planning is always superior; he merely considered that there are some advantages inherent in public enterprise as well as in private enterprise. Public enterprise can do away with the instability of investment that is forced on private entrepreneurs.[9]

Unemployment and international trade

Again in 1980 Kaldor participated in the International Economic Association conference in France on "Unemployment in Western Countries." Speaking on the general topic of international trade and unemployment, Kaldor chose to consider the "foundations of free trade theory and their implications for the current world recession." His object was to show that, in spite of free trade theory, conditions can and are likely to exist in which unrestricted trade may lead to a loss of welfare to particular regions or countries and even to the world as a whole: "The world will be worse off under free trade than it could be under some system of regulated trade."[10]

After reviewing economic theory on the subject of free trade, he noted that the factor price equalization theorem did not work if one allowed for either diminishing returns, as in a land constraint, or increasing returns, as in industry. He asserted that, therefore, international or interregional trade is capable of enlarging differences in living standards between areas as well as diminishing them. The question was which tendency will be dominant. Of the three types of trade—between manufacturing countries and primary producers, between manufacturing countries and each other, and between primary producers and each other—only the third type seems to follow the classical theory of mutual advantage of free trade. This gives rise to what Jan Fagerberg has called the "Kaldor paradox," in which the fastest growing countries in terms of exports and GDP since World War II have at the same time actually experienced faster growth in relative unit labour costs than other countries, and vice versa.[11] The evidence that free trade may be detrimental led Kaldor to call for "new rules of the game." He quoted Raymond Barre, the French prime minister, who said, "Free trade is nothing more than a pretext for the strongest and least scrupulous as well as being a trap for the weakest." Kaldor believed that the restoration of full employment and prosperity requires that trade imbalances be removed preferably by the creation of these new rules of the game.[12] In 1977 he had expressed his dismay that American economists had declared themselves against anything "that smacks of interference with the unhindered operation of free markets." He wrote to Pechman:

> If Japan sells manufacturing and takes nothing in return, manufacturing output in the United States will be reduced and taking the multiplier into effect, the reduction will be greater than the value of displaced output (by imports). So how can [anyone] maintain that free trade is an ideal policy which maximizes welfare?[13]

He argued that American economists must be assuming full employment, adding, "I cannot see the case against protectionist proposals once it is admitted that the effect of free imports is not to improve the allocation of resources but to reduce their utilization."[14]

In terms of policy, Kaldor not only called for new rules of the game but also arrived at the conclusion that exchange rate adjustments, which were supposed to exert their influence through changes in relative prices, had not been effective in changing the relative competitive positions of industrial countries during the 1970s. He was less optimistic than he had been in the 1960s about the effects of an employment subsidy, because it is "like an indirect change in the exchange rate" and therefore still dependent on the effectiveness of devaluation as an instrument. What was more important was income elasticity, as distinguished from price elasticities—"It was variations in levels of income and output which were the main cause of changes in imports relative to exports." He had concluded, in part relying on studies by T. F. Cripps, that the answer was that countries that were not constrained by a negative balance of payments should accept more imports from the "constrained" countries.[15] Kaldor said the problem he was tackling was one of structural disproportions between the import propensities and the export abilities of different countries: the "cause of a good deal of depression in world trade and world production. Its removal would help every country."[16]

As both a theorist and a policy maker, Kaldor had thought long and hard on these problems. While some of his views had changed, the intractable problems were still on his mind. In 1958, he had told the American Committee for Economic Development that the most important economic problem to be faced was "the growing disparity between rich and poor countries." He was certain that this growing disparity threatened the political and economic stability and cohesion of the noncommunist world.[17] His only optimism was that because of the cumulative effects of growing world demand, there need be no conflict of interest between the economic interests of advanced and developing nations. But he would not leave the solution of the problems of trade and unemployment to "the market." Rules were needed. Seeing that the continuing disparity between rich and poor nations is part and parcel of the economics of domestic employment levels and of international trade, Kaldor took the broad view toward economic analysis. And when he rejected equilibrium analysis and laissez-faire, he did not neglect to provide a different paradigm for approaching these problems.

NK

CHAPTER FOURTEEN

The Watershed of 1966

Kaldor's inaugural lecture as professor of economics in the University of Cambridge in 1966 marks the beginning of the next stage of his theorizing and the end of his reliance on "equilibrium methodology." He took as his subject the "causes of high and low rates of economic growth under capitalism," putting forth what he later insisted was "a complex thesis."[1] He began with comparative growth rates, noting that the United Kingdom invariably was "near the bottom of league-tables." He reviewed the allegations of blame that were generally offered, such as the inefficiency of management or the educational system. He felt that while many of these contained truth, they were generally "not capable of being tested." He suggested an alternative approach that sought to explain the differences in growth rates in terms of the *stage* of economic development of the different countries, arguing that the British economy had reached a high stage of maturity earlier than others. He then offered evidence of his thesis. He eschewed any temptation to attribute causal significance to a statistical relationship "unless it can be shown to be consistent with some general hypothesis, which can be supported by other evidence." He found that the different growth rates were largely accounted for by differences in the rates of growth of productivity, and that this was related to technology. And he asked, "Is there some general reason which makes the rate of increase of output-per-man . . . dependent on the rate of growth of manufacturing production?" Does the *size* of the manufacturing sector explain the facts? Does the existence of economies of scale or increasing returns?

He reviewed the contributions of Adam Smith, Alfred Marshall, and Allyn Young, who emphasized "the interplay of static and dynamic factors in causing returns to increase with an increase in the scale of industrial activities," and relied on Kenneth Arrow, who had shown that "productivity tends to grow the faster, the faster output expands." He emphasized Young's argument that "increasing returns is a 'macrophenomenon.' " But he did not offer a model.[2] Kaldor concluded, "It is a dynamic rather than a static relationship—between the rates of change of productivity and of output, rather than between the *level* of productivity and the *scale* of output," which explains the "Verdoorn Law."[3]

The Verdoorn controversy

The Verdoorn Law that Kaldor had in mind "asserts that, with a higher rate of growth of output, both productivity and employment increase at a faster rate."[4] However, without suggesting that the Verdoorn relationship applied *only* to manufacturing, Kaldor insisted that its application outside the manufacturing industry was "clearly far more limited"—it did not apply to agriculture and mining, and probably not to services. Then he attempted to explain why some countries had managed to increase their rates of manufacturing production faster than others. He admitted that complexities were involved and suggested that both supply and demand factors were important.[5] He argued that the evidence suggested that the major reason that Britain had failed to keep up was a manpower shortage. He thought this suggested policies to concentrate "our efforts on a more rational use of manpower in *all* fields, and to limit the absorption of labour into those sectors in which—if I may use a Pigovian phrase—the marginal social product is likely to be appreciably below the marginal private product."[6]

Much of what Kaldor said in this lecture became a permanent part of his thinking, though the shortage of labor arguments did not.[7] In this address he gave a theoretical framework to numerous testable hypotheses. Those have interested econometricians, who have produced too large a literature to be reviewed here. The point is not so much whether Kaldor was in 1966 right or wrong in his explanation; it is that he generated testable hypotheses by which economists can learn and had done so without reliance on what he called "equilibrium methodology." He had examined facts and tried to explain them in such a way that his explanations could be tested. This was the watershed of his career.

Extending the analysis to developing countries

In October of the same year, Kaldor gave the Frank W. Pierce Memorial Lectures at Cornell University, entitled "Strategic Factors in Economic Development." He continued to argue the mature economy thesis, stating that, yes, that thesis meant that someday the rate of growth of the world economy was bound to slow down. However, he did not see that as any immediate problem.[8] Looking at the world economy as a unit, he saw "a vast underdeveloped area with certain 'growth points.' "[9]

Having extended his analysis to the industrialization of the "underdeveloped countries," Kaldor concluded that restrictions on trade remained the major obstacle to the fast economic progress of the underdeveloped parts of the world. Their failure to develop in turn limited the markets for the goods of the industrialized sectors. He offered many policy suggestions, condemning efforts to cure balance of payments deficits of underdeveloped countries through devaluation because this only resulted in inflation.[10] The one "general" economic cause of "backwardness" and stagnation he attributed to the failure of underdeveloped countries to create an agricultural surplus. Kaldor admitted that the world's economic problems had causes other than economic ones and that what was needed was "a general theory of social and cultural development" rather than just economic policies. He called for "land-saving innovations" as a key to development in the underdeveloped areas.[11]

A shocked response to the inaugural address

J.N. Wolfe of the University of Edinburgh questioned nearly every point that Kaldor made in his inaugural address, and a few that he had not. Fundamentally, Wolfe objected to Kaldor's method and stated his preference for the "traditional method of estimating the production function." He challenged Kaldor's argument regarding the shortage of labor in Britain. He also indicated his anti-Keynesian or perhaps pre-Keynesian views by stating, "It is . . . difficult to increase capital formation or exports without increasing savings." One curiosity was his statement that there was nothing in the evidence Kaldor offered to support the Selective Employment Tax, a policy alternative that Kaldor had not mentioned. One of his worries was that Kaldor's thesis had "proved remarkably influential." Wolfe seemed alarmed that Kaldor might have misled the profession: "There is nothing in Professor Kaldor's lecture which should make us alter our view that the main burden of economic growth will continue to fall on technical progress and capital formation, as it does now."[12]

Kaldor responded with a quotation from Alexander Pope, urging readers to consider the whole, "not th'exactness of peculiar parts." In defending his approach, he noted that the neoclassical framework cannot accommodate concepts like "disguised unemployment," the "dual economy," or the distinction between "capitalist and pre-capitalist enterprise." He reiterated that "the rate of growth of industrialization fundamentally depends on the exogenous components of demand." He was not yet ready to surrender his belief in the maturity of the British economy or the importance of the shortage of labor. He refused to comment on issues such as the Selective Employment Tax and other policy matters he had not mentioned in his lecture.[13]

What remains of Kaldor's law?

Nearly ten years later, R.E. Rowthorn, also of Cambridge, asked "What Remains of Kaldor's Law?" meaning Kaldor's use of the role of labor supply as a constraint on potential productivity. Rowthorn reviewed a study by Stanislaw Gomulka that, he said, questioned Kaldor's law and one by T.F. Cripps and R.J. Tarling that seemed to support it.[14] Rowthorn's paper initiated a discussion that has continued into the 1990s. First, he challenged Kaldor's "unconventional and seriously misleading method of estimation" and concluded from his own investigation "that there is no empirical evidence that Kaldor's law has operated during the post-war period in manufacturing."[15]

In response, Kaldor defended his method and decried the unfortunate fact that "Rowthorn (and others)" had taken from his inaugural address only the idea that the slow rate of economic growth in Britain was mainly due to the shortage of labor resulting from economic maturity. He announced that he had since abandoned this argument "as a result of fresh statistical evidence, as well as further historical experience."[16] And in a discussion in 1981, Kaldor declared, "The assumption that labour is not a constraint on output as a whole or on the output of any particular sector such as manufacturing is basic to my whole approach in economics. It is, of course, a denial of the basic neo-classical hypothesis according to which in a market economy there is both full employment and a 'pareto-optimal' allocation of the labour force."[17] Kaldor no longer believed that the United Kingdom "*had* attained the state of 'economic maturity' . . . and that her comparatively poor performance was to be explained by inability to recruit sufficient labour to manufacturing." His main point had been missed. The real difference between the neoclassical and Keynesian schools of thought was rather "the question . . . whether one regards economic growth as the resultant of demand . . . or of changes in resource-endowment."[18] As for modifying his "story concerning the United Kingdom," he would definitely not do so in the direction of Rowthorn or the neoclassicals but would instead "now place more, rather than less, emphasis on the exogenous components of demand, and in particular on the role of exports in determining the trend rate of productivity growth." This indicates the evolution of Kaldor's ideas.

Rowthorn's views were also affected by the exchanges. He replied that he had never intended his article as a rebuttal of Kaldor's entire writings on economic growth, only of his method and his attempts to validate the Verdoorn Law. Now he was objecting to Kaldor's belief that there were "unlimited supplies of labor in the countries of his sample." However, Rowthorn thanked Kaldor for making him "realise, as I did not before, the importance of interaction and simultaneity in the economic processes concerned."[19] Then in 1979 Rowthorn, in "A Note on Verdoorn's Law," said that his own views had changed and that "returns to scale are more likely to be the result of a dynamic learning process than of a purely static choice between already known techniques."[20]

This did not end the matter of Verdoorn's law,[21] and Kaldor, in one discussion, was moved to declare his loyalty to the law as he understood it: The Verdoorn law is "essential for the existence of 'circular and cumulative causation' which I regard as critical for understanding the nature of the process of economic development, but the assumption of which is incompatible with neo-classical economic theory (i.e., the theory of general equilibrium)." He agreed with M. Chatterji and M. Wickens that the difference between economists like himself and those who believe in neo-classical theory is essentially a difference in empirical assumptions.[22]

A year after Kaldor's death, Erkin I. Bairam reviewed the literature in an article entitled, "The Verdoorn Law, Returns to Scale, and Industrial Growth" for the *Australian Economic Papers*. Bairam relied on a bibliography of seventy-three articles written by economists from many countries, testimony to the interest in the question. In 1991 John Battaile Hall reminded the Berkeley Roundtable on the International Economy (BRIE), that their arguments that the manufacturing sector plays a crucial role in the United States had been previously thought out in some detail by Kaldor and others of the Cambridge school.[23] Through his articles on economic growth and the theory of distribution, Kaldor had shown himself to be one of the most stimulating thinkers in the history of economic thought. This talent for challenge continued in his work after 1966.

Kaldor's story: The role of increasing returns, technical progress, and cumulative causation in the theory of international trade and economic growth

While gathering many honors, Kaldor continued to clarify his "story" of economic growth. Already a fellow of the British Academy, he served as president of Section F of the British Association for the Advancement of Science in 1970 and of the Royal Economic Society in 1974. He was made an honorary fellow of the London School of Economics in 1970, an honorary member of the American Economic Association in 1975, foreign honorary member of the American Academy of Arts and Sciences in 1977, elected honorary member of the Hungarian Academy of Sciences in 1979, and received an honorary doctorate at Frankfurt University in 1982.

Kaldor was not one to sit around and bask in this recognition. He continued his interest in the effort to provide an economic explanation of the differences in growth rates, in the world economy as a unit, and in the need for a method other than "equilibrium methodology." One of his earliest and best statements on "cumulative causation" appeared in a much quoted article, "The Case for Regional Policies" mentioned earlier.[24] In 1981, Kaldor's then current views on the role of increasing returns, technical progress, and cumulative causation in the theory of international trade and economic growth appeared in the French journal *Économie Appliquée*. Kaldor argued that the case of increasing returns, in spite of its existence having been understood even by Adam Smith, had never been properly explored in economic theory. The only attention to increasing returns came about when it was thought that economies of scale might lead to monopoly. When the imperfect competition analyses suggested that falling costs and competition can coexist, "economists in general shied away from exploring the consequences." This neglect, coupled with the traditional assertion that free trade is always to the advantage of each trading country, has led to the concentration of manufacturing production in certain areas. In turn, this "polarisation process" has inhibited growth of manufacturing in some areas and concentrated it in others. This is what he had meant about an underdeveloped world with "growth points." While polarization first occurred in the Industrial Revolution, it did not stop the spread of industrialization because all the countries that became industrialized did so with the aid of protective tariffs high enough to induce a substitution of home-produced goods for imports. Britain started the industrialization process and did not have to rely on protection in the initial phases. Kaldor was here reviewing history, not advocating policy. He added, the history of Britain "provides an excellent example of both the need for, and the practical limits of restructuring the economy in the face of adverse changes in the world market."[25]

All this, he noted, was explicable in "Keynesian (or rather Harrodian) terms" but not in neoclassical terms—i.e., "*not* in terms of a theory which assumes continuous full employment and a situation in which output in general is 'resource constrained.' "[26]

Casual readers may have trouble with Kaldor's argument unless they note: (1) that economic growth of any one country is not resource constrained so much as demand constrained and, in some arguments, policy or balance of payments constrained, (2) that exogenous demand is most often the constraining element in the economic growth of an individual economy, and (3) that there are, however, limits to world resources that may in the long run come into play to limit economic growth but whose effects may be delayed by resource-saving inventions.

He concluded that the further spread of industrialization in developing countries involves an outward strategy, which is the development of export potential and not just import substitution. He believed that rising incomes in developing countries would stimulate exports from industrial countries, but he noted there is "no guarantee that the reduced export share of the older industrialised countries and the increase in total world demand will fully offset one another." He placed great emphasis on the need for a rising rate of growth of total world trade (i.e., world demand). Speaking in the midst of a world recession of the early 1980s, Kaldor said that the world was suffering from an insufficiency of demand for industrial products, but that it did not follow that free trade would lead to the maximum development of trade. Instead, "if it involves chronic imbalances, it might lead to a situation in which the world economy is in a state of continuous recession which cannot be effectively counterbalanced by national policies of economic management" because of the need to avoid deficits in their balance of payments.

Kaldor's plan was to introduce a system of planned trade among the industrially developed countries on a multilateral basis—an agreed pattern of surpluses and deficits in the trading of manufactures between developed countries, so as to remove the balance of payments constraint on their internal expansion. As for the policies now used, which put trade restrictions mostly on imports from low-wage developing countries, Kaldor would recommend that such imports be freely accepted, since these countries have an unlimited appetite for manufactured imports of capital goods. He saw no necessary conflict of interest between accelerated industrialization of the developing countries and the economic interest of the developed countries, provided that the developed countries pursued full employment policies and avoided trade-induced balance of payments constraints among themselves. However, a conflict can only be avoided if world industrial production continually accelerates, so that the emergence of each new center of industry is a net addition to the existing rates of growth of the other industrial countries.[27]

Then Kaldor noted that, "It is surely true to say that the growth in the output of primary products (food, fuel, and raw materials) . . . governs the rate of economic growth generally"; that from the point of view of the world as a whole, "it is by no means . . . evident that poverty and underdevelopment are not basically due to scarcity of natural resources rather than to the insufficient availability of capital goods." He concluded that this "dilemma of Nature's constraint" can only be avoided if future technical progress is reoriented from its current labor-saving bias to one with natural-resource-saving bias. It is "no good having silicon chips if we do not also invent ways in which land-content or rather the natural resources content of a unit of final product is reduced at the same time." His fear was that as a result of new inventions, labor productivity might rise dramatically, but the growth of total output will be constrained by the scarcity of natural resources such as oil.[28]

This idea of switching emphasis toward land- and resource-saving technology and away from labor-saving technology is an important one, and it deserves, as many other of Kaldor's statements do, more attention. When E.F. Schumacher had first presented his views at Cambridge in 1964 on "intermediate technology," Kaldor was reportedly one of his most vociferous critics. While land- and resource-saving technology is not the same as "intermediate technology," Barbara Wood does claim that Kaldor came to accept that there was value in Schumacher's idea.[29]

In any case, Kaldor wrapped himself fully in the cloak of classical economists Adam Smith, Karl Marx, David Ricardo, Robert Malthus, and of course Allyn Young. He claimed that his views were "in stark contrast to the neo-classical view that the natural rate of growth of any closed economy is determined by the growth of the labour force plus the growth of labour productivity due to technical progress." He thought this was because modern economics had been developed from the viewpoint of the advanced industrial countries, and his economics was from a world viewpoint.

Kaldor's broad view of economic growth and its potential effects on standards of living is validated through world experience. Nicholas Stern, in "The Determinants of Growth," written in 1991 for the hundred-year anniversary of the *Economic Journal*, agreed that experience has shown that "there is no guarantee that growth will eliminate destitution and hunger ... or protect the environment."[30] Furthermore, Stern thought that so far "only a limited aspect of what Kaldor had in mind" had been captured by the new growth theories. Stern predicted "a resurgence of interest in the work of Kaldor, including his emphasis on both static and dynamic increasing returns."[31]

Kaldor and Young in retrospect

Ideas about increasing returns had been with Kaldor throughout his career, but it is interesting that they bubbled to the forefront during his process of freeing himself from "equilibrium methodology." Kaldor was Allyn Young's pupil when Young made his famous presidential address, "Increasing Returns and Economic Progress," to Section F (Economics) of the British Association for the Advancement of Science in 1928. Kaldor took extensive notes of Young's lectures, which is fortunate, since many of Young's papers were lost after his premature death in 1929.[32]

Roger J. Sandilands, who edited Kaldor's notes for publication says, "It is clear from Kaldor's LSE notes that many of his later contributions to economics—for example, on the role of speculation, on community indifference curves, and on the irrelevance of much of 'equilibrium' theory to an understanding of the dynamics of growth—were inspired by what he learned from Young."[33] Kaldor has said as much himself, but it is interesting to have another source of Kaldor's claim of Young's brilliance. One is particularly pleased to know from Kaldor's notes that he had learned as a graduate student that "Seeking for equilibrium conditions under increasing returns is as good as looking for a mare's nest."[34]

Young had other famous pupils. Among them was Frank H. Knight, with whom Kaldor debated capital theory in 1937, later changing his mind and saying Knight was correct. Another was Edward H. Chamberlin, whose book, *The Theory of Monopolistic Competition*, Kaldor favorably reviewed and with whom Kaldor argued whether Chamberlin's theory was really different from Joan Robinson's concept of imperfect competition. Chamberlin students think there was a concession eventually by Kaldor of a meaningful difference.[35]

Still another famous pupil of Young's was Lauchlin Currie, who studied under Young while Young was still at Harvard. Currie and Kaldor met in Dubrovnik in November 1977 and carried on a correspondence which has now been published.[36]

Currie believed that Kaldor had misinterpreted Young's "increasing returns" and distorted the meaning. He particularly objected to Kaldor's using the concept "increasing returns to scale" as a Youngian idea, because he thought Young's broader concept of increasing returns could apply equally to agriculture. Currie, who spent most of his professional life in Colombia, thought this broader concept more appropriate.[37] He also objected to Kaldor's alleged addition of Keynesian analysis to Young's. Young was discussing a "macroeconomic" *real* increasing returns, according to Currie, whereas Keynes introduced monetary factors into the picture. Currie also felt Keynes's definition of Investment, which was applied by Kaldor, was too broad. However both agreed that economic growth is demand induced.[38] On the other hand, Charles P. Blitch, who has made important studies of Young, believes that Kaldor was following Young's insights and conclusions faithfully.[39]

In short, Kaldor, forsaking models, following Young, and incorporating what had been learned from Keynes, provided a vision based on a venerable classical tradition. That vision and approach has reopened heretofore unexplored vistas for economists.

Part V

Where Kaldor Stood

NK

CHAPTER FIFTEEN

Economics Without Equilibrium

Nicholas Kaldor's eventful approach to economic theory and policy had led him to a confrontation with the orthodox economics he had learned from Lionel Robbins so long ago at the London School of Economics. He saw the problem of theoretical economics not as the allocation of scarce resources, but as the understanding of economic growth and income distribution. The problem of policy was how to balance the conflicting objectives so that economic growth could continue apace. Economic growth was not just the provision of employment and the piling up of material goods, but a synonym for rising standards of living. In a search for a more encompassing understanding of the economic real world, Kaldor had returned to his earlier teaching from Allyn Young, who had drawn inspiration from Adam Smith. It is a curiosity that this trend of thought was considered "destructive" by mainstream economists.

Kaldor's arguments parallel those being worked through in another field—artificial intelligence (AI), the effort to create machines that think. According to the *Economist*, Herbert Simon has been struck with how easy it is to work out the difficult problems such as logical theorems, while how seemingly impossible it is to create machines that have common sense. Accordingly, most AI researchers have "given up the dream of finding a general theory of intelligence" and have settled for "a toolbox of problem-solving techniques, each one suited to different jobs."[1] Kaldor was merely asking economists to do the same.

The irrelevance of equilibrium economics

In "The Irrelevance of Equilibrium Economics" Kaldor attacked the hegemonious "neo-classical model," the idea that "general equilibrium theory is the one and only starting point for any logically consistent explanation of the behaviour of de-centralised economic systems." His quarrel was that the basic assumptions of the theory were either provably wrong or unverifiable. Increasingly this had led to the fact that the "'theorist' and the 'empiricist' operate in two separate compartments and the challenge of anomalous observations is ignored by the theorist." He observed that in econometrics, where empirical material was applied to the standard theoretical model, "the role of empirical estimation is to 'illustrate' or to 'decorate' the theory" rather than to provide support to the basic hypothesis.[2] Over the years Kaldor had suggested an alternative methodology: start with the stylized facts rather than with the neoclassical model.[3]

Economics without equilibrium defined

In his three Arthur M. Okun Memorial Lectures at Yale University in 1983, three years before his death, Kaldor offered a different approach— "economics without equilibrium." Applauding Okun's efforts to discover "methods or policies to improve the performance of the economy in terms of the twin objectives of efficiency and equality," he called for beginning with observation rather than intuition. Kaldor's favored metaphor of Walrasian economics was that, "The ship is no nearer to the shore, but considerably farther off," adding, "though in a logical, mathematical sense, the present system of derived tautologies is enormously superior to Walras's original effort."[4]

In its negative view, economics without equilibrium is economics without constant returns, without perfect competition, without perfect knowledge, without the maximization principle, without a set of blueprints, and without a certain tendency toward equilibrium.

But in positive terms, economics without equilibrium is economics in time, "a continuing and irreversible process."[5] There may be stages of development through time; there may be imperfect competition; and there may be increasing as well as decreasing returns. Technical progress is endogenous to the system, rather than outside it. There are not only producers and consumers, but also dealers, middlemen, speculators, and government. In the private markets in industrial societies, producers are price-makers rather than price-takers. Quantity signals are more important in causing an economic agent to change his policy than are price signals. With these stylized understandings, economics can flourish. Of the "equilibrium model," Kaldor said flatly, "A theoretical approach that ignores the way markets are organized in the real world for the sake of logical or mathematical purity is not likely to come up with conclusions that will improve our understanding of how things work."[6]

However, in emphasizing the market adjustment of production to quantity signals, Kaldor did not deny the importance of prices. He was, instead, seeing the constraint in economics without equilibrium as demand rather than resources. And since it is through budget constraints that demand constraints are made effective, prices are still important. But even under "full employment" the individual economy is demand constrained rather than resource constrained, because there is, inevitably with imperfect competition, a large amount of "disguised unemployment."[7]

Economics without equilibrium is Marshallian economics, for, "Marshall realized that human societies are subject to continuous evolution, the precise direction of which can never be predicted . . . ."[8] In orthodox neoclassical economics, we have, instead, a Heisenberg-type "mathematical crystal . . . some rigid thing, which may be correct or incorrect but without an intermediate case." Kaldor thought general equilibrium theory had achieved this moribund state by 1954 and that "nothing has come of the original intention to gradually 'dismantle the scaffolding.' "[9]

Most important, economics without equilibrium has deep roots. It is the increasing returns economics of Smith and Young. And the world of increasing returns is one of the cumulative causation of Myrdal and of the multiplier of Keynes, where differences in productivity and well-being may be enlarged by trade.

Economics without equilibrium is thus not an economics to be left to the Unseen Hand. In his address, Kaldor once again paid tribute to Okun's recognition that conflicting economic objectives required the use of more than fiscal and monetary policies. So that, finally, economics without equilibrium is an invitation to economic policies tailored to the needs of the society for efficiency and equality.

The twenty-first century

For the hundredth anniversary of the *Economic Journal* in 1991, twenty notable economists wrote their predictions of what economics might be like in the century ahead. Reading their projections satisfies me that Kaldor was one of the few economists of his generation who tried to make his work meaningful to what William Baumol called "the newer economics" in research method, teaching matter, subjects for pure research, and topics for applied economics.[10] Jagdish Bhagwati predicted a reversal of the trend that had taken economics out of the realm of moral philosophy. He found economists now reaching out to politics, psychology, sociology, and philosophy. In his opinion, the growing integration of the world economy must force "a dramatic shift in the nature of the questions posed and consequently in the content of Economics. . . ."[11]

Nicholas Stern, as we have seen, predicted a resurgence of interest in the work of Kaldor, including his emphasis on both static and dynamic increasing returns.[12]

Frank Hahn, Michio Morishima, and Edmond Malinvaud wrote on the fate of the general equilibrium theory (GET) in the years ahead. Without mentioning Kaldor, they gave credence to his arguments. Malinvaud made a small concession, saying that "more and more people among us will recognise the limits of the dominant concepts of economic rationality and economic equilibrium; without abjuring their faith in the value of these concepts, they will realise that exclusive reliance on them is not always warranted."[13]

Morishima feared that GET economists had "sunk into excessive mental aestheticism," forming a bad habit that needed to be corrected in order to avoid the degeneration of their subject. He noted that models focusing on "pricetakers" are applicable to industries such as agriculture whose outputs account for only 20 percent of the gross domestic product of industrial societies; that methods of determining prices differ according to the stage of technological development; that the "number of actors on the stage" in the GET world are "far too few." Of the two "pillars of economics—mathematical analysis and social scientific analysis"—the latter would become relatively more important in the twenty-first century. He was not engaging in "anti-mathematics" sentiment, but following Walras, who wanted to entrust "the social sciences to men of general culture who are accustomed to thinking *both* inductively and deductively and who are familiar with reason *as well as* experience." Morishima found works like Okun's *Prices and Quantities*, which Kaldor had so admired, especially encouraging. He asked for models built "on the basis of empirical observation," and thought "axiomatisation and mathematical refinement must be the second stage."[14]

Hahn foresaw "an increasing realisation by theorists that rather radical changes in questions and methods are required if they are to deliver, not practical, but theoretically useful, results." He recognized that this adjustment would be painful to some theorists. There was a need for simulations rather than theorems, for psychological, sociological, and historical "postulates" instead of "simple transparent axioms." He thought there were signs that "the subject will return to its Marshallian affinities to biology," that "the learning stage cannot be skipped," that these are "some of the 'grand' questions which most theorists know to be next on the agenda." Addressing these questions would "inevitably lead to deep changes in the manner of theorising." Hahn found some recent maximization theory illustrative of the fact that "the habits of proof and argument are gone." He noted the serious difficulties for theory when markets are not perfect, when firms have transaction costs and/or increasing returns. Hahn had consistently defended GET[15] and was not writing off its contributions, but he predicted that it "will increasingly be found to be too faint in the search for answers to questions which have quite naturally arisen from twentieth-century theoretical developments." He expected future economists to be far less concerned with general theory, but "to bring to the particular problems they will study particular histories and methods capable of dealing with the complexity of the particular." Hahn ended majestically: "Not for them the grand unifying theory. . . . Not for them, or at least less frequently for them, the pleasures of theorems and proof. Instead the uncertain embrace of history and sociology and biology."[16]

Mark Blaug may criticize Kaldor, as he did, for asking the "Big Questions" and for trying to answer them in a "Big Way." Yet, judging by this prophetic issue of the *Economic Journal*, it is Kaldor's questions and answers which will be of interest to economists of the twenty-first century.[17]

A parting word

A year before he died, Kaldor gave the second annual Hicks lecture at Oxford University, speaking on the limits on growth. This provided an opportunity for praising his long-time friend, John Hicks, who was in attendance, and for expressing admiration for his "pursuit of knowledge as such."[18] Kaldor offered a prescient insight into the growing inequality of incomes between rich and poor countries: "Any benefit of labour saving technical progress in the primary sector tends to get passed on to the consumers in the secondary sector in lower prices, whereas in the industrial sector its benefits are retained *within* the sector through higher wages and profits." This circumstance had shifted the terms of trade against the primary producing areas.

What then are the limits of growth according to Kaldor? To know this, Kaldor says we need another measure of technical progress—"land saving" or "natural resource saving." Indeed the physical limits on growth are distinct from the actual limits, which are "increasingly dependent on a complex of policy objectives."[19]

Kaldor, who had begun his economics as an enthusiast for laissez-faire and standard economics, had evolved through study and theory and policy-making, toward a view of the world economy in which opportunities that would not be brought forth by the Unseen Hand could nevertheless be achieved through formulating new rules of the game.

NK

CHAPTER SIXTEEN

Kaldor's View of the World

Where did Nicholas Kaldor stand at the end of his life? He continued to believe that economics could be a force for good and that good meant improving the lot of most people. He understood markets and their limitations in providing equity. He recognized the complexity of a government's facing conflicting economic objectives. These givens are important to our understanding of his conception of the role of the economist.

He had mastered received economic theory, but he believed that future improvements in economic understanding must use methods that differ from those adhered to by orthodox economists. He wanted economists to build from what little understanding we have of the real world rather than from *a priori* assumptions. He thought we could learn through constructing and testing hypotheses as distinguished from trying to fit the facts to neoclassical models.

The possibility of economic growth became his central interest simply because economists had understood since Adam Smith's *Wealth of Nations* that the material well-being of people could be improved through economic growth. He understood also that there are physical limits to growth, but he thought that even in the long run those limits might be ameliorated through resource-saving inventions in the same way that we have relied on labor-saving inventions. As his explanations and theories and hypotheses of the growth of an economy evolved, they did so within the framework of an open or world economy rather than a closed model. He saw that there was not only competition and conflict present but also some complementarity of interest. However, he never wrote that final book which might have summarized his views.

Kaldor has been damned by some as destructive for having departed from established method and by others for having attempted too much.

While he had honors heaped upon him during his lifetime, there is a chance that his work may be neglected now that he is gone. Instead his articles deserve a careful rereading by anyone working along the ethical, methodological, theoretical, problematic, or policy lines that he pronounced upon. Throughout this book I have given citations of those who agree with this opinion. The following is my summary of Kaldor's views as I think these stood toward the end of his life.

Domestic policy

In order to work toward the conflicting objectives of targeted employment levels, growth rates, balance of payments, and wages growth, and thus equity in a society, several economic quantities must be managed by a government:

1. Money must be managed both domestically and internationally. Once you have a credit system utilizing bank lending, the people who want to use money (to borrow it for investment or to employ it for expenditures) ultimately determine the amount of money in circulation. If banks refuse to grant liquidity when money is demanded, then the credit system will collapse. This would not necessarily be true of a commodity-money system, but Kaldor was talking about the economic world as it exists. Readers will recall the American stock market crash of October 1987, when the banking system was called on to provide liquidity.

The demand for money domestically cannot be entirely separated from the international standing of the currency. Kaldor would not exclude the use of floating exchange rates or other market devices in managing this relationship, but he would not *limit* policy to market solutions. One of his fears of a single European currency was that the ecu would be managed without consideration of British domestic needs. However, he had long advocated an international currency backed by commodities, one that would facilitate growth of trade within the world economy.

2. Total demand for goods and services must be managed, and preferably in a particular way—through export-led growth. This would mean that investment, that centerpiece of Keynesianism, would be fostered, leading in turn to growth of real income. This would permit increases in consumption that would not be constrained by balance of payments problems. Kaldor's argument that it is external demand (and thus balance of payments problems) that constrain the growth of a domestic economy is contrary to the traditional economists' belief that domestic growth is resource constrained and that in any case prior savings are necessary to growth. Acceptance of investment rather than savings as the

originator of growth was part of the Keynesian revolution, but Kaldor goes beyond Keynesianism and argues that the increasing returns associated with export led-growth are the means to growth. Traditional theory, monetarist theory, even the New Classical theory of the 1980s have held that all markets clear, so that supply occasions transactions. This argument between supply and demand factors is one of the oldest arguments in economic theory. Since all these variables are interrelated (that is, supply and demand are not as distinct as precise theory would require), the difference between economists turns on which variable they emphasize. When Kaldor emphasized effective demand, he lined up with Malthus, Marx, Sismondi, Keynes, and others. Traditional, Walrasian, and New Classical theory, as well as Say's Law in its simplest statement, hold that supply creates its own demand, and that savings creates supply. Traditional Keynesians saw the sequence as spending for investment creating savings through increases in income. (The investment dog wagging the savings tail and not the other way around, because investment causes the level of employment and income to grow. Given a stable propensity to consume, savings are made out of the increase.) For Keynesians, since you can have equilibrium at less than full employment, demand growth is crucial to economic growth. For continuous growth, demand must increase, and this should be translated into investment-led rather than consumption-led growth. Kaldor went beyond the closed Keynesian model to include international trade and the need for export-led growth.

3. The distribution of income must be managed through fiscal (taxing and expenditure) policy and through incomes policies. The distribution of income is inextricably linked to economic growth. Given a distribution of income to groups or individuals, growth means that the pie and thus the pieces of the pie get larger. For Kaldor and other post Keynesians there was a hitch. Wage earners in the real world would not necessarily be satisfied with merely a larger piece but the same percentage share: they might want a larger percentage share of the pie. This leads to the next point.

Domestically induced inflation is ordinarily cost-push, initiated by groups who want a larger share and resisted by groups who have the power to pass along the increased costs to the consumer through increases in prices. This creates a barrier to growth, either because the consumer rebels against rising prices or because the monetary authority restricts credit because of inflation. By restricting credit, the central bank causes interest rates to rise and thus restricts investments (which become more costly) and so restricts economic growth. The alternative to credit restrictions is to have both a planned growth and an incomes policy by which wages increase through planning and system-wide negotiated settlements rather than through power. Incomes policy is the means to avoiding credit restrictions on economic growth.

4. Increasing returns must be fostered. Technological progress and the increase in productivity is more important than the amount of savings. Increasing returns are associated mainly with manufacturing and the widening of markets through international trade, so the domestic economy must be oriented toward the production of and export of manufactured goods. Policy must be directed toward fostering investment in those areas that stimulate increasing returns and exports. Domestic consumption, particularly of imported goods, must be balanced through international agreement among the industrialized nations. This is because of the principle of circular and cumulative causation, which otherwise might lead to growing disparities in the distribution of world income.

5. Policy must watch for constraints on growth. A common restraint on economic growth in an industrial society is a balance of payments where imports exceed exports. It is less likely that a shortage of either the supply of labor or raw materials will restrain growth. However, in an industrial society that has no incomes policy, inflation created by a wages-push may trigger banking constraints, such as policies of higher interest rates which in turn will constrain growth.

In summary, Kaldor believed the prerequisites of stable growth in Britain could be as complex as requiring an incomes policy, an industrial relations system in which workers participated in decisions and thus favored domestic over foreign investment, a fair tax system based on expenditure taxes or perhaps income and supplementary expenditure taxes, a managed currency, and so on. Given these as the rules of the game, the private economy could generate domestic private investment whereby savings are stimulated through rises in income, ameliorating any tendency toward balance of payments constraints due to excessive imports.

Though Kaldor thought that a government must have economic objectives and a plan for achieving them through a kind of social contract, he did not think that socialist aims such as ownership of the means of production were necessary. In fact, he advised Latin American countries that private rather than public industries might function more efficiently in a poor, overpopulated country where there would be tremendous pressure on the government and its publicly owned company to place social aims higher than the economic aim of covering all costs and providing for new investments. Indeed, public investment might be reserved for "pilot industries" and for maintaining an appropriate level of investment.

Hence, while he faced the reality of the necessity of public planning to reach national objectives, Kaldor offered no pat policies that would work at all times for all objectives. His "story" of an economy is best described as one in which the history of an economy, including its resource pattern, will determine not only the objectives but also the possibilities of fulfilling them. As he had no ideological requirements, he might find himself at times agreeing with Milton Friedman on the issue of floating exchange rates and disagreeing with him on the policy of fixed increments to the supply of money (which Kaldor ruled impossible to achieve, as indeed it proved to be when tried).

Negotiated solutions, given strong economic objectives, were Kaldor's program. While he advised the Labour party and could see political arguments, his advice was based on economics. Thus, if he thought devaluation of the pound would help, he recommended it and fought for it, regardless of whether such would be a politically popular program at the moment. If he thought entering the European Community would be detrimental to British interests, he said so, opposing both parties. If he thought a tax program was right for the country though it might hurt him personally, he would still be for it.

International considerations

Kaldor's values led him to argue that the world should rely on negotiation rather than war to settle economic disputes. Again, he faced the complexities of this underdeveloped world with its isolated "growth points." Because of his reliance on promoting exports in the domestic economy, he had to answer the question of what the appropriate international trade policies might be. In every case, money, resources, markets, he promoted internationally negotiated agreements over the fiction of free trade and laissez-faire market solutions. Did this, therefore, make him favor protection? Not necessarily. He might favor moderate survival protection for some industries in some developing nations, but no protectionist trade wars, particularly among industrial nations. Rather, he promoted stable and regulated trade among all nations. Since increasing world trade allowed for increasing returns and extended the life of any given economic growth cycle, Kaldor thought the interests of all parties could be made ultimately complementary through agreements. He had been an internationalist at least since his service with the Economic Commission for Europe, and everything he had learned further convinced him of the complementarity of interests in world economic growth. But he also recognized that each nation has its own history, resources, and path of development, and he was knowledgeable regarding the different growth paces and patterns of the British economy. Like Keynes he believed that only through international organizations could the interests of industrial, underdeveloped, slow- and fast-growing economies be meshed. There was no unseen hand to do it.

The North-South model

Kaldor led us to expect to see a complex of interrelationships. Some have called it the North-South model, roughly referring to the fact that global industrialization has taken place mainly in the Northern Hemisphere, while the Southern Hemisphere mainly produces raw materials.

North

Economic growth in an industrial country need not be constrained by a shortage of labor, because labor can migrate to industry from agriculture or immigrate from the poorer countries of the world. Ordinarily an industrial country also has an educational system that can provide suitable workers. Nor are land and natural resources constraints in the short run to economic growth in an industrial nation. (There may at times be bottlenecks.) Through technical progress an industrial country can look forward for some time to putting off the dismal predictions of the law of diminishing returns, though Kaldor strongly recommended research in land- and resource-saving techniques, such as solar energy.

What is likely to limit economic growth in an industrial country? (1) Internally, the central bank's response to rising prices by restricting credit, so that a recession is caused, will deliberately stop or slow economic growth; (2) Externally, an imbalance of payments caused by imports growing too quickly or exports too slowly creates a balance of payments constraint on growth; (3) Limitations on world markets for goods will limit growth.

Hence, in an industrial nation, policy should be directed toward fostering manufacturing for exports, international support for expanding markets (that is, rising world income), and discouragement of domestic consumer purchases of imports beyond a certain point. Since expanding markets are needed at the same time that domestic imports are to be kept in line, international management of credit and trade is implied.

South

In an underdeveloped country, often overpopulated, with too many workers on the land for agriculture to be efficient, labor need not be a constraint, though education is needed. Other requirements are new capital and infrastructure, including roads, buildings, and communications, obtainable, to some extent, through credit from abroad. Should such a society be managed differently? Kaldor says no. This society, in order to take advantage of increasing returns, must also emphasize export industries. And in order to pay for imported capital, a fair price must be paid each year by the industrial societies for the country's primary products. Stabilization of prices and supplies of the primary products of developing countries require that all countries participate in international trading and price agreements. An international agency may be needed to oversee "granary" storage procedures and "buffer stocks" when shortages or bumper crops occur. Kaldor concluded that the limits to continuous and worldwide economic growth in the foreseeable future are not real (labor and raw materials) but political (a failure of policy).

Kaldor's view of the world was that of a master theoretician and practicing political economist who believed in human equality, economic justice, and the possibility of improving economic institutions. His education, motivation, and experience took him over a rocky road of intellectual development—from laissez-faire to economic management; from neoclassicism to economics without equilibrium. His views can give us hope and reassurance. Rather than being doomed, we can, with foresight and good will, negotiate some amelioration of many worldwide economic problems.

NK

APPENDIX

The notes in the Appendix provide background material on some of the subjects touched upon in the course of this book.

[For complete citations, refer by author and year to References. Abbreviations used are APT: Anthony P. Thirlwall's *Nicholas Kaldor*; CEE: Kaldor's *Collected Economic Essays*; and JMK: *The Collected Writings of John Maynard Keynes*.]

Chapter note 6.1 American tax debates and the expenditure tax

In 1942, Treasury Secretary Henry Morgenthau proposed an expenditure tax, his motivation being the wartime restriction of consumption. In 1977, the Treasury was facing the unfairness of the income tax in an inflationary economy and issued a *Blueprint of Tax Reform*. Harvey Galper, a senior fellow at Brookings Institution who served as director of the Office of Tax Analysis, U.S. Treasury Department, from 1976 to 1981, played a major role in the preparation of *Blueprint*. Later, with Henry J. Aaron, also a senior fellow at Brookings, he proposed a "cash flow tax system," which is essentially an expenditure tax proposal. Their colleague, Joseph A. Pechman (1985, 10, 17, 113–19) also a senior fellow and formerly director of economic studies of the Brookings Institution, opposed these proposals as a sort of wage tax. Joseph J. Minarik (1989) tells us that in 1986, both Gary Hart, in his brief ascendancy as a presidential candidate, and Senator Bill Bradley, a Democrat of New Jersey, in his role as tax reformer, considered an expenditure tax as an option. Tax attorneys such as William D. Andrews of Harvard Law School and economists like David F. Bradford have defended the idea. (In 1991 Bradford was appointed a member of the Council of Economic Advisers by President George Bush.) By 1992, such disparate sources as Democratic Senator Sam Nunn, Republican Senator Pete V. Domenici, (*Los Angeles Times*, October 1, 1992, p.16) and the *Economist* (November 14–20, 1992, p. 14) looked with favor on a "progressive expenditure tax—i.e., an income tax levied only on the part of income that is spent." Conservatives who have advocated a national value-added tax are also drawn to some of the arguments. The expenditure tax is certainly not dead.

Interest in the expenditure base for taxation in both the United States and the United Kingdom during the 1970s was stimulated by stagflation, that condition in which unemployment and inflation go hand in hand. The British considered the Meade Committee report which proposed an expenditure tax, in 1978. Also, by the 1970s, a great deal was known about the defects in the comprehensive income tax as practiced in the United States. In the 1950s, Pechman had quantified the effects of selective tax preferences so that the tradeoffs involved in legislating preferences were well known.

Minarik reports that Stanley S. Surrey, a lawyer, insisted such preferences were really "tax expenditures" or an "upside-down subsidy." There were many studies of the effects on various income groups of such "tax expenditures" or deductions. According to Minarik, in the United States in the 1960s, during a robust growth period and at the time of the Kennedy-Johnson tax cuts, the question of the fairness of the distribution of tax cuts was the overriding political issue. However, with the stagflation of the mid-1970s, economists recognized that inflation was distorting the measurement of income from capital—overstating the income of lenders and understating the income of borrowers. The wrong incentives were thus created: Accumulate debt, whether you are an individual or a corporation. Consume existing capital rather than reinvest it. There was also concern over the double taxation of corporate source income in first profits taxes and then individual dividends. At this juncture, Kaldor's proposal for converting the tax base to expenditures became intriguing to both economists and other tax experts.

The conference sponsored by the Fund for Public Policy Research and the Brookings Institution in September 1978 was attended by fifty-three invited scholars, including Kaldor. Three of the five papers on the subject "What Should Be Taxed: Income or Expenditure?" were on the expenditure tax (Pechman 1980).

David F. Bradford of Princeton University presented "The Case for a Personal Consumption Tax" (1980, 75–113). Like Kaldor, Bradford saw problems in the income tax's capacity to deal with inflation, depreciation, capital gains, and other accruing gains (1980, 82), whereas the consumption tax (as Bradford called his expenditure tax) did not require depreciation or estimates of accruing capital. Nor was there any need to measure the effect on wealthy shareholders of retained earnings if a consumption base were employed. Bradford felt that income taxes simply failed to function equitably when prices were changing (1980, 86). On the other hand, inflation poses no problem for the consumption tax because calculation of the base involves only the current year transactions. He thought that the main defects of the United States income tax were the measurement problems and that it was not and probably would never be comprehensive, so that given the definition of income, the federal government continued to tax savings lightly (1980, 88–90). Bradford also thought that using an income base for taxation led to profound effects, and not benign ones, on the financial structure of the United States (1980, 92). With the consumption tax, the disincentive to save is eliminated (1980, 96). Bradford thought such a tax more practical and believed that if it were established many problems would vanish and there would be no new problems (1980, 109). With Bradford on the Council of Economic Advisers in 1991, these ideas spread in Washington.

Instead of a total turnover from income to an expenditure base, William D. Andrews (1980, 127–51) proposed a supplemental personal expenditure tax, much like that of Kaldor's original compromise proposal. That was because Andrews was unsure whether complete substitution of the expenditure tax for the income tax was practical. The supplemental expenditure tax would be used to cut the marginal rates on income tax, which then exceeded 40 percent and to eliminate the minimum tax (1980, 133, 136, 139). He proposed to start with low rates, which would avoid hurting groups who had already "paid" for their capital, like retirees. He thought this would give relief to savers, because the current income tax was seen as a tax not only on income saved but also on the return for investing it (1980, 141). Unlike Musgrave and Domar, Andrews saw the current tax relief for capital gains as creating "a pointless inducement to try to cast income in that form" (1980, 148). He said this was concentrated in the high brackets and tended to undermine progressivity. Finally, the expenditure tax as a supplement would allow a decrease in the tax on inflationary gains (1980, 150).

Kaldor commented on Andrews's presentation and wrote two letters to Pechman clarifying his position (KPP). He still believed that the expenditure tax system would be both different and superior to the income tax system (1980c, 151). He made clear that he was in favor of the expenditure tax principle not because some existing system of income taxation was defective but because "the basic limitations of the income concept make it impossible to implement the Haig-Simons formulation, *no matter how the tax laws are framed*" (1980, 153, his italics). On other grounds, he was "fully in agreement with Andrews that, for theoretical as well as practical reasons, it is better to use an expenditure tax as a supplement to an income tax than as a replacement." However, he thought Andrews's paper showed a "lack of awareness of the political and sociological problems involved in closing tax loopholes. . . . [Andrews] gives the impression that most if not all of these distortions arise from the choice of income tax as a base, not from the political process by which tax laws are framed. . . . There is no reason to suppose that these same pressure groups would take an expenditure tax 'lying down' and permit the new tax to get onto the statute book in a pristine form. Indeed, they did not in 1957, when the Expenditure Tax Bill was passed by the Indian parliament" (1980c, 154–55).

Soon after the Brookings Conference, historical forces in the United States overcame the deliberative ones. In the 1960s and 1970s, European countries had increasingly turned to a consumption tax, the value-added tax (VAT), though none had adopted an expenditure tax as a base. In the United States in 1981, the Reagan tax cut rolled through Congress, reducing income tax rates across the board and narrowing the tax base. Associated with the tax cuts of President Reagan's first term in 1981 was a revenue loss of $162 billion (Pechman 1987, 41). The promised increase in economic growth rates did not occur. The national debt which had been $935 billion in 1981, stood at $1.823 trillion by 1985.

The interpretation of which of these factors "explains" the increasing indebtedness defines the interpreter's politics in the United States. For an economist, the major factor was that the promised estimated growth in the economy did not accompany the reduction in tax rates and thus did not pay in revenues what was promised. The Laffer curve would have been best left on the cocktail napkin where it originated, rather than being written into national policy. Nevertheless, the U.S. Economic Recovery Tax Act of 1981 set off a worldwide movement for lowering income taxes.

The 1981, or Reagan, tax cut cost so much in revenue that tax reform, as distinguished from just cutting tax rates, became a priority in the United States. It was at this point that Senator Bill Bradley seriously considered the expenditure tax option. He rejected it, according to Minarik, for several reasons. Explaining the expenditure tax to members of Congress so they could explain it to their constituents seemed difficult. Bradley knew that a fair expenditure tax must include taxes on gifts and bequests and that that might be difficult to legislate. He feared that the expenditure tax base could become "even more leaky" than the present income tax base. In addition, the changeover would unfairly tax people who had already paid income tax on accumulations of wealth. Congress might get a strong reaction from older people in this category. There were doubts as to whether shifting the tax burden away from capital was such a good idea. Finally, no country had such a tax, since India and Sri Lanka had long since repealed their expenditure taxes. The administrative problems were unknown, but it is interesting that it was the tax collector, the Treasury, that had earlier issued a blueprint of an expenditure tax proposal in 1977 (Minarik 1989 141–44).

As for the world picture, rather than the personal expenditure tax gaining support, the value-added tax, which is a tax on consumption but not a "base" for taxation, spread to England from Europe and was widely discussed in the United States.

By 1986, with Reagan still in power but the Democratic party in control of Congress, the United States Congress found it possible to take away some of the selective preferences embedded in the income tax. However, this loss of some "upside-down subsidies" was accompanied by still lower rates. One of the preferences that fell was that of lower rates for long-term capital gains. The Tax Reform Bill of 1986 was clearly along the "old-line economic ideal of a comprehensive income" tax, according to Minarik (1989, 142), and represented a "downgrading" of the consumption tax principle of deferring tax on the income from capital until it is finally consumed. (Kaldor thought taxing of capital gains was essential if income base was to be used.) Thus the changes in the American income tax in 1986 were somewhat in line with Kaldor's suggested reforms in *An Expenditure Tax* (1955), though short of his expenditure proposal. As Minarik suggests, the 1986 reforms in the United States tax system continued the dominance of the Haig-Simons income tax principle. Nevertheless, they did not stop the arguments.

In 1989, when Joseph Pechman was to give the presidential address to the American Economic Association, he chose as his topic "The Future of the Income Tax." Unfortunately his death on August 19 preceded the association's meeting in December, and his address had to be read by someone else. Pechman had continued to support the comprehensive income tax and also the base-broadening reforms of 1986. But, he said, "The reduction in the redistributive effect of the income tax has gone too far" (1990, 1–20). He thought the tax cuts of 1981 and 1986 had little effect on the labor supply and no effect on saving. According to him, incentives are not the problem, equity is. The only restoration of equity had been in the increasing ratio of transfers to income, but these transfer payments had been financed by the low- and middle-income groups. He strongly opposed omitting savings from the tax base and accused "several expenditure tax advocates" of proposing a tax on labor income, a kind of wage tax. He summarized what had happened to equity in the United States in the last decade: The 1981 act increased inequality by reducing income tax rates 23 percent across the board (with a top rate on ordinary income of 50 percent), lowering the capital gains rate to a maximum of 20 percent, introducing general deductions for individual retirement accounts, and providing very liberal depreciation allowances for business investment on top of previously enacted investment tax credit. After 1981, income inequality began to widen. The Reform Act of 1986 reduced inequality by increasing personal exemptions and the standard deduction, equalizing the tax rates on capital gains and ordinary income, and closing numerous loopholes; but maximum income tax rates were reduced to 33 percent on individuals and 34 percent on corporations. The bill was supposedly revenue neutral, so that additional revenues were not expected.

The discussion inevitably has continued. By 1990, the congressionally authorized debt ceiling had been raised twenty times in the last ten years, and the debt exceeded three trillion dollars. In the summer of 1990, President Bush invited consultation with Congress about what should be done to remove not the tremendous debt, which is economically impossible short of revolution, but the current and menacing annual deficit. His remarks and subsequent signature on the budget bill were interpreted as a resignation from his "Read my Lips" remark which promised "No new Taxes." Bush instead proposed the reduction of taxes on capital gains, which was not passed, and he was defeated in his reelection bid in 1992.

Looking to Europe, one can see that seventeen of the twenty-four OECD countries had by 1990 adopted some form of a value-added tax, beginning during the 1960s. Japan and Australia have had proposals for a VAT, and Canada, after long debate, adopted VAT (Cnossen 1988, 261–8).

Given the circumstances, some reform of the American tax system is inevitable. Were the United States to follow suit of the Europeans, adopting a VAT, and were taxes on capital gains repealed, the United States would have a bastardized version of the income tax base teeming with upside-down tax subsidies supplemented by a regressive consumption tax, the worst of all worlds and a wretchedly discriminatory tax system taken as a whole.

As an alternative, were the United States to do what Andrews had suggested—forego the specific capital gains tax, treating capital gains as ordinary income but at the reduced tax rates, and place, instead, a supplemental tax on expenditures which was progressive among households—some equity would be restored. Tax the expenditures of the rich and repeal the minimum tax. Strengthen gift and inheritance taxes. (See chapter note 6.2, Outline of the Expenditure Tax.) The VAT would not come into the picture (Andrews 1980, 148–50). Andrews makes the point that unrealized gains would be unaffected by such a change, inflation would have a smaller impact, and sales of assets would be treated as any other source of funds.

Kaldor raised no objection to the use of the expenditure tax as a supplement in his remarks on Andrews's 1978 proposal except to ask, "If, as Andrews argues, 'the current political climate is not hospitable to a simple increase in a tax on capital gains,' why does he suppose that it will be hospitable to the introduction of a progressive expenditure tax?" (1980c, 156).

The possibility of supplementing the multibased income tax with a progressive expenditures tax base remains a powerful idea for economists and tax experts to contemplate. In the postwar world, it was Nicholas Kaldor who raised this debate from the annals of economic doctrine.

Chapter note 6.2 **Outline of the expenditure tax**

Essentially, Kaldor was arguing for an expenditure tax *principle* that would avoid the inequities of the income tax and the adverse effect of income and company taxes on investment. As visualized by Kaldor, the expenditure tax would be levied on individuals and family units. The reporting would be via self-assessment, as is the income tax in the United States. In summary, persons/units would establish a cash-flow statement of their income and expenditures, paying a tax on their expenditures according to a graduated base that takes into account the number of persons in a unit and the level of wealth. All gifts would be taxed as expenditures, and there would be heavy inheritance taxes. The object would be in part to change the incentive system. People could save for major expenditures, education, or retirement without paying taxes on those savings or on the income from those savings. The capital and savings would be taxed when spent or gifted. Kaldor did not work out a universal system to be applied, leaving room for institutional flexibility. In his report on India (CEE 8:49–50), he recommended "a single, comprehensive return," covering wealth, property transactions, income, and personal expenditures, that would produce a "self-checking system" for income tax, capital gains tax, annual wealth tax, personal expenditure tax, and gift tax.

In the reporting system each taxpayer would have a code number to be used in all property transfers. Each seller and buyer would report property transfers by code number, providing the self-checking element.

A simpler method was proposed in the United States by William D. Andrews, who suggested a cash-flow reporting system. He called his tax "a consumption-type or cash flow personal income tax" (*Harvard Law Review* 1974). Richard Goode (1980, 70) thinks that a balance sheet would be necessary, though he notes that Peter Mieszkowski developed a cash-flow system for the United States Treasury Department. Actually, the expenditure tax could be collected with no more difficulty than the current income tax.

The major obstacle of changing from the income tax base to the expenditure base is that persons have paid income taxes on past savings and would therefore object to paying on the expenditure from those savings. The other difficulty is that the tax rates on expenditures would be high if sufficient revenue were to be raised. However, the inequities of the income tax as levied plus the anti-savings and investment aspects of the whole tax system undermine belief in its fairness. The replacement of the expenditure tax for the British surtax or for the American minimum tax, both supplementary taxes on the rich, would not create the same problems. Economists are increasingly concerned with the distortion to investment created by our tax system and may someday surrender the myth that the income tax is, as applied, a progressive and fair tax.

The real problem is whether either the United States or the United Kingdom, given their current distribution of income and power, can levy a fair tax. But that should not and does not mean that economists need not consider what a fair, progressive, and economically justified tax would be.

Chapter note 8.1 **Politics and North Sea oil**

The first finds of gas by British Petroleum (BP) in the British North Sea were in 1965. By 1967, natural gas was piped to British homes and by 1978 provided 97 percent of British gas needs, and North Sea oil was making a contribution to the British balance of payments (Arnold 1978, 36).

The Conservative government had in 1964 extended to offshore areas the oil and gas licensing and regulatory powers granted in 1934 by the Petroleum Production Act, but it did not contest the division of the North Sea between the UK and Norway, which gave UK only 35 percent of the North Sea. This Continental Shelf Act established state ownership of the North Sea reserves. The first licensing round came in 1964, and fifty-three licenses were granted.

In the October 1964 election, the major difference between Conservatives and Labour regarding oil was whether to have a regulatory agency or a state corporation. They agreed that the government should have direct access to information and the ability to interpret the information for either purpose (Hann 1986, 11).

Having won the election, Labour was in power when the 1965 discovery of gas in the West Sole Field made it a proven rather than a potential field, and also when the first discoveries of oil were made in 1969 by Amoco and the Gas Corporation. However, production was not immediate. Guy Arnold (1978, 36–7) notes that it is common in the industry to allow discoveries to lie dormant before companies decide they are "commercial." Production of oil in these fields did not commence until 1976. In the 1960s, OPEC had provided an early stimulus for further exploration by pressing the oil companies for more revenue from the Middle-East fields, a policy in which Libya, the source of much European-sold oil, was successful (Hann 1986, 6–7).

The rounds of licensing continued under both Labour and Conservative governments. Edward Heath was the Conservative prime minister when, in the winter of 1973–74, the world price of oil was quadrupled. Labour came to power again in 1974, and immediately called for a fairer share of oil profits for the government in order to maximize the gain to the balance of payments. Labour sought greater public control of British minerals and proposed a British National Oil Corporation (BNOC) that would participate in both exploration and exploitation of oil and gas (Hann 1986, 9–10). BNOC was established in 1976, just as oil came into production, the same year that Harold Wilson resigned and turned over Labour's reins to James Callaghan. BNOC soon became the largest world trader in North Sea oil. For the remaining three years of Labour under Callaghan, oil would make an increasing contribution to the balance of payments, and once again, Labour handed a healthy balance of payments over to the Conservatives in 1979.

Although Margaret Thatcher's government privatized most of its functions (creating Britoil), BNOC remained as an oil trader, since this was valuable to the Conservative government for both revenue and policy purposes (Hann 1986, 18–19). The Conservatives under Thatcher even implemented taxes proposed by Labour to recapture for the nation any windfall profits arising because of the 1973–74 oil crisis. It was the Conservatives, then, who benefited most by the development of North Sea oil. Production had begun in 1976, and by 1981 was considerably greater than what was needed for home consumption, thus making large contributions to the balance of payments (Atkinson and Hall 1983, 7). Given these developments, it is evident that the wild card had not come into play during the payments crises in 1964 and 1974. Nor was it in view during the discussions of whether to join the Common Market or not. (Britain became a member of EEC in 1972, with her entry effective in 1973.)

Chapter note 10.1 **Political economics of the quantity theory of money**

The quantity theory of money in several variations was widely accepted during the 1920s and when Nicholas Kaldor began to study economics. Generally, it was applied in trade cycle or business cycle theory, but it was the monetary theory of the day. The relationships established in the theory were that the amount of money (M) times its velocity of circulation (V) varies directly with the price level (P) and the volume of trade (T), or MV = PT. If you assume the velocity of circulation is a stable condition in a society and assume full employment, as traditional theory did, then changes in the amount of money will cause changes in the price level. Thus governmental action to increase the supply of money was the cause of inflation, and governmental action to decrease the supply was the cause of deflation. As expressed, MV = PT is a tautology. Changes in the amount of money were considered exogenous to the economy. Obviously, if the velocity of circulation of money is not stable and full employment is not given, then other outcomes are possible. And if the supply of money is endogenous, then the whole argument falls.

In quantity theory of money circles, Keynes lived rather a double life. R.F. Kahn (1984, 41) called Keynes of the 1920s, "a fanatical believer in the Quantity Theory" as evidenced in Keynes's obituary of Alfred Marshall written in 1924. Kahn (1984, 47) thought him a supporter of the theory in his *Tract on Monetary Reform*, though Joan Robinson (1978, viii) thought that in his *Tract*, Keynes had exposed the theory as useless for policy-making purposes. Kahn (1984, 52) made the point that Keynes wrote the *Tract* during the post World War I period of hyperinflation. He suggested that Keynes "was going to spend a considerable part of the next twelve years of his life in a struggle to escape from the stranglehold of the Quantity Theory—success being heralded by the publication of his *General Theory*, the *Treatise on Money* representing an intermediate phase." Kahn's account of the quantity theory should be read for its clarity of expression as well as its historical value. He added, "The great innovation of the *Treatise* (1930) was the abandonment of the Quantity Theory— apart from a few parting gestures—in favour of the idea of the flow of expenditure" (1984, 64–5). But he marked the great change as coming in the summer of 1932, when Keynes changed the title of his lectures from "The Pure Theory of Money," last given in 1929, to "The Monetary Theory of Production" (1984, 110–113, 171). This change was partly intellectual and partly in response to the work he was doing with the Macmillan Committee during the period November 1929 to June 1931. Keynes was appointed to this committee by the Ramsay MacDonald Labour government. By August 1931, Keynes became convinced of the necessity of going off the gold standard and thus devaluing the pound (Kahn 1984, 77–87).

In his *General Theory* Keynes (1936, 304–6) insisted that the assumptions that make the quantity theory of money a truism simply do not hold and that the relationship between the quantity of money and prices is much more complicated than the original theory suggests. He proposed the liquidity preference theories instead. This made the quantity of money of endogenous rather than exogenous origin. Keynesians generally, including Kaldor, accepted the implications of Keynes's theory making the quantity theory of money an unreliable guide to governmental policy. As Joan Robinson said in 1933, the quantity theory equations, no matter which one you used, were all "tautologies without causal significance" (1978, 53–4). And if you could not discern the cause, you could not guide the policy. This is not the same as saying that the tautology is of no use whatsoever descriptively, but in the *General Theory* the quantity theory was dropped.

Why did others continue to cling to the quantity theory? First and foremost, the quantity theory was *the* theory of money in traditional economics. Some thought it gave an explanation of the causes of business cycles and inflation/deflation; most important to others was the belief that it offered the key to appropriate governmental policy for stabilizing prices in order to provide the best possible climate for free enterprise. Acceptance of the quantity theory of money restricted the role of government in the management of the economy. Clearly, it was a governmental function to provide money to an economy. Since stable prices were considered advantageous to the functioning of the private, otherwise unregulated economy, the government, then, could use its power to control the supply of money in such a way that prices were stabilized. Government need do nothing else. The Unseen Hand would be in control.

Keynes, on the other hand, had argued in the *General Theory* that rather than limiting its role to controlling the supply of money and some unachievable policy of stable prices, a government should seek through fiscal policy to maintain a level of full employment. Stable prices could take a back seat, though still a policy goal. British Keynesians always understood that once full employment had been approached, inflationary pressures would be generated. Keynesians, unlike monetarists, recognized that inflationary pressures were being generated in the real economy, as distinguished from the "monetary" economy. British post-Keynesians accepted the idea that cost-push inflation was possible and were quite willing to apply an incomes policy—in the form of a tax and/or regulatory policy that maintained wages and profits at some level or allowed them to rise in concert, perhaps through negotiation. This was true also of European countries.

Anti-interventionists and monetarists objected to expanding the role of government into the area of distribution of income, which is far beyond a simple monetary role. American Keynesians did not stress the pressures generated by the maintenance of full employment, opting, apparently, for some inflation in preference to a lot of unemployment (Turner 1990). Acceptance of inflation as the lesser of two evils avoided the necessity of direct controls on incomes, a policy that is more unpopular in the United States than in Europe. (See chapter note 10.4, Incomes policy.)

Enter the Phillips curve (See chapter note 10.5) which argued that there was an inevitable tradeoff between unemployment and inflation. From the quantity theory, we have arrived at a series of problems best seen as embodying conflicting national objectives. (See Chapter 13 for Kaldor's statement on conflicting national objectives.)

However, other events were in the wings. In London on September 16, 1970, Milton Friedman (1970a) announced "The Counter-Revolution in Monetary Theory," in the first Wincott Memorial Lecture, delivered at the

Senate House, University of London, and published for the Wincott Foundation by the Institute of Economic Affairs. The reader may remember that it was Harold Wincott who considered Kaldor's tax views the new *Mein Kampf*. Wincott was, according to Lord Robbins, "a financial journalist of unique standing in his generation." When he died a memorial was established in his honor (Friedman 1970a, 4–5).

In brief, Friedman's counter-revolution was a return to the traditional quantity theory of money and its limited policy objectives. Gone would be the necessity of maintaining full employment because the Unseen Hand would do that. Gone would be the use of taxation or spending (fiscal policy) for economic purposes. Certainly, there would be no need for incomes policies. Remaining would be the role of the government, limited, for Friedman c. 1970, to maintaining a steady but limited increase in the quantity of money, just enough to satisfy the needs of population growth.

Friedman's counter-revolution was based on the following arguments: (1) Keynes was wrong when he said that monetary policy was ineffective; actually, monetary authorities had *caused* the Great Depression. (2) Keynes's argument that the collapse of investment was the cause of the Depression implied that monetary policy was of little importance except to keep interest rates down and that fiscal policy must be used, and this was wrong, too. (3) Keynes was wrong when he implied that inflation is a cost-push phenomenon and that therefore it is necessary to control costs. Friedman concluded that since Keynes had been wrong about the causes of the depression, the efficacy of monetary theory, and the origin of inflation, he had misled a generation of economists about fiscal policy being necessary to achieve economic objectives.

The upshot of this view is that only monetary policy is needed, and little of that. Government, except for monetary authorities, could retire from regulating the economy. Friedman continued his argument, saying: (1) that economists became disenchanted with Keynes when the predicted postwar depression did not come; (2) that both Britain and the United States had to give up on cheap money (low interest rate) policy; (3) that a reexamination of the monetary history of the Depression proved that it was bad monetary policy that had to be blamed (liquidity was not provided when needed); (4) new studies indicated that velocity of money was not as passive as Keynes had argued. Friedman's assertions are mostly questions of fact, and Keynesians have answered them. (cf., Hendry and Ericsson 1983). But as Samuelson has said, there is no man so deaf as one who does not wish to hear.

When making his speech in 1970, Friedman predicted that the United Kingdom would follow the United States in the policy of returning to what he called monetary doctrines—i.e., the reliance on control of the supply of money as the chief economic control of the economy. He was correct. Both the Conservative and Labour parties had been mainly Keynesian in their policies, attempting, with moderate success, to maintain full employment, and through incomes policies, with less success, to control wages. There were many changing circumstances beyond the control of government, especially when OPEC raised crude oil prices by multiples.

The rise in the popularity of monetarism within the economics profession followed a pattern that was noted by Harry G. Johnson (1971, 2–3) in his presidential address to the American Economic Association. He set out the social and intellectual conditions that had made the counter-revolution possible. He proposed an "as if" methodology to ask how one could go about making a counter-revolution. He admitted such an effort would "fly in the face of currently accepted professional ethics."

The way to go about a counter-revolution was to attack the central propositions of the current orthodoxy, then to make the aggressive theory appear to be new, yet absorbing much of current orthodoxy, giving new names to old ideas; the new theory had to be or seem to be complex and difficult in order to attract the young and hold the seniors of the profession up to criticism; the new theory must offer a new methodology to the young and some new important empirical relationships for the emerging econometricians to tackle. Keynes had done that in his day, and this is what Friedman tried to do. First, Friedman concentrated on inflation as a problem that Keynesian theory was not designed to deal with. Johnson (1971, 7) said that the history of the monetarist counter-revolution has, in fact, been characterized by a series of mostly vain "efforts to convince the profession and the public (a) that inflation is an important question and (b) that monetarism can provide an explanation and a policy whereas Keynesianism cannot." (Actually, monetarism did not become important, according to Johnson, until the United States experienced inflation associated with the Vietnam War.)

Second, by restating the quantity theory of money, Friedman presented an attractive degree of difficulty framed as "positive economics," which forsook the large Keynesian models for small studies making great predictions. The bait thrown to the econometricians was the testing of the stability of the demand function of money. Johnson (1971, 9–10) observed that "intelligent and gifted young men and women will persevere until they succeed in finding statistical validation of an allegedly important theoretical relationship, and will then interpret their results as evidence in favor of the theory that originally suggested the relationship"; thus, their efforts are likely to support the theory. He said that the counterists tried to meet criticisms of the earlier quantity theory regarding the assumption of full employment and stable velocity of money, first by denying that Chicago theorists—originators of the counter-revolution—relied on these assumptions, and second by holding that the question of the stability of the demand function was an empirical question. Friedman agreed that empirical questions are never settled. According to Johnson (1971, 10–11), Don Patinkin has shown that the early Chicago school theorists were indeed assuming full employment. Johnson thought, however, that the whole issue must be decided not on "scholarly chicanery," but on policy. He predicted (1971, 13) that monetarism would "peter out." He said that if we are lucky, we will just accord more importance to monetary factors; "if unlucky, then there will have to be a post-counter-revolution."

In terms of policy, then, the UK was probably unlucky: Kaldor (1985c, 257) set the beginning of the monetarist period in Britain as 1977, when Denis Healey, his former boss, initiated severe monetary restrictions. Furthermore, Thatcher's government was militantly monetarist in philosophy and policy from 1979 to at least 1981. Monetarism gripped the United States at about the same time, when Paul Volcker was appointed by President Jimmy Carter to be Chairman of the Federal Reserve System. Meanwhile, the International Monetary Fund had always placed emphasis on conservative monetary management, regardless of the domestic impact of restrictive policies, and during the upheaval of international credit adjustments in the 1970s and 1980s, the IMF enforced monetarism on developed and less developed countries alike.

The battle of Keynesianism and interventionism versus monetarism and laissez-faire continues; it is two-fold, involving both theory and politics, and forces economists to face the fact that the political element was at least as important as the theoretical arguments during the 1970s and 1980s. In a comment in the late 1970s, Harry Johnson (1978, 126) remarked that the popular use of monetarism owes a lot "to the desire of newspaper columnists and other fringe personnel to encapsulate scientific controversy into sloganized 'schools.'" He also referred to the danger of the debate over monetarism being "saddled with the dead weight of the historical luggage and political passions" of the so-called "new economics." He called his old teacher and colleague—Kaldor—one of the "illiterate monetary policy amateurs," along with Nobel Laureate J.R. Hicks, and added, "In Britain, in fact, the majority view bases itself on the axiom 'monetarism' = Milton Friedman = 'The Treasury View' = utter nonsense; in the same circles, incidentally, the corollary is 'Keynesianism' = incomes policy" (1971, 126).

Friedman (1970a, 20) considered himself a counter-revolutionary and conducted himself as one. In his Wincott lecture, he likened himself to the British economists who had brought "the message of Keynes" to America. Friedman said he was counting on the "very able and active group of economists" in the United Kingdom to bring off the counter-revolution, which he had in his speech announced. In a political sense, the counter-revolution had begun much earlier. In 1947, Friedman and Hayek had called together a group of thirty-nine economists, all of whom "were known as strong believers in political, economic and moral freedom" (Friedman 1976, xi-xxi). Afterward, Friedman reported his satisfaction at being at the founding of the Mont Pelerin Society, a group devoted "as intellectuals and citizens" to stemming and reversing the tide of what they believed to be threats to freedom. They were to meet annually "to renew our spirits and faith among a growing company of fellow believers." Warren Samuels (1976, 392) concluded that in order to carry out their self-appointed mission, the Chicago School converts—Friedman was hired in 1948 and Hayek in 1950—practiced "a mixture of science, social control, and psychic balm, including myth, all in the service of the explication and canonization of the market."

There was no such political coalition among post-Keynesians. In fact, post-Keynesians in the United States had to start their own journal to be heard even within the profession (Turner 1989, 195–99).

In England, the Cambridge Economic Policy Group might be said to have some political motivation, but it is doubtful that they retreat to a mountain for intellectual sustenance. There are "Think Tanks" of all persuasions in the United States.

However, so pluralistic is economics in the United States, that monetarism spread almost without resistance. Few economists recognized the revolutionary nature of a policy doctrine of such simplicity. Essentially, there was little that was new in the counter-revolution, so that the emphasis on the supply of money was absorbed into the fabric of teaching. Now the sometimes contradictory doctrines of Walras and Keynes were marching through the textbooks side by side with those of Friedman. As far as policy was concerned, the fad of monetarism merely strengthened the hand of those who questioned the value of governmental intervention in the first place without convincing those who opposed it. But monetarism did inspire the so-called New Classical Economics. More than anything, monetarism was a political rather than an economic thought change. Coming as it did after the McCarthy period in American politics, American academics, deathly afraid of even reading Marx, fearful of being accused of being sociologists, having dropped their own indigenous institutionalism in favor of mathematical models, began to rediscover the glories of laissez-faire. But in England, Nicholas Kaldor was not prepared to stand by and watch a counter-revolution in economic thought go unchallenged. Thirlwall (APT, 8–9 and Chapter 12) notes that, under Thatcher monetarism prevailed in spite of Kaldor but that Kaldor "won the theoretical war."

I certainly agree that this was so, but on another matter, with some dismay, I find my analysis differing from that of Thirlwall (APT, 301). He says that Kaldor's opposition to monetarism "had nothing to do with wanting to see more government control of the economy." My analysis challenges that. Kaldor objected to monetarism on theoretical grounds, certainly. He could not bear to see economists going down another blind, already explored, theoretical alley. However, in the arena of policy, since the monetarism of Friedman and, as Thirlwall has shown, that of the *Times* editors aimed at reining in government control by limiting it to a monetary growth role—and since the monetarism of the Thatcher government trumpeted the same aim—I see Kaldor as consistently in favor of a managed economy. Britain, unlike the United States, had a tradition of intervention, which had been carried on by both Conservative and Labour governments; monetarism promised a departure from that, relying instead on one monetary tool; Kaldor said it wouldn't work because the economics was all wrong, and it did not work. Clearly, he favored a more active role for the government than did the monetarists.

Chapter note 10.2 **Cambridge Economic Policy Group (CEPG)**

In the *Manchester Guardian* (October 1979), Martin Walker called the Cambridge Economic Policy Group (CEPG) "economists with a mission." Kaldor and Robert Neild were termed "key gurus of the Group." During the 1960s, Neild and Kaldor had been among those trying to convince governments that devaluation was an appropriate policy. Their mission in 1979 was to convince the Labour government and later the Thatcher government that import controls were needed to stop the run-down in Britain's industrial capacity. Neild argued that there was in fact some protection in disguised ways, such as paying subsidies to shipbuilders, and that this might be extended to other industries. Francis Cripps put the so-called absence of controls in this way: The 1.5 million who were unemployed due to the deflationary policy were the real import controls. The group published the *Cambridge Economic Policy Review* beginning in 1971 and were listed in 1981 as being comprised of Iain Begg, Kenneth Coutts, Francis Cripps, Michael Anyadike-Danes, Wynne Godley, Graham Gudgin, Barry Moore, John Rhodes, Roger Tarling, Terry Ward, and Frank Wilkinson.

Walker said that the New Cambridge group was ignored by the Labour government and derided by the far left, but that the public continued to associate its arguments with the left. Tarling, who had worked for Kaldor in the Treasury, said he had moved left politically "because of my economics." He left the Treasury in 1970 to found the Group. The *Review* was financed by the Social Science Research Council (60 percent), Cambridge University, and governmental contracts. Members of the New Cambridge group considered themselves pragmatic, empirically oriented, rather than ideological. One member, Graham Gudgin said, "We are the rude mechanicals of the profession." Walker said one of their converts was Professor Wilfred Beckerman of Oxford, who announced regarding his earlier contrary views: "I was wrong . . . ." Walker said the Group had became "one of the few clearly defined schools of thought in Britain."

In 1980, the *Cambridge Economic Policy Review* (Atkinson et al. 1980a) answered the "academic criticisms of the CEPG analysis." There were two questions that the "New Cambridge" was addressing: (1) Whether a country in fundamental payments disequilibrium is better off with protection than without it. (Their answer was yes.) (2) Whether a deficit country can regain internal and external equilibrium better through devaluation than through protection. (Their answer was no.)

The mainspring of "New Cambridge" was the realization that "vulgar Keynesianism had to go." The New Cambridge theorem is that "private expenditure as a whole (personal and company) is related to private disposable income as a whole." They differentiated themselves from "global monetarists" by saying that the global monetarists assumed continuous full employment and completely flexible market-clearing wages and prices, while New Cambridge assumed wages and prices to be unresponsive to changes in demand and domestic prices, even in the traded goods sector, and to be unresponsive to foreign prices of competing products. Rather than assuming full employment, New Cambridge saw employment and domestic activity as determined by the interrelationship between net export demand and domestic fiscal and monetary policy. The work of the CEPG had been for the previous ten years directed toward the characterization of the "increasingly serious predicament of the British economy" and had tried "to assess the strategic options for policy." They relied on a simulation model for their forecasts.

Chapter note 10.3 **House of Lords**

David Cannadine's *Decline and Fall of the British Aristocracy* (1990) shows that during most of the nineteenth century the House of Lords was made up of the landed gentry and that most new peers, those granted titles by the monarch, were from the same group. Nobility order is prince, duke, marquis, earl, viscount and baron. Lord is the informal title for those below the duke. A baronet or knight is addressed as "Sir."

During the nineteenth century politicians were often ennobled, though many of those had large properties. The granting of a peerage to persons of eminence (as distinguished from persons of property) began with Gladstone, who, in 1883, saw that Tennyson was made an earl. In 1891, Lord Salisbury obtained peerages for Sir Frederick Leighton, the president of the Royal Academy; physicist William Thompson; and Sir Joseph Lister, the first "medical man" to be made a peer. Salisbury argued that the House of Lords should be something other than a body of rich men and politicians.

The twentieth century ushered in a trend toward what Cannadine (1990, 202–4) calls "new plutocratic peers," who replaced the territorial peerage. From 1911 to 1940, of the 312 persons ennobled, more than half were former members of Parliament; 108 were from finance, industry, and commerce; 55 were from the professions, including lawyers; and 50 were from the home, armed, and colonial service. In the years 1916 to 1945, of 280 new peers, only 9 were men of great eminence, among those an occasional academic.

During the 1930s, the Labour party was hostile to the award of hereditary honors. The Parliament Bill, which became law in 1949, reduced the House of Lords' power to delay legislation from two years to one. Cannadine (1990, 663) calls the thirteen-year rule of the Conservative party following Churchill's election in 1951 the "last fling" of aristocratic government.

Cannadine (1990, 680) considers it an irony that the Conservatives under Harold Macmillan (1957–63) introduced life peerages, which would result in the Lords ceasing to be a hereditary chamber in time. When Anthony Wedgewood Benn, Labour MP who inherited his father's title in 1960, was to be forced to give up his seat in Commons, a law was passed that allowed hereditary peers to disclaim their titles. Another sign of the times was Churchill's refusal of a dukedom upon his retirement.

Since 1945, the creation of hereditary as distinguished from life peers has been 180 to 500. Between 1965 and 1983, no hereditary titles were created. Cannadine's estimate (1990, 681–83) is that by the year 2175 inherited titles will have died out.

Harold Wilson's government (1964–70) explored the possibility of reforming the House of Lords by removing the right of hereditary membership. Even Conservatives conceded that the hereditary principle and the overwhelming preponderance of one party must be abandoned. But this effort was doomed by a coalition between the far left who wanted abolition and the far right who wanted no changes (Cannadine 1990, 674–5).

By the time Kaldor was made Baron Kaldor of Newnham in the City of Cambridge in 1974 and took his place in the House of Lords in 1976, the House of Lords was no longer dominated by hereditary peers but was "essentially a chamber of nominated life senators."

Chapter note 10.4 **Incomes policy**

Government policy inevitably must deal with the problem of conflicting national objectives. When, in realizing rising and/or full employment levels, or perhaps just shortages in raw materials, an economy experiences inflationary pressures, what should be the response? For British Keynesians, the proper response was an incomes policy in which wages and prices are tied through some agreement, usually a tripartite agreement between government, labor, and industry. It may take the form of guidelines, freezes, laws, excess profits taxes, or some combination of these in a new social contract. There is no one form of incomes policy that is universally applicable. (For two different tax-based income policy proposals see Weintraub 1972 and Leasure 1974.) No one argues that incomes policies stand alone as cures of inflation. Instead, incomes policy in a free society is an experimental undertaking, like democracy, in concert with other governmental monetary and fiscal policies.

Because they are often partial and experimental, incomes policies are universally controversial. Samuel Brittan (who styles himself as an ex-Keynesian) and Peter Lilley (1977, 124–26) concluded that the cost of incomes policy in Britain exceeded the benefits. They thought that the only reason the Dutch and Swedish policies were thought to be successful was because they had survived.

Many efforts have been made to evaluate the experience with incomes policies, one of the best being a study issued by The Brookings Institution in 1983 (Flanagan, Soskice, and Ulman). As in the evaluation of the British joining the EEC, the problem is that of comparing actual with counterfactual conditions. Consequently, one goes either on what Brittan and Lilley call "a political judgment" or on the exigencies of a commitment to a certain economic theory.

The economic justification of incomes policy turns on the assumption of wage rigidities and structural conditions in a society. There is an implicit assumption that workers can affect their money wages. One has only to look at the miner's strikes in the Soviet Union while it was fully integrated to ascertain that working people in any society have some economic power, even in the absence of unions. That power is assumed to be used when the workers perceive that they are not getting a fair deal—their real income is falling or not rising fast enough. Workers do not have to be subject to the much debated monetary illusion. Their only redress may be in higher wages, so they turn to them. Nor does economic power have to be widespread to affect wages and thus prices; it may, instead, be concentrated in key industries.

Another assumption is that the companies involved are typically not in perfectly competitive industries. When companies are price makers, they may be tempted to give into wage demands and then charge what the traffic will bear. Post-Keynesians rely on both of these assumptions.

To defeat the need for incomes policies, then, one must attack its underpinnings; one must believe that most employers are in purely competitive industries and therefore cannot raise their prices, and that workers cannot in fact affect their wages through strikes against employers or the government. That is to say, one must defeat the idea that inflation can be, *even in part,* a cost-push phenomenon. One must insist, as Milton Friedman did, that unions are "toothless lions" and can only affect employment levels; that inflation is due to demand factors alone, or that increases in the supply of money are the *cause* of inflation; and that there is a natural rate of unemployment which cannot be changed.

A defense against the logic calling for incomes policies may also be made through a decision to forgo economic growth. Hayek (1960, 338–39) was willing to avoid what he called "expansionist policies" in order to avoid prompting inflation and thus government intervention. He asserted that those wishing to stop the drift toward increasing government control must rely only on monetary policy. He found nothing more "disheartening" than the views of those who are "induced by the immediate benefits of an expansionist policy to support what, in the long run, must destroy the foundations of a free society."

One other defense is the belief that the government has no business making *any* economic policy, but this is self defeating in that *not* making policy is itself a policy. This can only be ideology.

Furthermore, those economists who, like Kaldor, see that incomes policies can be a partial answer to problems of conflicting national objectives have never insisted that it is the role of the government to do more than mediate a new social contract and legislate such laws that will support it rather than undermine it.

As we have seen, British governments, both Conservative and Labour, were Keynesian enough to adopt the goal of full employment. Having done so, and in the face of the other problems of a declining empire and slow growth, they chose to experiment with some form of incomes policy in the 1960s and 1970s. In an early study of the years 1959–64, Elynor McPeak (1966, 212) notes that all types of policy solutions—monetary and fiscal restraint, the promotion of increased growth rates, and wage policy—were used by the British Conservative governments, but never the strict, legally enforceable policies such as those used in the Netherlands during that same period. As for monetary restraints, the British Cohen Committee found that those affected investment more than consumption, and thus had not been effective as anti-inflation policies only as anti-growth policies. McPeak concluded that although the wages policies used by the Conservative administrations before 1964 were not effective enough to eliminate inflation in the United Kingdom, that did not imply that wage policy has no part to play. She thought both demand restraint and wage policy were desirable, along with measures to increase growth.

That program is, of course, what the Wilson government between 1964 and 1970 attempted. Along with other policies, Wilson sought agreements between the government, labor, and management. After that, there were off and on programs, including Heath's rather bold program to tame cost-induced inflation.

There was a brief interlude of trial of incomes policies in the United States. Certain voluntary restraints were mandated under President Lyndon Johnson, but the real trial was under President Nixon in August 1971. Congress had given Nixon authority to freeze wages and prices in August of 1970, and although Nixon reiterated his opposition to doing so, he signed the bill. He rejected the idea of a wage-price board in spite of some pressure from the International Monetary Fund and Arthur Burns, then chairman of the Federal Reserve Board. Even the Organization of European Economic Cooperation suggested that the United States consider some form of incomes policy. In May 1971, the authority to impose wage-price controls was extended, and in August Nixon made his move. After floating the dollar by going off the gold exchange standard, he called for a ninety day freeze on wages and prices. The experiment was short-lived.

Robert Flanagan et al. (1983, 3, 6, 40) claim that by the end of the 1960s, most of the first generation of experimental incomes policies ended with wage explosions, strikes, and sharp increases in prices of food and raw materials accompanying the quadrupling of the price of oil in 1973. Most of the emphasis had been on guidelines based on consensus or social contract. There had been more of an effect on wages than on prices, resulting in a decline in real wages.

The leading successful examples of the consensus approach were in Norway and Austria. Their programs were largely voluntary restraint requiring formal consultations with the governments. Their goals were to maintain the country's share of international markets, full employment with "extremely accommodative fiscal and monetary policy," and some income redistribution. Norwegian economists argued that the determination of wage rates should be subject to government influence (Flanagan 1983, 155). M. Ingham (1981) thinks that the Austrian experiment limited layoffs and unemployment by relying on the hard currency option and price surveillance to restrain price increases, and upon trade union cooperation to dampen wage claims in return for minimizing unemployment. According to Flanagan, et al. (1983, 298), the Federal Republic of Germany has considered an incomes policy as an adjunct to demand management since the 1950s.

Flanagan, et al. (1983, 688) see incomes policy as an important component of overall macroeconomic policy on a continuing basis because "the structural characteristics of contemporary economies are not likely to disappear." They attribute the policy failures after 1973 in part to the exceptionally severe shocks associated with oil prices.

Chapter note 10.5 **Phillips curve**

The Phillips curve refers to the probable tradeoff between levels of employment and levels of prices, relating unemployment to the rate of change of prices. As an economy approaches full employment, there is pressure on prices to rise, so that the question is, at what level of unemployment will prices remain stable?

Economists in the United States seem to have accepted the idea that inflation could be avoided only through allowing serious unemployment, or stated differently, that stable prices could be bought only with high unemployment. It was on this issue that Joan Robinson accused American Keynesians of being "Bastard Keynesians" (cf. Turner 1990).

For the history of the belief in the tradeoff, I am indebted to Neil W. Chamberlain and Donald E. Cullen (1971, 628–30). Their reconstruction is this: Gottfried Haberler (see Wright 1951, 39) argued that there is a certain limit beyond which the money wage level cannot be pushed without either a rise in prices or the appearance of unemployment. He thought that unemployment was inevitable in the United States, since our society will not tolerate inflation beyond a certain limit and will use monetary or fiscal policy or direct controls to counteract inflation, while, at the same time, labor unions would never be satisfied with wage increases within the critical limit. A.W. Phillips (1958) found that in Britain, when wage increases remained within the increase in productivity, prices remained stable with as low an unemployment rate as 2½ percent; but if the productivity increases were passed along in lower prices, unemployment rates rose to approximately 5½ percent. (Under traditional theory with perfect competition, such productivity increases were expected to be passed along through lower prices.) All this led to the widely expressed belief that there had to be a certain "tradeoff" between unemployment and wage changes. Robert M. Solow and Paul A. Samuelson (1960) made a limited study for the United States and concluded that after World War II, it took a high unemployment rate of perhaps 8 percent to keep wages stable. William G. Bowen (1960) came to the even more pessimistic conclusion that the unemployment rate must be at least 9 percent if the rate of increase in wages is to be held to increases in productivity of about 2½ percent. Kaldor did not challenge the idea that there is some value in keeping wage increases within the boundary of productivity increases, but he did question whether stable prices were a more important goal than some others.

NK

E N D N O T E S

These endnotes are cited by author, date, and page number and are intended to be used in conjunction with the references. If an author has more than one publication during a year, these are referenced, for example, as 1980a, 1980b, and so on. Publications of joint authors are listed separately, after the publications by a single author. The following abbreviations have been used:

APT: *Nicholas Kaldor* (Thirwall 1987b)

CEE: *Collected Economic Essays* by Nicholas Kaldor, 8 vols., cited by volume rather than year, and are listed in the references as 1:1960a, 2:960b, 3:1964a, 4:1964b, 5:1978a, 6:1978b, 7:1980a, and 8:1980b.

JMK: *The Collected Writings of John Maynard Keynes,* 28 vols., cited by volume number.

KPP: Kaldor's private papers, which are under the supervision of Anthony P. Thirlwall.

Chapter 1

1. Kaldor 1986a, 3. Hungary was separated from the Austro-Hungarian Empire in 1920 by the Treaty of Trianon. Kaldor was then twelve years of age. Hungary lost much territory, resources, and access to the sea, and went through a series of political changes during his formative years.

2. In 1927, Vambery was the dramaturge of the experimental Theater am Schiffbaudamm in Berlin. He became famous for discovering, adapting, and staging the Threepenny Opera, thereby launching it and its previously unknown authors (including Berthold Brecht) into worldwide success. I am grateful to Tibor Scitovsky for explaining this to me.

3. Pasinetti 1983, 335.

4. Kaldor 1986a, 4.

5. By increasing returns, economists mean that output (and profits) may be increased more than in proportion to increased inputs—a rather obvious point, since it would include mass production. But for traditional equilibrium economic theory, that is a damaging admission, since one of the essential assumptions of traditional theory is that returns to scale are constant. If plant is fixed, traditional theory assumes diminishing returns set in as production is increased. While modern equilibrium theorists make many adjustments in their models, fundamentally they are tied to constant rather than increasing returns.

6. Blaug 1990, 12, 205.
7. Kaldor 1986a, 4–5.
8. Kaldor to Hicks, April 20, 1943, KPP.
9. APT, 24–25.
10. CEE 1:xi.
11. Robbins [1932] 1940.
12. Kaldor 1986a, 7. Young supervised the thesis of Edward H. Chamberlin. Kaldor's notes on Young's lectures have been reproduced and cover discussions of various forms of monopoly. See Sandilands 1990a.
13. Cf. Clapham 1922 and Sraffa 1926.
14. Kaldor 1986a, 7.
15. APT, 23.
16. London *Times* December 6, 1932 14e. There were 2,799,806 unemployed and 9,373,000 employed. Rates were not given in those days, but if the unemployed are added to the employed to equal a labor force of 12,172,806, then the rate was 23 percent. However, of the unemployed, 2,189,258 were wholly unemployed; 512,998 were "temporarily stopped," and 97,550 were "normally in casual employment."
17. Robinson [1933] 1969b; Chamberlin 1933; Kaldor 1934; 1938. Letters from Chamberlin April 23, 1938 and September 20, 1942; from Kaldor October 8, 1938 are detailed and would be of interest to some scholars. KPP.
18. These took place c. 1933 and involved Joan and Austin Robinson, James Meade, and Richard Kahn of Cambridge; and Abba Lerner, Sol Adler, Ralph Arakie, and Aaron Emanuel of the London School. JMK 14:148.
19. Kaldor 1986a, 7 and APT, 25. Myrdal's book was first published in German. When Keynes's *General Theory* appeared in 1936, Kaldor was in the United States on a Rockefeller Research Fellowship.
20. Kaldor 1936, 723.
21. Blaug 1991, 181, referring to Kaldor 1936.
22. Samuelson 1946, 192.
23. Hicks 1982, 3. See also Hicks 1981. Dieter Helm (1984, 4) claims this to be the only group of which Hicks was a member.
24. Letter to Hicks, April 20, 1943, KPP.
25. Kaldor 1986a, 7.
26. APT, 40.
27. Blaug 1968, 544.

Chapter 2

1. APT, 6, 10.
2. Kaldor to Hicks, April 20, 1943, KPP.
3. Lieberman 1956. Kaldor's distaste for communism is also indicated by a letter he wrote to his friend Theodor Prager in response to the news that Prager had resigned from the Communist party. Kaldor replied, "I am afraid I did not even know that you were a member of the C.P. (which shows my unworldliness and ignorance) but I am sure you have done the right thing." Letter dated March 3, 1970, KPP.
4. CEE 2:243–58.
5. While working in Geneva for the Economic Commission for Europe (then a subsidiary body of the Economic and Social Council of the United Nations), Kaldor learned of British moves to exclude the Russians from the benefits of the

Marshall Plan and passed the information on to his boss, Gunnar Myrdal. Myrdal's English assistant, Ronald Grierson, told the British Foreign Office of these "indiscretions," and the Foreign Office persuaded Robbins to recall Kaldor to LSE. Robbins gave him nine months' notice to return. Kaldor resigned from the London School in 1947. APT, 105.

6. APT, 7 and interview with Clarissa Kaldor, 1986.

7. APT, 228. Kaldor exhibited pride in his wife's achievements. He wrote to Theodor Prager, a friend and Austrian journalist, that Clarissa had been returned to the Council with a very large majority. This was the same year that Margaret Thatcher became prime minister. Letter dated May 8, 1979, KPP.

8. Taylor 1965, 246, 250.

9. APT, 31 says of Kaldor "he was a complete convert to the Keynesian revolution, and never deviated from the faith." Kaldor himself admitted being an easy convert to Keynes" (Kaldor 1986a, 7). Perhaps I am merely quibbling when I say he was not a convert. As Thirlwall has shown Kaldor had come to these ideas in part via Myrdal's essay "Monetary Equilibrium." A convert is to me a "believer" and I do not find "belief" other than in egalitarian values prominent in Kaldor's work. If the question is whether he was convinced of the efficacy of Keynes's general analysis, then, of course, the answer is yes. Thirlwall says "[Kaldor] was a convert in the sense that having embraced one doctrine (like everybody else) he then embraced the alternative theoretical structure laid out by Keynes. To be a convert to a doctrine does not require belief in all its elements." (Letter to me dated July 3, 1991.) Let the reader decide.

10. APT, 10–11.

11. Steindl 1990, 286. I am grateful to Professor Scitovsky for pointing me toward this reference, which helped me in my interpretation.

12. Steindl 1990, 300.

Chapter 3

1. Kaldor 1932a.

2. Keynes to Kaldor, May 17, 1932; Kaldor to Keynes, May 18, 1932, KPP.

3. Kaldor 1932b. This article, which appeared in the *Harvard Business Review*, may have been different from the one submitted to Keynes.

4. Kaldor 1939. Cf. Stevenson 1989, 102, for opinion that Hicks and Kaldor reached the conclusion that compensation criteria could be based on measurements of the loss of consumer surplus "at about the same time." However, Hicks (1981, 66) gives Kaldor more credit, indicating that he owed the device used in his analysis "to Mr Kaldor." Also see quote from Hicks in text. V. Kerry Smith (1990, 870) in his presidential address to the Southern Economic Association states affirmatively that if the Kaldor-Hicks compensation test is accepted, it is possible to arrive at a consistent gauge of potential Pareto improvements for policies involving price changes. Smith refers us to Just, Hueth, and Smith, 1982, and Boadway and Bruce, 1984, for a discussion of the "Kaldor tests."

5. Hicks 1981, xi.

6. Harrod (1938, 389) called himself "a tyro from a University [Oxford] which must in the modern period recognise its own juniority of status" to Cambridge. Cambridge had the highest status not so much because of Keynes but because of Marshall. Oxford was second and LSE below that. However, Harrod was questioning Robbins (1940) of LSE.

7. Robbins 1940, 137, vii.

8. Harrod 1938, 390, 393.

9. Harrod 1938, 396–97.
10. Robbins 1938, 635–36, 639.
11. Kaldor 1939, 550–52 or CEE 1:144–46.
12. Kaldor 1940a, 380.
13. Scitovsky 1941. In a letter dated January 10, 1992, Scitovsky kindly aided my phrasing of his complex argument.
14. Young 1987, 175. Young says the split was evidenced in publications by Joan Robinson and James Meade in 1937.
15. Young 1987, 173, 178.
16. Young 1987, 108–9.
17. Young 1987, 115, quoting from his 1986 interview with Kaldor.
18. Hicks to Kaldor, April 14, 1982, KPP.
19. JMK 14:238.
20. JMK 14:250.
21. JMK 14:240.
22. Young 1987, 185. Note 13 points out that the equations presented in Hicks's paper were originated by Harrod.
23. Young 1987, 110–11.
24. JMK 14:240.
25. JMK 14:241–42.
26. JMK 14:243–47.
27. JMK 14:255.
28. JMK 14:256.
29. JMK 14:247–49.
30. JMK 14:260.
31. JMK 14:262 and Young 1987, 111.
32. JMK 14:266–67 and Young 1987, 112.
33. Young 1987, 112, and JMK 14:267. Also see letter from Dennis Robertson to Kaldor quoted by Young (1987, 174) saying that the General Theory must have merit if economists "of the calibre" of Hicks, Harrod, and Kaldor saw something in it.
34. Young 1987, 94–125, especially 116–17. Young notes that these events preceded the publication of Alvin Hansen's reinterpretation of Keynes "through what is essentially the 'looking-glass' of Hicks's 1937 paper."
35. Samuelson 1946, 188.
36. Young 1987, 52–53.
37. Young 1987, 113.
38. Hicks to Kaldor, May 20, 1986, KPP.
39. Samuelson to Clarissa Kaldor, October 17, 1986, KPP.

Chapter 4

1. This was not an idle fear. Immediately after France's surrender in June 1940, German troops were massed at the coast poised for an invasion of England. It was not until November 1940 that this invasion was called off according to General Franz Halder, who was later interviewed by Kaldor. See *US Strategic Bombing Survey* Interview #52, U.S. Archives.
2. At one time, Kaldor's sister and her family and his mother were actually in a lineup to be deported on an outgoing train bound for a concentration camp and certain death. Since the Nazis had recruited Hungarian policemen as escorts, the family members were individually able to escape—the women by "fainting" and

being left behind, the brother-in-law by walking away when he passed his former residence. Some young cousins also narrowly escaped a German massacre of children being sheltered by a Red Cross-type agency. Because of illness they failed to join the others in the bomb shelter as Allied bombs rained down. The other children were taken from the shelter, shot, and thrown into the Volga by the Nazis. The father and uncle of these young cousins were, however, deported and murdered. After the war, only Kaldor's mother agreed to leave Hungary. Under the Communist regime, Varannai was sentenced to prison and his wife and daughter to a work camp in 1948 because he wrote in a story for Reuters: "Victor Chornoky who for several days had been under police supervision, attempted to leave his house and was shot in the leg by the police." It was allegedly a crime to "spread a false report as defined in paragraph 171 of the Penal Code." Reuters intervened on his behalf, but he was sentenced nevertheless and denied the promised visa to leave for England. Kaldor was able through intermediaries occasionally to get aid to his relations during the many years of privation. From the 1960s on, he was able to visit them, and they visited England several times.

3. Craver 1986; Craver and Leijonhufvud 1987.
4. Scitovsky to Kaldor April 27, 1942, KPP.
5. APT, 77–78.
6. Numerous letters from U. Hicks to Kaldor during the summer of 1939. KPP.
7. Kaldor CEE 2:3–4.
8. Kaldor 1940b.
9. This paper was not published at the time but is in CEE 2.
10. Deane (1978, 181) quotes James Meade as saying that before Keynes, economists had thought "a dog called savings wagged his tail labelled investment."
11. Kaldor 1986a, 12.
12. E.g., U. Hicks to Kaldor, September 17, 1939, KPP, and APT, 70. While Ursula and John Hicks thus recognized the importance of the paper from the beginning, the contents may have been forgotten by John Hicks. In 1977 Kaldor wrote to him of his annoyance that Hicks had attributed some of Kaldor's ideas from this paper to Axel Leijonhufvud (Kaldor to Hicks, February 14, 1977, KPP). Kaldor was referring to the paper Hicks had sent him from the Festschrift for Georgescue (Tang, Westfield, and Worley 1976). Kaldor said that while Hicks's and his own "thoughts seem to be converging" on the possibilities of "stock demand," he was annoyed that his ideas were "invariably attributed to Leijonhufvud, when in fact I made the same points thirty years earlier." Hicks replied (February 23, 1977, KPP) accepting this criticism and promising that in his "Preface (and Survey)" at the beginning of his forthcoming book of essays (Hicks 1977) he would rectify the reference. He did so in a footnote. In a valuable footnote quoting Keynes on Walras, Hicks notes in harmony with Kaldor's beliefs, "It is much to be desired that the methods of trading on organised markets, in different countries and at different times, should be studied systematically" (Hicks 1976, 151).
13. Kaldor to Hicks, February 14, 1977, KPP.
14. Kaldor 1986a, 13.
15. Wood 1984, 162.
16. Beveridge 1960, 14.
17. Kaldor 1960d.
18. *Manchester Guardian*, February 10, 11, 1943.
19. APT, 101.

Chapter 5

1. APT, 81. Tibor Scitovsky had written to Kaldor from America that his articles on war finance were "regarded as classics in this country."
2. Once classified as secret, the original survey is now available in the National Archives. For a summary of the overall economic report and some others
consult *The United States Strategic Bombing Survey* 1987. See also Daniels
1981. Kaldor participated in the Overall Economic Effects Division.
3. Phone interview with Scitovsky, August 27, 1991. On a minor point,
Scitovsky said they were in the field by May 1945, although Daniels (1981) said it
was July.
4. Daniels 1981, xx–xxii. Scitovsky was amused by this statement in my manuscript which I gleaned from the *Guide*. Apparently, he was responsible for order-
ing two IBM machines. Washington sent twelve instead. Scitovsky had been
apprised that the German economic ministry, which had been evacuated from its
offices, had a complete inventory of all the German capital equipment and that
this was stored on punch cards. Since he was focusing on the question of the
destruction of capital equipment that occurred because of Allied bombing, he
wanted these cards for his research. The outcome was that he was given a truck to
pick up the punch cards and bring them back to Bad Nauheim. Realizing that the
cards would be decipherable only on German machines, he brought back German
machines and technicians along with the cards. Then no one knew what to do
with the IBM machines, so Scitovsky suggested that they be used to record all of
the bombings of industrial targets by the Allies.
5. Wood 1984, 180. Schumacher accused Kaldor of "pointless personal quar-
rels which overshadowed his abilities."
6. *United States Strategic Bombing Survey* (1987, 24–32) points out that Speer
became the minister for weapons and ammunition after the defeat at Moscow in
February 1942, but not head of the German war economy, because Goering
wanted to control not only the air force but the aircraft industry as well. He was
allowed to do so until 1944. There was an economic minister who supervised the
production of basic materials, textiles, leather and so on.
7. Phone conversation with Scitovsky, August 27, 1991.
8. In a letter to the *Times*, August 10, 1970, Kaldor said that he interviewed
General Halder in June 1945. This interview, now declassified, was conducted
also by Mr. K. Mandelbaum, and is filed as #52a in the National Archives. Interested scholars will find some 36 boxes of these materials and pictures in the
National Archives. There is a statement attributed to John Kenneth Galbraith to
the effect that he restrained Kaldor from flying back to England to tell candidate
Clement Attlee that Halder had told them that plans of the Army to take over the
Reich in September, 1938 to forestall war over the Sudetenland were dropped
when, on September 15, news came that Neville Chamberlain was flying to
Berchtesgaden which would have meant that the British were caving in. Kaldor
thought it might tip the election in Atlee's favor. Galbraith argued with him and
did not allow Kaldor to go. In any case, Galbraith was inclined not to believe
Halder. (Galbraith's statement marked TRO–16, TRO–17, National Archives.)
9. London *Times* letters: Kaldor's letter August 10, 1970 and Josef Kosina,
same date; Dr. Otto John, August 21, 1970; Kaldor's reply, September 4, 1970;
George Ingr, September 8, 1970; and Lord Boothby, same date. In the interview,
Halder claimed to Kaldor and Mandelbaum that Hitler had only twenty or
twenty-one divisions including one or two panzer divisions, whereas Czechoslo-

vakia had strong frontier defenses and some thirty-five divisions (*U.S. Strategic Bombing Survey* 1945, Interview #52A, p. 2.)

10. The *United States Strategic Bombing Survey*, 1945, Overall Economic Effects Division, gave an over-all account of the effects of strategic bombing on the German economy," summarizing the findings of many participants, but the acknowledgment noted the following as carrying the major responsibility of this report: J. Kenneth Galbraith, director; Burton H. Klein, asst. director; Paul Baran; James P. Cavin; Edward F. Denison; Samuel J. Dennis; Thomas Dennis; G. Griffith Johnson, Jr.; Nicholas Kaldor; James W. McNally; and Roderick H. Riley. Scitovsky, who used a psuedo name, and E. F. Schumacher were also there. See also APT, 102 and Galbraith 1981 and 1986, 299 where Galbraith remarked of these years, "I, like others, took pride in my access to privileged if not terribly secret information and made evident my pleasure in my superior knowledge."

11. Scitovsky told me that one of the remarkable discoveries made by the economists was that the Germans, unlike the British and Americans, seldom worked more than one shift in war production. The intelligence community in charge of interrogating prisoners of war had never asked this question (Phone interview). The manpower figures are intriguing. According to the report, the increase from September 1939 to September 1944 in the number of German men and women employed, including those in the armed forces, was less than 1 million and fell short of the natural growth of the working-age population over the period. The armed forces mobilized 11.5 million men in that period, and their place in the civilian labor force was but partially filled by 7 million foreign workers and prisoners of war and the 1 million newly mobilized Germans, a net loss to the labor force of 10 per cent. With few exceptions, the German armament industries worked only a single shift throughout the war (*USSBS* 1945, 8-9). The report grouped all foreigners together "including Jews, both German and foreign, and prisoners of war." Their proportion in the labor force increased from .8 percent in 1939 to 19.7 percent in 1944. In 1944 the industrial percentage breakdown of "foreigners" was agriculture 22.1; industry 29.3; handwork 16.4; transport 17.4; power 12.7; trade banking and insurance 6.5; administration and services 4.1; armed forces administration 11.2; domestic service 5.2; home work .4. (Table 5, p. 206).

The average weekly hours were overall averages and "conceal divergent tendencies in individual industries." However, the highest computed was 49.5 hours for September 1941 and was down to 48.3 by March 1944. The conclusion was "it is probable that at least in production goods and armament industries full time men workers put in average hours in excess of 50 per week, with 60 hours worked in the key armament industries as the war moved into its final stage"(p. 35).

No specific mention was made in the report of labor camps. Scitovsky suggests that the Germans had limited housing and did not build barracks as did the Americans and British, and this limited the availability of labor. Also the Germans themselves seemed to object strenuously to working night shifts, which meant that the "foreign workers" could not be worked, lacking supervision. Finally, the Germans had plenty of machine tools for the amount of production they planned.

12. Kaldor 1945–46, 33–44.

13. *United States Strategic Bombing Survey* 1945, p.1. Overall Economic Effects Division divides the war into four phases: (1) the early period until the end of 1942; (2) the period of limited capabilities (January 1943–February 1944); (3) the aircraft period (February 1944–June 1944); and (4) the period of full-scale offensive (July 1944–April 1945).

14. This according to Halder in an interview June 25, 1945 by E. F. Denison, G. G. Johnson, and T/Sgt P. A. Baran (*United States Strategic Bombing Survey* file, National Archives).

15. *United States Strategic Bombing Survey* 1987, 11–12 and 39.

16. Unlike the British and Americans, the Germans had sufficient machine tools to restore production without an increase in shifts worked. Scitovsky noted that the Germans had about twice the inventory of machine tools that the Allied researchers expected to find.

17. Kaldor (1945–46, 52) and *United States Strategic Bombing Survey* (1987, 18) refer to the "seeming paradox" that though production recovered in the air industry, the German air force became ineffective. This was due to their losses of fighter personnel.

18. Monnet 1978, 238.

19. Monnet, who was educated in Cognac but never attended a university, sold brandy for the family firm in Canada. He spent a year in China and then had a career in international banking, making a fortune, which he lost in 1929. He is said to have had a leading part in Winston Churchill's 1940 proposal for a Franco-British unity, and to have conceived of the "lend-lease" idea, and to have coined Roosevelt's slogan, "Arsenal of democracy." (Moyne 1972, 35–37).

20. Monnet 1978, 144.

21. E.g., Harrod 1948 had not yet appeared.

22. APT, 104.

23. Toye 1989, 197. For example, Kaldor was asked to comment in 1963 on the possibility of substituting the VAT for the British profits tax and purchase tax. As Toye points out, Kaldor was not enthusiastic (see "A Memorandum on the Value-Added Tax" in CEE 3:266–93 particularly). But as J.G. Palma and M. Marcel indicate, VAT was enthusiastically supported by Kaldor at the 1962 meeting in Santiago, Chile, of the Conference on Taxation held by the Economic Commission of Latin America, the International Development Bank, and the Organization of American States (Palma 1989, 264–65). The tax was included in the Christian Democrat Manifesto of the 1970 presidential election in Chile and "became a highly efficient tax and a regular source of public revenue," according to Palma and Marcel.

24. APT, 105–6. Myrdal's introduction to the March 1948 survey says: "The Survey is the work of the Research and Planning Division of the Secretariat under the direction of Mr. Nicholas Kaldor, who was mainly assisted in this task by Mr. Hal B. Lary and Mr. H. Staehle." And in April 1949: "The present Survey, like its predecessor, is the work of the Research and Planning Division of the Secretariat, under the general direction of Mr. Nicholas Kaldor (Director), and Mr. Hal B. Lary (Assistant Director). Acknowledgments should also be made to the following senior members of the Division for their share in the analytical and statistical work: Tibor Barna, Esther Boserup, Mogens Boserup, Karl Brunner, Machiel Jansen, Albert Kervyn, Bengt Metelius, Robert Neild, Rudolf Nötel, Gizelle Podbielski, Hans Staehle, Sergio Steve and Pieter Verdoorn." Kaldor was also cited in the May 1950 report.

25. One of the important friendships Kaldor made while at the ECE was with the young Dutchman P.J. Verdoorn, who later did some work on increasing returns that Kaldor saw as extending Allyn Young's ideas.

26. APT, 109–10.

27. Pasinetti 1983, 334.

Chapter 6

1. Kaldor 1955, 242. The book was dedicated "To C.," undoubtedly his wife Clarissa.
2. According to Thirlwall in comments to author, September 1991.
3. Kaldor 1955, 11, 53.
4. Kaldor 1955, 8, 11–12.
5. Kaldor 1955, 7–8.
6. Reddaway 1989, 142.
7. APT, 120.
8. Kaldor 1955, 8.
9. CEE 7:230–31.
10. CEE 7:231. In this view, current income is consumption plus savings.
11. CEE 7:235–36. California and probably other governments have attempted to ameliorate the unfairness of the impact of inflation on progressive income taxes by indexing income tax; however, this does not remove all the problems associated with capital gains.
12. Kaldor to Pechman, January 19, 1979, KPP.
13. Reddaway 1989, 142.
14. Kaldor 1955, 13–15.
15. Kaldor 1955, 14–15.
16. Kaldor 1955, 173–74.
17. Kaldor 1955, 208.
18. Kaldor 1955, 220.
19. Kaldor 1955: Chapter 6, "Taxation and Economic Progress," is well worth reading. Kaldor was seeking a tax base that promoted stability and economic progress.
20. Kaldor 1955, 223.
21. Kaldor 1955, 146.
22. Kaldor 1955, 100–101.
23. Kaldor 1955, 151.
24. Kaldor 1955, 159.
25. Kaldor 1955, 162–63.
26. APT, 120. The unsigned review appears in the *Economist* December 10, 1955, p. 933. Little 1956, 120.
27. Kahn to Balogh, November 19, 1951, and Balogh to Kahn, November 21, 1951, KPP.
28. Musgrave 1957, 201.
29. Musgrave 1957, 205. It was only later (Kaldor 1958b) that Kaldor came to grips with Musgrave's and Evsey Domar's 1944 article that he had not seen earlier. Musgrave and Domar had argued that a comprehensive income tax with full loss offsets does not discriminate against risk taking at all. But Kaldor (1958b, 206) said income tax-based systems still favored spending over savings. And he remained convinced that there was some bias against risk taking even in a comprehensive income tax, although he conceded that it was possible to avoid it. His original argument (1955, 204) was that the tax should be leveled on "persons" rather than on "income" or "money" as such.
30. Harberger 1958.
31. Palma and Marcel 1989, 249, 264.
32. Phrase taken from Heilbroner (1990) who uses the term "Not Socialism, Not Capitalism" to describe the emergence of Eastern European economic systems from communism.

33. Kaldor to Mihály, March 12, 1985, KPP.

Chapter 7

1. CEE 2:235–36. As the reader will see, the problem of differential growth rates continued to interest Kaldor throughout his professional career.
2. CEE 3:xx.
3. CEE 3:264.
4. Chakravarty 1989, 237.
5. CEE 8:viii and 31–189 for Kaldor's proposals in India. See also CEE 3:216–24 for Kaldor's address given to the Informal Consultative Committee of the Parliament in New Delhi, December 16, 1958; and CEE 4:299–305.
6. CEE 8:ix.
7. CEE 3:217 and CEE 8:ix.
8. U. Hicks 1958, 160.
9. APT, 139.
10. Chakravarty (1989, 238–39) pointed out that Kaldor elsewhere strongly emphasized the vital necessity for an effective land tax both for increasing the efficiency of land use and for diverting the agricultural surplus to uses in productive investment outside of agriculture. Chakravarty estimated that 80 percent of the population was engaged in agriculture in India in the mid-fifties when Kaldor was there.
11. U. Hicks 1958, 163.
12. CEE 7:236.
13. These problems had not been resolved as of 1991, when Rajid Gandhi of India was assassinated allegedly by a Tamil terrorist group because of his intervention in Sri Lanka on behalf of the government. In the year after Kaldor's visit, Ceylonese Prime Minister S.W.R.D Bandaranaike, whom Kaldor had advised, was assassinated, and his widow assumed leadership.
14. CEE 8:190.
15. APT, 142.
16. Toye (1989, 189) presents in tabular form a useful summary of Kaldor's tax reform activities in developing countries.
17. CEE 8:ix-x.
18. APT, 142. Lopez-Mateos was President of Mexico 1958–64.
19. CEE 8:264.
20. CEE 3:xix.
21. CEE 8:x.
22. Toye 1989, 188.
23. CEE 8:306.
24. CEE 8:xi-xii. Kaldor here says that this resulted in "a sudden end to my association with Dr. Nkrumah." But Thirlwall reports that Kaldor "continued to advise Nkrumah by correspondence from Cambridge" (APT, 147).
25. Letter to *Times*, February 17, 1962, 8a. The cost of living had increased at least 10 percent since the last salary raise for the civil service workers. The Civil Service Commission had recommended allowances calling for $2.5 million, but Jagan had not yet acted. According to Peter Simms (1966, 156) all grades of the civil service were on the verge of striking. It was at this point that the budget recommended by Kaldor was introduced.
26. See Thomas J. Spinner, Jr., (1984, 91–97) and Jagan (1966, 303–9) where Jagan quotes from Drew Pearson's syndicated article published March 22, 1964,

entitled "Castro and Jagan" and from testimony given before a subcommitte of the Committee on Appropriations of the House of Representatives of the United States Congress on March 12, 1963.

27. Quoted by Jagan (1966, 255–56) from paragraph 45 of the report of the Commonwealth Commission of Enquiry into Disturbances in February 1962.

28. Jagan 1966, 255.

29. London *Times*, February 20, 1962.

30. Ibid.

31. Letter to *Times*, March 1, 1962.

32. Naipaul 1991.

33. Jagan 1966, 309, quoting.

34. Naipaul 1991.

35. *Economist* 322:46 February 19–March 6, 1992. According to the *Economist* the jointly owned management company, Booker Tate, immediately negotiated with the unions (which had not been done for ten years), and doubled wage levels, persuading cane cutters to return to the fields. The *Economist* claimed that "out-of-office politicians" (which probably meant Jagan) talk about selling out to former slavemasters."

36. APT, 151–52.

37. CEE 8:313.

38. CEE 8:333.

39. CEE 8:310.

40. Toye 1989, 192.

41. CEE 8:337–38.

42. CEE 8:344–45.

43. CEE 8:349.

44. CEE 8:364–65.

45. CEE 8:361–63.

46. Palma and Marcel 1989, 245–46, 248. Kaldor's article was written in 1956 and finally appeared in the Mexican journal *El Trimestre Economico*, April 1959.

47. Palma and Marcel 1989, 261, 265.

48. CEE 7:xxiii. See also Reddaway 1989, 148.

49. CEE 7:viii.

50. Kaldor to Rosenstein-Rodan, April 2, 1962, KPP.

51. Toye 1989, 188–90.

Chapter 8

1. Letter to *Times*, April 28, 1950. This was a very early statement of a theme to which Kaldor returned with increasing emphasis.

2. Letter to *Times*, September 27, 1957.

3. Letter to *Times*, January 13, 1958.

4. Letter to *Times*, February 19, 1963.

5. Letter to *Times*, February 28, 1963.

6. Letter to *Times*, March 11, 1963.

7. Letter to *Times*, July 28, 1964.

8. Letter to *Times*, October 8, 1964.

9. "Observer" 1964, KPP. Other economists advising the government were Sir Donald MacDougall; Professor Alexander Cairncross, from within the Treasury; and Robert Neild, who had been a student of Piero Sraffa at Cambridge. "Observer Weekend" (*Financial Times*, April 4, 1965, KPP) said that "as usual, it seems,

everything except the final Wilsonian decisions have centered on the Treasury." Sir Eric Roll was also associated with Wilson's government. According to Thirlwall, initially Balogh was against devaluation, Kaldor in favor of floating, Neild and MacDougall in favor of some sort of exchange rate adjustment; Cairncross was skeptical of the success of a floating policy and feared that devaluation would lead the United States to devalue and thus undermine the Bretton Woods system (APT, 233). Thirlwall thinks that Cairncross was inherited by the Labour administration and later deposed (letter to author, 1991).

10. APT, 231 and *Times* Industry Page Notes, November 3, 1964.

11. "Observer" 1964 (KPP).

12. Sunday *Times*, November 1, 1964.

13. APT, 231 and *Times*, November 30, 1964.

14. Letter to *Times*, December 15, 1964, and APT, 237.

15. Undated letter to *Times* (KPP) signed D.G. Champernowne, F.H. Hahn, R.F. Kahn, R.C.O. Matthews, J.E. Meade, W.B. Reddaway, E.A.G. Robinson, A. Silberston, J.R.N. Stone. Meade and Stone were Nobel Laureates in 1977 and 1984, respectively.

16. Letter to *Financial Times*, December 21, 1964.

17. Letter to *Times*, December 22, 1964.

18. Letter to *Times*, February 18, 1964.

19. "Observer" 1964 (KPP).

20. APT, 239.

21. Pelling 1972. David Steel (1980, 134) says that a majority of five was reduced to three in 1964 because of by-elections and the appointment of Michael Stewart to the cabinet.

22. Thirlwall (APT, 233) says that orders were given on Wilson's instructions "to destroy all copies of papers advocating devaluation and to refrain from mentioning the idea."

23. APT, 232. Derbyshire and Derbyshire (1988, 26) say it is also true that Callaghan opposed devaluation and resigned soon after it was finally undertaken in 1967.

24. New York *Times*, November 3, 1964.

25. Whiteley 1983, 144–46.

26. APT, 234.

27. Kaldor 1974a, 11. Roy Jenkins followed Callaghan as chancellor of the exchequer.

28. Steel 1980, 128.

29. Reddaway 1970 and 1973.

30. Reddaway 1989, 150–53. Reddaway said he had spent five years working to determine the effects of SET.

31. Kaldor 1974b.

32. I am struck by the similarity of this question by Kaldor and Milton Friedman's 1970a allegations against Keynesianism. However, their answers on what should be done differed.

33. CEE 5:100–38.

34. The foreign trade multiplier refers to the theory that new exports have exactly the same effects on Gross National Product—that is, output and income— as net new domestic investment. However, the stimulative effect is moderated and/or reduced by imports. Thirlwall told me that Kaldor did not begin talking about balance of payments constrained growth until the 1970s.

35. Kaldor 1974b, 287–88. During this same period Friedman was insisting that the problem was inflation, to be cured only by controlling the supply of money.

36. Steel 1980, 139–40.
37. Whiteley 1983, 151.
38. Kaldor 1977.
39. Kaldor 1974a, 1.

Chapter 9

1. De la Mohotiere (1970, 11) gives an excellent chronology of the major European trade events 1946–70, and I have relied on it.
2. Lipgens 1982, 185.
3. Jones 1977, 191, quoting Ernest Bevin.
4. Mezerik 1962.
5. Holt 1972, 76.
6. Pelling 1972, 127–28.
7. Kaldor to Mishan, September 14, 1961, and Mishan to Kaldor, September 20, 1961, KPP.
8. Letter to *Times*, October 15, 1962. See also de la Mohotiere 1970, 16.
9. Letter to *Times*, October 19, 1962.
10. Besides opposing the enlargement of the community, France of the de Gaulle period was often at odds with the other five countries. In 1953, France rejected the European Defence Community treaty signed in Paris the year before. In 1965, the French delegates walked out of the Council of Europe meeting because of its opposition to majority voting. Then France boycotted all of the EEC institutions for the next seven months. But in 1966, France returned to the EEC and the common agricultural policy was agreed to (de la Mohotiere 1970, 12–16).
11. The year 1968 was one of widespread unrest in France after which de Gaulle lost power and resigned, opening the way for enlargement of the European Community.
12. In 1969, after the election of Pompidou as president of France, the franc was devalued. To avoid the consequent bonus to the farmers, French agriculture was isolated from the Common Market for two years. Then the Germans revalued the Deutsche mark, and more negotiations for CAP were undertaken in a marathon session (de la Mohotiere 1970, 16).
13. De la Mohotiere (1970, 140–41) estimated that in 1964 the percentages of the labor force employed in farming were France 19 percent, Italy 25 percent, Germany 11 percent, Netherlands 11 percent, Belgium 6 percent, and Luxembourg 14 percent. Parker (1979, 59) estimated the percentages for the late 1970s as UK 3 percent, Germany 8 percent, France 13 percent, and Italy 18 percent.
14. De la Mohotiere 1970, 146–47. Germany, Belgium, and Luxembourg came off the worst in the operation of the Farm Fund.
15. Johnson 1973, 129–43.
16. Barnes (1991) provides a delightful account of Thatcher's behavior at the two-day summit in Rome of the European Community leaders in October 1990, which led to her resignation under fire. Thatcher refused to associate herself with the decision to make January 1994 the start of the next stage of economic and monetary union. She called the agreement "like cloud-cuckoo land" and added, "If anyone is suggesting that I would go to Parliament and suggest the abolition of the pound sterling—no!" This behavior was discussed in the British press and prompted the subsequent changes in the Conservative party that made John Major successor to Thatcher.
17. APT, 258.

18. Johnson letter to the *Times*, February 12, 1970, discussing a Labour party White Paper. The 1970 election was not until June 18. Kaldor letter to the *Times*, February 15, 1970. White Papers are government policy papers.

19. *New Statesman*, April 3, 1970.

20. Brassley (1988, 599–600) says that in addition, structural problems seem to have been aggravated, in that the rich get richer, individually and by country. The overuse of pesticides and expansion of production into formerly unused areas like wetlands have increased the surpluses.

21. Negotiations of the so-called Uruguay round broke off December 8, 1990. Hector Gros Espiell, foreign minister of Uruguay was chairman of the 107-nation talks. See *New York Times*, December 8, 1990, pp. 1, 44. The United States was joined by the Cairns Group, including Canada, Argentina, Brazil, and Australia, in demanding cuts to CAP internal and export subsidies. The *Economist* (December 1, 1990) called that meeting "GATT's last gasp." But meetings continued. Elections and political controversies in both France and Germany played a role in the disagreements. But a year later (November 1991), the negotiators were at it again in what the *Economist* called "The final stretch?" (November 9, 1991). In March 1992, Kohl and Bush were still declaring that some solution would be found, but in November 1992, Bush raised tariffs on French white wines by two hundred percent, probably in a bargaining threat (Cf. *Economist* November 7–13, 1992). The point is that this is a long-term problem, and Kaldor was prescient in his opinion of CAP and its effects on international trade.

22. Letter to *Times*, October 9, 1970.

23. *New Statesman*, March 12, 1971.

24. Cf. Kaldor 1971b and 1966b.

25. According to the *Economist* (March 13, 1971), Britain had offered 3 percent for 1973, and there had been counter proposals. *Economist* reviewed Evans 1971.

26. Kaldor in a letter to the *Economist* (July 31, 1971) in response to the review of Evans 1971 in which Kaldor's article had been reprinted. The Werner Plan (1970) was one of a series of plans made for monetary union. These included the Barre Plan (1969) and the European monetary "snake" (1972), which linked currency values. (Cf. David Overton 1983, 96). At the time of this exchange between the *Economist* and Kaldor, nothing was settled, and the Six were still acting relatively independently in setting exchange rates. The *Economist* assumed that the decision to proceed to a common currency would require unanimity, and that Britain would be in the catbird seat. Kaldor thought otherwise, and he turned out to be correct. After a series of meetings, the European Council at Brussels in December 1978 adopted a resolution on the introduction of a European monetary system (EMS). All countries except Britain took part. In March 1979, the EMS with the countries in the snake (Germany, Denmark, Holland, Belgium, and Luxembourg) established certain central rates. The Republic of Ireland, Italy, and France derived their exchange rates from market rates. The UK, though not participating in the EMS's exchange rate mechanism, selected a national central rate, so it could calculate the divergence indicators. The European Commission, of which Roy Jenkins (Labour) was president, emphasized in a public lecture (the first Jean Monnet Lecture, in Florence on October 17, 1977) the need for the economic and monetary union of community countries. Clearly, it was intended to bring the UK into the EMS and to proceed in introduction of a European currency. The current date for establishing the common currency is January 1, 1999.

27. Kaldor letter to the *Economist*, March 10, 1971.

28. *Times*, May 14, 1971.

29. Kaldor letter to the *Times*, May 27, 1971. See also Kaldor 1971c.
30. Johnson 1973, 134.
31. Benn and Kaldor letters to the *Times*, May 27, 1971.
32. Kaldor 1971d.
33. *Economist*, July 31, 1971.
34. Kaldor letters to the *Times*, August 4 and August 16, 1971.
35. *Times*, September 6, 7, 8, 1971. Negotiations followed Nixon's decision, resulting in the Smithsonian Agreement of December 1971 and almost continual adjustments and maneuvers in individual countries' currency values. The British did not float the pound until June 1972.
36. Cf. *Times*, October 22, 1971.
37. Kaldor letter to *Times*, February 22, 1972.
38. Kaldor letter to *Times*, March 24, 1972.
39. Kaldor letters to *Times*, April 7 and April 24, 1972.
40. Cf. *New Statesman*, June 9, 1972.
41. Kaldor letter to *New Statesman*, June 23, 1972.
42. Kaldor letters to *Times*, October 2 and 10, 1972.
43. Kaldor 1972b.
44. Kaldor letter to *Times*, October 24, 1972.
45. Parker 1979, 88.
46. *Manchester Guardian Weekly*, December 1, 1991.
47. *Parade*, November 3, 1991, p. 5.
48. *Economist*, December 14–20, 1991, p. 51. See also p. 70 where Andre Swings, the director of monetary operations at the Kredietbank in Brussels is reported as saying it would not make sense for British firms to accept the transaction costs of operating in a separate currency when their European competitors were using the ecu. Prime Minister Major also was able to avoid "opting in" to the new social legislation, which led Volker Hoffmann of the EC employers' organization to worry that the rejection would lead to a "two-speed Europe," where Britain might attract foreign investment because of lower social costs, "becoming the Hong Kong of Europe."
49. Cf. Atkinson, Begg, Cripps,and Anydike-Danes 1980a, 1980b, and 1980c.
50. Cf. Beggs, Cripps, and Ward 1981.
51. El-Agraa 1984, 315.
52. Pomfret 1985, 706.
53. El-Agraa 1985, 94.
54. Thirlwall in a letter to author September 1991 said, "I think Kaldor would have been very much opposed to monetary integration. He wouldn't have liked the loss of sovereignty and he was opposed to a common currency. He was merely making the point that a political union would have to precede a monetary union if the monetary union was not to break down."
55. Johnson 1973, 129–43.
56. Barnes 1991, 60.

Chapter 10

1. Thirlwall 1983a.
2. For the Treasury view, see JMK 9:115: "It is the orthodox Treasury dogma, steadfastly held, [. . .] that whatever might be the political or social advantages, very little additional employment and no permanent additional employment, can, in fact, and as a general rule, be created by State borrowing and State expenditure," quoted by R. F. Kahn (1984, 79).

3. Quote from Keynes 1925 by Kaldor 1982, ix. Kaldor argues that this statement "was far ahead of the times and ahead of much of his (Keynes's) own writings on the subject." Keynes served on the Macmillan Committee on Finance and Industry from 1929 to 1931, appointed by Ramsay MacDonald, Labour prime minister. When the committee report was issued in June, Keynes still favored the fixed parity of the gold standard, but by August he had changed his mind and favored devaluation. The country was "pushed off the pre-War parity" September 21, 1931, according to Kahn (1984, 86–88).

4. CEE 3:154.

5. See APT, 294–99 for full discussion of this evidence. Kaldor's memorandum can be found in CEE 3:128–53.

6. APT, 294.

7. CEE 3:128.

8. CEE 3:131.

9. CEE 3:139.

10. CEE 3:141.

11. CEE 3:141–49.

12. Kaldor 1982, 8.

13. Kaldor 1982, 2.

14. CEE 3:163.

15. Kaldor 1970c discussing in part Friedman and Schwartz 1963 and Friedman 1968 and 1969, Friedman's response 1970b, and Kaldor's rejoinder 1970d.

16. Kaldor 1970c, 1.

17. Kaldor 1970c, 8, 10, 17.

18. Friedman 1970c, 195.

19. Kaldor 1970d, 54.

20. Kaldor to Henry C. Wallich, September 29, 1970, KPP.

21. Weissman to Kaldor, August 26, 1970, KPP.

22. Friedman 1970b, 52–53.

23. Friedman 1970b, 53.

24. Kaldor 1970d, 54.

25. Hicks 1975b, 1–13, and Johnson 1976, 13.

26. Kaldor 1982, 39–111.

27. Kaldor 1982, 39–40.

28. Kaldor 1982, 42–47.

29. Kaldor 1982, 48–60.

30. Kaldor 1982, 68–69. See also Hendry and Ericsson 1983.

31. Kaldor 1982, 74.

32. Kaldor 1982, 83–86.

33. Kaldor 1982, 60–64.

34. Kaldor 1985a.

35. *Times*, October 8, 1972.

36. Kaldor to the *Times*, November 6, 1972.

37. Kaldor to the *Times*, March 3 and March 30, 1973.

38. *Financial Times*, April 10, 1973.

39. *Times*, February 13, 1974.

40. Ibid.

41. *Times*, February 8, 1974.

42. Kaldor to the *Times*, February 12, 1974.

43. Hahn to the *Times*, February 14, 1974.

44. Kaldor to the *Times*, February 20, 1974.

45. *Times*, October 5, 1974. Kaldor was a consultant to the Treasury and an adviser to the Department of Health and Social Security 1968–70.

46. *Times*, February 13, 1976.

47. "Diary" in *Times*, March 15, 1974.

48. *Economist*, April 23, 1974.

49. *Times* article,"Cambridge Economics and the Balance of Payments II: Theory dogged by its assumptions," April 18, 1974, p. 19. See also "Challenging the elegant and striking paradoxes of the New School," which is Part I, p. 19 April 17, 1974.

50. *Economist*, April 27, 1974, pp. 13–14.

51. *Times* Business News, July 14, 1976.

52. According to Thirlwall in letter to author, September 1991.

53. *Times*, September 1, 1976.

54. Kaldor letter to the *Times*, October 12, 1976.

55. Kaldor's address, "Debate on the Address" House of Lords, November 25, 1976.

56. *Journal of Commerce*, December 27, 1977.

57. Ibid.

58. *Times* article by David Freud, February 18, 1978 in which he quotes Kaldor.

59. Kaldor 1985c.

60. CEE 3:xiii-xiv. This paper was first published in 1964 in the 1st ed. In 1979, Kaldor (CEE 1:xxix-xxx) said that this article had been recently described to him "by an official dealing with this particular subject as 'very good—but rather utopian—the time is not yet ripe for it.'"

61. Kaldor letter to the *Times*, February 15, 1978.

62. Congdon article in the *Times, September* 20, 1978.

63. Seers letter to the *Times*, September 29, 1978.

64. Congdon letter to the *Times*, October 16, 1978.

65. Kaldor letter to the *Times* October 18, 1978.

66. *Times*, October 28, 1978.

67. Kaldor letter to the *Times, November* 1, 1978.

68. Kaldor letter to the *Times*, November 16, 1978.

69. House of Lords, June 13, 1979. Kaldor continued to see this ideological element in Thatcher's administration (cf. House of Lords, November 10, 1982 and November 14, 1985.) Unlike Heath, who had at first attempted laissez-faire and then turned pragmatic, embracing an incomes policy, Thatcher never relented. However, there was little discussion of Thatcher's determination to rely on monetarism after 1981, though money supply targets were maintained into the mid-eighties.

70. House of Lords, June 13, 1979.

71. House of Lords, June 19, 1979.

72. House of Lords, July 4, 1979.

73. House of Lords, November 7, 1979.

74. *Times*, reminiscing about Kaldor November 19, 1990.

75. House of Lords, November 7, 1979.

76. House of Lords, July 11, 1979.

77. House of Lords, February 13, 1980.

78. W. M. Corden (1984, 359) says that the first printed reference to the "Dutch disease" was in the *Economist*, November 27, 1977. There is now a large literature on "booming sector economics" including Corden and Neary 1982 and Corden 1984.

79. House of Lords, February 3, 1982.

80. House of Lords, July 11, 1979.
81. House of Lords, April 16, 1980.
82. House of Lords, June 11, 1980.
83. Ibid.
84. House of Lords, November 12, 1981.
85. House of Lords, November 10, 1982.
86. House of Lords, March 17, 1982.
87. Friedman 1977a. Friedman argued (459–64) that there could be a "transitional phenomenon" of a positively sloped Phillips curve, lasting until all agents adjust their expectations and institutional and political arrangements to "a new reality." He also thought that economic theory was affected more by the force of events than by political beliefs.
88. Friedman said that printing money to pay for war had, historically, been a major source of inflation, but that a full employment policy is "a modern invention for producing inflation." He argued that inflation was a tax that required no legislative approval and thus was relied on when government funds were short (*Times,* January 3, 1981).
89. House of Lords, July 20, 1977.
90. Ibid., referring to Friedman 1977a.
91. House of Lords, July 14, 1980.
92. House of Lords, November 12, 1981.
93. House of Lords, June 29, 1983.
94. House of Lords, November 13, 1984.
95. House of Lords, November 14, 1985.
96. House of Lords, June 29, 1983.
97. House of Lords, November 7, 1979.
98. Reflation refers to the effort opposite of deflation. You raise interest rates and allow the exchange rate to rise in order to deflate. You lower interest and exchange rates in order to reflate.
99. House of Lords, November 27, 1980.
100. House of Lords, January 17, 1979. Kaldor pointed out that for the first two years of the Labour government, workers had supported the government's incomes policy.
101. House of Lords, December 5, 1979.
102. House of Lords, January 30, 1980. Kaldor thought that subsidies could ensure the medium-term demand for coal during the current recession, permit the continuance of the coal mining industry, and offset the uncompetitiveness of much of British industry, including steel.
103. House of Lords, May 20, 1980.
104. House of Lords, February 3, 1982.
105. House of Lords, January 23, 1985.
106. Ibid. This statement was made twelve years after joining the Common Market and within two years of Kaldor's death. Kaldor added, "I know that there are Euro-fanatics who think that the future of Europe is far more important than prosperity, full employment or even the fate of this country . . . ."
107. House of Lords, March 4, 1981.
108. House of Lords, January 23, 1985. Kaldor thought that business was mainly interested not in trading in the Common Market but in the right to emigrate and do business there.
109. House of Lords, November 7, 1979.
110. House of Lords, December 3, 1985.

111. House of Lords, May 20, 1980.
112. House of Lords, November 19, 1982. This speech is part of the collection in Butler 1983.

Chapter 11

1. Targetti and Thirlwall 1989, 23. Kaldor (CEE 1:xxviii) muddies the water even more when he says that "throughout my academic life economic theory has remained my basic interest."
2. Interview with Lord Kaldor, 1984.
3. Turner 1989, 71–72.
4. APT, 320; Kornai 1971, 332; and Turner 1989, 108. It seems to me that many critics of Kaldor fail to appreciate this point. I would include Blaug in this indictment. Is the theory the method? This philosophical question, extensively treated by philosophers of science, cannot be allowed to detain us. But Geoff Hodgson (1989, 80) argues that Kaldor's growth models that include cumulative causation represent "a direct challenge to the equilibrium theorising of orthodoxy, where it is often supposed that the market economy contains self-righting mechanisms to bring recovery from any downturn, and an effective price mechanism to compensate for imbalances in development. This central methodological difference accounts in part for the reluctance of orthodox theorists to embrace Kaldor's arguments."
5. CEE 5:xvii.
6. CEE 5:xviii.
7. APT, 316.
8. Blaug (1990, 205–6) says that the repudiation of equilibrium economics would involve abandoning not only orthodox microeconomics but also Keynesian macroeconomics and all varieties of growth theory (including Joan Robinson's), "leaving little else but Kaldor III growth laws as the sum of the content of economics." One gathers that the theory *is* the method for Blaug. Furthermore, Blaug thinks that the schools that have repudiated neoclassical economics, such as neo-Austrians, evolutionary and new institutional economists, have not been followers of Kaldor. Blaug concludes that "by academic, rather than political, standards," Kaldor's ideas have failed to take off.
9. Pasinetti 1979, 368.
10. Lawson, Palma, and Sender 1989, 1.
11. CEE 5:xviii.
12. CEE 1:209–36.
13. CEE 1:153–205.
14. Pasinetti 1979, 368.
15. Quoted by Kaldor in CEE 1:227. See his footnote 1 also.
16. CEE 1:228n.
17. APT, 160. See also Kaldor's letter to R.F. Kahn June 15, 1962. KPP.
18. CEE 2:214.
19. Ibid.
20. CEE 1:235.
21. CEE 2:295. In the first stage, profits were determined in the Marxian manner, as a surplus over subsistence wages.
22. CEE 2:263–4. The assumption of "Keynesian" full employment is thus employed. Kaldor (CEE 1:xxv) says that Dennis Robertson named it Mark I.
23. CEE 5:ix.

24. CEE 5:ix-x.
25. CEE 2:273, especially n. But "blueprints" and capital versus labor-using techniques also interested Joan Robinson, who did not rely on marginal productivity theory.
26. Kaldor 1986b.
27. CEE 2:271–72.
28. CEE 2:293–97.
29. Hicks 1960.
30. CEE 5:x.
31. CEE 5:xiii.
32. Lutz 1961.
33. CEE 5:2–3.
34. The assumptions to be removed were absence of technical progress, market-clearing prices, all profits saved and wages spent, complementarity between capital and labor, and an unlimited supply of labor at a constant wage (CEE 5:9).
35. CEE 5:41.
36. Lutz 1961, xii-xiii.
37. Lutz 1961, 296.
38. Lutz 1961, 367.
39. Hicks 1960, 124, 128–29, 132.
40. Kaldor 1961, 1–2.
41. Hicks 1975a, 365–67. Hicks remained suspicious of the "anti-production function people" who asserted a "technology frontier" without naming names. He may have meant to include Kaldor, but this does not seem to me a proper understanding of what Kaldor argued in his technical progress function.
42. Hahn 1989, 48, 55.
43. Blaug 1990, 194–95 referring to Hacche 1979.
44. Hacche 1979, 280.
45. Hacche 1979, 296–98, 300.
46. CEE 5:xiii.
47. CEE 5:31–36. Kaldor objected that the production function assumes: (1) that the capital stock in existence is perfectly adapted to any capital-labor ratio; (2) that there is a curve that continually shifts upwards; (3) that the slope of the curve determines the share of profits; and (4) that the production function is independent of time.
48. APT, 180. Champernowne programmed the calculations (CEE 5:72n).
49. CEE 5:xiv.
50. Deane 1978, 242–44.
51. Hahn 1989, 56.
52. CEE 5:xvi.
53. CEE 5:81.
54. CEE 5:81–83. Both Thirlwall 1987b and Targetti and Thirlwall 1989 quote this.
55. CEE 5:93.
56. Kaldor 1970a. This was the fifth annual Scottish Economic Society Lecture delivered at the University of Aberdeen on February 18, 1970.
57. Dixon and Thirlwall 1975 and Thirlwall 1979.
  Curiously, Thirlwall (1979) does not mention Kaldor (Davidson 1990–91).
58. Scott 1989 and Hacche 1979.
59. Scott 1989, vii.
60. Ibid., 48–49. Solow also started some of his models with a steady state

analysis: Scott is agreeing with Kaldor and Solow that it is a good place to begin and disagreeing with Hacche 1979, 298.

61. Scott 1989, 348.
62. Scott 1989, 70–71. The three works are R.G.D. Allen 1967, M.G. Mueller 1971, P.A. Samuelson 1973. Scott also mentioned Ott, Ott, and Yoo 1975, and W. H. Branson 1979, indicating that these books had referred to Kaldor's savings theory but not his growth theory.
63. Scott 1989, 358.
64. Robinson 1991, 1509.
65. Thirlwall 1983b.

Chapter 12

1. Atsumi 1960, 117–18.
2. Tobin 1960, 119–20.
3. Tobin (1989, 37) quoting from an earlier publication.
4. Kaldor 1960c, 122.
5. Pasinetti 1962, especially note 2. The widow's cruse reference that so impressed the Cantabrigians is a note on p. 139 of Keynes's *Treatise on Money*, Vol I. See also Joan Robinson 1978, 55. Kaldor (CEE 1:227n.) says that according to this principle, "profits as a source of capital increment for entrepreneurs, are a widow's cruse which remains undepleted however much of them may be devoted to riotous living." On the other hand, saving becomes a "Danaid jar which can never be filled up." Kaldor considered this passage in the *Treatise* "the true seed of the ideas developed in the *General Theory*."
6. Pasinetti 1962, 267.
7. Lutz 1961, 294.
8. Samuelson and Modigliani 1966a, 269–70.
9. Samuelson and Modigliani 1966a, 269. In a footnote they questioned "the imperialistic notion that the 'neo-Keynesian' results hold in general" if "neo-Keynesian" is interpreted to involve any or all of the following notions: "investment is in some sense autonomous; marginalism is a modern irrelevancy; effective demand problems are always vital; income shares alter (in the long or short run) to equilibrate full employment; causation of interest or profit determination runs from growth rate of labor and not from impatience, thriftiness, and technical productivity." They added, "Many of these elements enter into certain models that we often choose to analyse, but there is nothing universal about such behaviour equations."
10. Pasinetti 1966, 303. Pasinetti said they admitted it in Samuelson and Modigliani 1966a, 287.
11. Pasinetti 1966, 306.
12. Robinson 1966, 308.
13. Kaldor 1966a, 309.
14. Kaldor 1966a, 316.
15. Samuelson and Modigliani 1966b, 321.
16. Samuelson 1991, 177–78.
17. Kubota 1968, 358–60.
18. Nuti 1969, 257–59.
19. Robinson 1969a.
20. Kaldor 1970b, 1–7, especially 4–5.
21. Tobin (1989, 38–39) was, however, called to account for a "muddle"

by Ian Steedman (1990). Tobin (1990) apologized, saying he had been trying to pay tribute to Kaldor and to exhibit a simple model that was compatible with Kaldor's. He offered to send a corrected version to the readers. Steedman felt that the recent decades had seen good progress in the analysis of the choice of technique and the dependence of relative commodity prices on distribution, a question on which Cantabrigians Kaldor, Robinson, and Sraffa had made important early statements.

22. For example, in the same 1991 issue of *Oxford Economic Papers* as Samuelson (1991) there are two articles on the Pasinetti and Anti-Pasinetti theorems: Koichi Miyazaki 1991 and Mauro Baranzini 1991.

23. Rothschild 1965, 656, 660.

24. Rothschild 1965, 652.

25. Gallaway 1964, 586–7. M. Reder (1959, 201) notes that he did not think the Kaldorian and marginal productivity theories inconsistent with each other. He thought that Kaldor's theory explained the secular rise in the share of employee compensation in the United States, while his [Reder's] version of the marginal productivity theory explained the secular constancy of labor's functional share. The difference between "employee compensation" and "labor's functional share" is the self-employment of wage earners, an indication of how difficult it is to empirically test from data collected for other purposes. Reder (1959, 205) thought the testing of such corollaries, however, would improve our understanding of the operation of the economy. We should remember that Kaldor did not claim short-run predictability for his theory.

Chapter 13

1. Kaldor 1971a, 2–3.
2. Kaldor 1971a, 6.
3. Kaldor 1971a, 16–17.
4. Baumol 1980, ix.
5. Kaldor 1980d, 8–10.
6. Kaldor 1980d, 13–14.
7. Kaldor 1980d, 33.
8. Kaldor 1980d, 208–209.
9. Kaldor 1980d, 284.
10. Kaldor 1980e, 85–92 and in discussion 93–100.
11. Fagerberg 1988, 355.
12. Kaldor 1980e, 89–91.
13. Kaldor to Pechman, June 6, 1977, KPP.
14. Kaldor to Pechman, October 12, 1977, KPP.
15. Cripps 1978; Kaldor 1980e, 92. As noted earlier, Thirlwall (1979) has made a model using balance of payments constraints to explain economic growth patterns. See also Thirlwall (1992) for a popular article on balance of payments and economic performance.
16. Kaldor 1980e, 99.
17. Kaldor 1958a, 91–98.

Chapter 14

1. Kaldor 1968, 385.

2. Kaldor 1966b, 6–8. See also CEE 5.
3. Kaldor 1966b, 10–12.
4. Kaldor 1966b, 75.
5. Kaldor 1966b, 16–19.
6. Kaldor 1966b, 31.
7. Kaldor gave up the shortage of labor arguments in the 1970s. While he seemed to have resurrected the view that labor might be an ultimate limit (1986b), Thirlwall assures me that he thought it was the rate of land saving innovations that ultimately constrained growth. Letter to author, May 28, 1992.
8. Kaldor 1967, 47.
9. Kaldor 1967, 68–69.
10. Kaldor 1967, 62–63.
11. Kaldor 1967, 56.
12. Wolfe 1968.
13. Kaldor 1968.
14. Rowthorn 1975a, Gomulka 1971, Cripps and Tarling 1973.
15. Rowthorn 1975a, 18–19.
16. Kaldor 1975, 891.
17. Kaldor 1981a, 432.
18. Kaldor 1975, 895–96.
19. Rowthorn 1975b.
20. Rowthorn 1979, 133.
21. Verdoorn (1980, 385) replied to Rowthorn that he had decided that "the 'law' that has been given my name appears . . . to be much less generally valid than I was led to believe in 1949." In the same volume, Thirlwall (1980) objected to Rowthorn's interpretation and offered copies of his translation of Verdoorn's article, which had appeared in Italian. See also Chatterji and Wickens 1981.
22. Kaldor 1981a, 432–33.
23. Bairam 1987, Hall 1991, 229.
24. Kaldor 1970a, 340–44.
25. Kaldor 1981b, 596–98.
26. Kaldor 1981b, 601.
27. Kaldor 1981b, 605–9.
28. Kaldor 1981b, 611–14.
29. Wood 1984, 323, 328. Wood (1984, 230–31) notes that after World War II Schumacher came into contact with Indian and Chinese philosophy and began to take flying saucer tales seriously. Kaldor thought it so out of character that he assumed it was all a big joke. In any case, he was not ready to listen to Schumacher's ideas on intermediate technology in 1964.
30. Stern 1991, 123
31. Stern 1991, 131.
32. Sandilands (1990a, 3) says that upon Young's sudden death of influenza when he was only fifty-two years of age, his wife, who was blind, departed hastily from London. Many of Young's papers were lost, including a book on money and credit, which he had in preparation, and notes for a book on the fundamentals of economic theory.
33. Sandilands 1990a, 6. Also, see 103–5.
34. Sandilands 1990a, 45.
35. The apparent reference for this is Kaldor's appendix, "Indivisibilities and Increasing Returns," CEE 5:196–201.
36. Sandilands 1990b, 296–303.

37. Sandilands 1990b. Currie received his Ph.d. from Harvard University in 1932. His dissertation competed for the Well's Prize with that of Harry Dexter White, whom he considered brilliant. His ideas were controversial, even at Harvard, and when Young died, he lost his faculty sponsor. He worked for the Federal Reserve Board and then became in 1939 the first professional economist to work in the White House, as adviser to President Franklin D. Roosevelt. During the McCarthy period he was accused by Elizabeth Bentley of being connected with one or two alleged espionage rings in Washington. He moved into advising developing countries, and immigrated and became a citizen of Colombia. Sandilands's account of his work history deserves to be read for its content and as an indication of how and when American economics turned away from institutionalism and toward a more conservative view of the economy. The public attacks on Currie in the United States were thus more successful than those on Kaldor in the United Kingdom, in effect depriving Currie of his domestic career.

38. Sandilands 1990b, 197–99.

39. Blitch 1983a and 1983b, 360.

Chapter 15

1. *Economist* 322: Survey 5, 6 (March 14–20, 1992).

2. Kaldor 1972a, 1239. Kaldor is not alone in this view. Clive W.J. Granger (1992, 4) in "Fellow's Opinion" complained among other things that "Many economic theory papers have no empirical implications and are thus of very little potential use to applied economists and are not possible to evaluate with data."

3. Ibid. Granger considered modeling of stylized facts "learning efforts by theorists."

4. Kaldor 1985b, 8, 13.

5. Kaldor 1985b, 61.

6. Kaldor 1985b, 20.

7. Kaldor 1985b, 35.

8. Kaldor 1985b, 59.

9. Kaldor may have borrowed this metaphor from Kornai 1971, for it also appears in Hahn 1973, 327–28, a review of Kornai 1971.

10. Baumol 1991, 1.

11. Bhagwati 1991, 9.

12. Stern 1991, 131.

13. Malinvaud 1991, 68. See also Hahn 1991 and Morishima 1991.

14. Morishima 1991.

15. Hahn 1984b.

16. Hahn 1991.

17. Blaug 1990.

18. Kaldor 1986b, 187–98.

19. Kaldor 1986b, 188, 197. Kaldor (1986b, 193–95) worked Hicks's distinction between the "fix-price and Flex-price markets" into his presentation and referred to Hicks 1973, which is part of the "John Hicks" tradition in its emphasis on the sequential character of production.

NK

REFERENCES

Abramovitz, Moses et al. (1959) *The Allocation of Economic Resources: Essays in Honor of Bernard Francis Haley*, (Stanford Studies in History, Economics and Politics, vol. 17). Stanford, California: Stanford University Press.

Allen, R.G.D. (1967) *Macroeconomic Theory*. London: Macmillan.

Andrews, William D. (1980) "A Supplemental Personal Expenditure Tax," in Pechman (1980).

Anydike-Danes, Michael (1982) "The 'New Cambridge' Hypothesis and Fiscal Planning," *Cambridge Economic Policy Review* 8:33-8 (April).

Arnold, Guy (1978) *Britain's Oil*. London: Hamish Hamilton.

Arrow, Kenneth J. and Scitovsky, Tibor, eds. (1969) *Readings in Welfare Economics*. Homewood, Illinois: Richard D. Irwin.

Assorodobraj-Kula, N.; Bobrowski, C.; Hagemejer, H.; Kula, W.; and Los, J., eds. (1981) *Studies in Economic Theory and Practice: Essays in Honor of Edward Lipinski*. New York: North-Holland Publishing.

Atkinson, Fred and Hall, Stephen (1983) *Oil and the British Economy*. New York: St. Martin's Press.

Atkinson, Paul; Begg, Iain; Cripps, Francis; and Anydike-Danes, Michael (1980a) "Academic Criticisms of the CEPG Analysis," *Cambridge Economic Policy Review* 6:35-42 (April).

——(1980b) "Britain's Economic Crisis and Possible Remedies," *Cambridge Economic Policy Review* 6:5-18 (April).

——(1980c) "Policy Assessment," *Cambridge Economic Policy Review* 6:1-8 (December).

Atsumi, Hiroshi (1960) "Mr. Kaldor's Theory of Income Distribution," *Review of Economic Studies* 27:109-18 (February).

Bairam, Erkin I. (1987) "The Verdoorn Law, Returns to Scale and Industrial Growth: A Review of the Literature," *Australian Economic Papers* 26:20-42 (June).

Baranzini, Mauro (1991) "The Pasinetti and Anti-Pasinetti Theorems: A Reply to K. Miyazaki and P. A. Samuelson," *Oxford Economic Papers* 43:195-98 (April).

Barnes, Julian (1991) "Letter from London," *The New Yorker* 66:57-69 (January 7).

Baumol, William J. (1980) *Public and Private Enterprise*. New York: St. Martin's Press.

——(1991) "Toward a Newer Economics: The Future Lies Ahead," *Economic Journal* 101:1-8 (January).

Beggs, Iain; Cripps, Francis; and Ward, Terry (1981) "The European Community: Problems and Prospects," *Cambridge Economic Policy Review* 7. No 2.

Beveridge, William (1960) *Full Employment in a Free Society*, 2nd ed. London: George Allen and Unwin.

Bhagwati, Jagdish (1991) "Economics Beyond the Horizon," *Economic Journal* 101:9-14 (January).

Blaug, Mark (1968) *Economic Theory in Retrospect*, Rev. ed. Homewood, Illinois: Richard D. Irwin.
——(1990) *Economic Theories, True or False?* England and Vermont: Edward Elgar.
——(1991) "Second Thoughts on the Keynesian Revolution," *History of Political Economy* 23:171-92 (Summer).
Blitch, Charles P. (1983a) "Allyn A. Young: A Curious Case of Professional Neglect," *History of Political Economy* 15:1-24 (Spring).
——(1983b) "Allyn Young on Increasing Returns," *Journal of Post Keynesian Economics* 5:359-72 (Spring).
Boadway, Robin and Bruce, Neil (1984) *Welfare Economics.* Oxford: Basil Blackwell.
Bourguignon, François; de Melo, Jaime; and Morrisson, Christian, eds. (1991) *Adjustment with Growth and Equity*, Vol. 19. Special issue of *World Development* (November).
Bowen, William G. (1960) *Wage Behavior in the Postwar Period: An Empirical Analysis.* Princeton, New Jersey: Princeton University Industrial Relations Section.
Bradford, David F. (1980) "The Case for a Personal Consumption Tax," in Pechman (1980).
Branson, W.H. (1979) *Macroeconomic Theory.* New York: Harper and Row.
Brassley, Paul (1988) "The Common Agricultural Policy of the European Economic Community," in McConnell (1988).
Brittan, Samuel and Lilley, Peter (1977) *The Delusion of Incomes Policy.* London: Temple Smith.
Bronfenbrenner, Martin (1957) "Academic Methods for Marxian Problems," *Journal of Political Economy* 65:535-42 (December).
Butler, Nick, ed. (1983) *The Economic Consequences of Mrs. Thatcher.* London: Gerald Duckworth.
Cannadine, David (1990) *Decline and Fall of the British Aristocracy.* New Haven: Yale University Press.
Canning, David (1988) "Increasing Returns in Industry and the Role of Agriculture in Growth," *Oxford Economic Papers* 40:463-76 (September).
Chakravarty, Sukhamoy (1989) "Nicholas Kaldor on Indian Economic Problems," *Cambridge Journal of Economics* 13:237-44 (March).
Chamberlain, Neil W. (1971) *The Labor Sector*, 2nd ed. New York: McGraw Hill.
Chamberlain, Neil W. and Cullen, Donald E. (1951) *The Impact of the Union.* New York: Harcourt Brace and World.
Chamberlin, Edward H. (1933) *The Theory of Monopolistic Competition.* Cambridge: Harvard University Press.
Chatterji, M. and Wickens, M. (1981) "Verdoorn's Law—the Externalities Hypothesis and Economic Growth in the United Kingdom," in Currie, Nobay and Peters (1981).
Clapham, Sir John Harold (1922) "Of Empty Economic Boxes," *Economic Journal* 32:305-14.
Cnossen, Sijbren (1988) "Overview," in Pechman (1988).
Colander, David C. and Coats, A.W., eds. (1989) *The Spread of Economic Ideas.* Cambridge: Cambridge University Press.
Committee on Economic Development (1958) *Problems of United States Economic Development*, Vol. 1. New York: Committee on Economic Development.
Congdon, Tim (1978) *Chile: the Rule of the Chicago Boys.* United Kingdom: World University Service.
Cook, Cris and Taylor, Ian (1980) *The Labour Party.* New York: Longman.

Corden, W. Max (1984) "Booming Sector and Dutch Disease Economics," *Oxford Economic Papers* 36:359-80.

Corden, W. Max and Neary, J. Peter (1982) "Booming Sector and De-Industrialisation in a Small Open Economy," *Economic Journal* 9 2:825-48 (December).

Craver, Earlene (1986) "The Emigration of Austrian Economists," *History of Political Economy* 18:1-32 (Spring).

Craver, Earlene and Leijonhufvud, Axel (1987) "Economics in America: The Continental Influence," *History of Political Economy* 19:173-82 (Summer).

Cripps, T. F. (1978) "Causes of Growth and Recession in World Trade," *Cambridge Economic Policy Review* 4:37-43 (March).

Cripps, T.F. and Tarling, R.J. (1973) *Advanced Capitalist Economics 1950-1970*. Cambridge: Cambridge University Press.

Currie, D.; Nobay, A.R.; and Peel, D., eds. (1981) *Microeconomic Analysis*. London: Croom Helm.

Daniels, Gordon, ed. (1981) *A Guide to the Reports of the United States Strategic Bombing Survey: I Europe, II Pacific*. London: Offices of the Royal Historical Society, University College.

Dasgupta, Partha and Stiglitz, Joseph (1988) "Learning by Doing, Market Structure and Industrial and Trade Policies," *Oxford Economic Papers* 40:246-68.

Davidson, Paul (1990-91) "A Post Keynesian Positive Contribution to 'Theory'," *Journal of Post Keynesian Economics* 13:298-303 (Winter).

Deane, Phyllis (1978) *The Evolution of Economic Ideas*. Cambridge: Cambridge University Press.

de la Mohotiere, Stuart (1970) *Towards One Europe*. New York: Penguin Books.

Derbyshire, J. Denis and Derbyshire, Ian (1988) *Politics in Britain from Callaghan to Thatcher*. Edinburgh: W. and R. Chambers.

Dixon, R. J. and Thirlwall, A. P. (1975) "A Model of Regional Growth Rate Differences on Kaldorian Lines," Oxford Economic Papers 27:201-14 (July).

Eatwell, John and Milgate, Murray, eds. (1983) *Keynes's Economics and the Theory of Value and Distribution*. London: Gerald Duckworth.

Economic Commission for Europe (1947, 1948, 1949) *Economic Surveys of Europe*. Geneva.

El-Agraa, Ali M. (1984) "Has Membership of the European Communities Been a Disaster for Britain?" *Applied Economics* 16:299-315 (April).

—— ed. (1985) *The Economics of the European Community*, 2nd ed. Philip Allan New York: St. Martin's Press.

Evans, Douglas, ed. (1971) *Destiny or Delusion*. London: Victor Gollancz.

—— ed. (1973) *Britain in the EEC*. London: Victor Gollancz.

Fagerberg, Jan (1988) "International Competitiveness," *Economic Journal* 98:355-74 (June).

Fallick, J. L. and Elliott, R. F., eds. (1981) *Incomes Policies, Inflation and Relative Pay*. London: George Allen and Unwin.

Flanagan, Robert J.; Soskice, David W.; and Ulman, Lloyd (1983) *Unionism, Economic Stabilization and Incomes Policies*. Washington, D. C.: Brookings Institution.

Freud, David (1978) in London *Times*, February 18.

Friedman, Milton (1968) "The Role of Monetary Policy," *American Economic Review* 58:1-17 (March).

——(1969) *The Optimum Quantity of Money*. Chicago: Aldine.

——(1970a) *The Counter Revolution in Monetary Theory*. (First Wincott Memorial Lecture). London: Institute of Economic Affairs.

——(1970b) "The New Monetarism: Comment," *Lloyds Bank Review* 98:52-3 (October).

———(1970c) "A Theoretical Framework for Monetary Analysis," *Journal of Political Economy* 78:193-238 (March/April).
———(1970d) "Money and Income: Post hoc and ergo propter hoc? Comment," *Quarterly Journal of Economics* 84:318-27 (May).
———(1976) "Introduction" in Machlup (1976).
———(1977a) "Inflation and Unemployment" (Nobel Lecture), *Journal of Political Economy* 85:451-72 (June).
———(1977b) *From Galbraith to Economic Freedom* (Occasional Paper No. 4). London: Institute of Economic Affairs.
Friedman, Milton and Heller, Walter W. (1969) *Monetary vs. Fiscal Policy*. New York: W. W. Norton.
Friedman, Milton and Schwartz, Anna Jacobson (1963) *Monetary History of the United States 1867-1960*. Princeton, New Jersey: Princeton University Press.
———(1965) *The Great Contraction 1929-1933*. Princeton, New Jersey: Princeton University Press.
———(1982) *Monetary Trends in U.S. and U.K. 1967-1975*. Chicago: University of Chicago Press.
Galbraith, John Kenneth (1981) *A Life in Our Times*. Boston: Houghton Mifflin.
———(1986) *A View from the Stands*. Boston: Houghton Mifflin.
Gallaway, Lowell E. (1964) "The Theory of Relative Shares,"*Quarterly Journal of Economics* 78:574-91 (November).
Geithman, David T. (1974) *Fiscal Policy for Industrialization and Development in Latin America*. Gainesville: University Presses of Florida.
Godley, Wynne, ed. (1981) "Economic Policy in the United Kingdom," *Cambridge Economic Policy Review* 7 No.1.
Gomulka, Stanislaw (1971) *Inventive Activity, Diffusion, and the Stages of Economic Growth*. Aarhus, Denmark: Aarhus University, Institute of Economics.
Goode, Richard (1980) "The Superiority of the Income Tax," in Pechman (1980).
Goss, B.A. and Yamey, B.D., eds. (1976) *The Economics of Futures Trading*. New York: John Wiley and Sons.
Granger, Clive W. J. (1992) "Fellow's Opinion," "Evaluating Economic Theory," *Journal of Econometrics* 51:3-5 (January/February).
Hacche, Graham (1979) *The Theory of Economic Growth, An Introduction*. New York: St. Martin's Press.
Hahn, Frank H. (1973) "The Winter of Our Discontent," *Economica* N.S 40:322-30 (August).
———(1984a) *Equilibrium and Macroeconomics*. Cambridge: MIT Press.
———(1984b) "In Praise of Economic Theory," (Jevons Lecture). London: University College.
———(1989) "Kaldor on Growth," *Cambridge Journal of Economics* 13:47-58 (March).
———(1991) "The Next Hundred Years," *Economic Journal* 101:47-50 (January).
Hahn, Frank H. and Matthews, R.C.O. (1964) "The Theory of Economic Growth: A Survey," *Economic Journal* 74:779-902 (December).
Hall, John Battaile (1991) "Sectoral Transformation and Economic Decline: Views from Berkeley and Cambridge" in *Cambridge Journal of Economics* 15:229-37 (June).
Hann, Danny (1986) *Government and North Sea Oil*. Basingstoke, Hampshire: Macmillan.
Harberger, Arnold C. (1958) Review of Kaldor's *Expenditure Tax, Journal of Political Economy* 66:84-5 (February).

Harcourt, G. C. (1986) Review of Kaldor's *Economics Without Equilibrium, Economic Journal* 96:540-41 (June).

Harrod, R. F. (1938) "Scope and Method of Economics," *Economic Journal* 48:383-412 (September).

——(1948) *Towards a Dynamic Economics*. London: Macmillan.

——(1964) Review of Kaldor's *Essays on Economic Policy Volumes 1 and 2, Economic Journal* 75:794-803 (December).

——(1969) *Life of John Maynard Keynes*. New York: Augustus M. Kelley.

Hayek, Freidrich A. von (1960) *The Constitution of Liberty*. Chicago: University of Chicago Press.

Heilbroner, Robert L. (1990) "Reflections after Communism," *The New Yorker* 6:91-100 (September 10).

Helm, Dieter, ed. (1984) "Introduction" to *The Economics of John Hicks*. Oxford: Basil Blackwell.

Hendry, David F. and Ericsson, Neil R. (1983) "Assertions without Empirical Basis: An Econometric Appraisal of Friedman and Schwartz," (Bank of England Panel of Academic Consultants, Panel Paper No. 22). London: Bank of England.

Hicks, John R. (1937) "Mr. Keynes and the 'Classics'; A Suggested Interpretation," *Econometrica* 5:147-59 (April).

——(1939) "Foundations of Welfare Economics," *Economic Journal* 49:701-16.

——(1946) *Value and Capital*, 2nd ed. Oxford: Clarendon Press.

——(1960) "Thoughts on the Theory of Capital—the Corfu Conference," *Oxford Economic Papers* 12:123- 32 (June).

——(1973) *Capital and Time: A Neo-Austrian Theory*. Oxford: Clarendon Press.

——(1975a) "Revival of Political Economy: The Old and the New" *Economic Record* 51:365-67 (September).

——(1975b) "What is Wrong with Monetarism?" *Lloyds Bank Review* 118:1-13 (October).

——(1976) "Some Questions of Time in Economics," in Tang (1976).

——(1977) *Economic Perspectives*. Oxford: Clarendon Press.

——(1981) *Wealth and Welfare*, Collected Essays on Economic Theory. Vol. 1. Cambridge: Harvard University Press.

——(1982) *Money, Interest and Wages*, Collected Essays on Economic Theory. Vol. 2. Cambridge: Harvard University Press.

——(1983) *Classics and Moderns*, Collected Essays on Economic Theory. Vol. 3. Oxford: Basil Blackwell.

Hicks, Ursula (1958) "Mr. Kaldor's Plan for the Reform of Indian Taxes," *Economic Journal* 68:160-69 (March).

Hobbes, Thomas (1909) *Leviathan*. Oxford: Clarendon Press (from 1651 edition).

Hodges, Wayne L. and Kelly, Matthew A., eds. (1970) *Technological Change and Human Development*. Ithaca: Cornell University, New York School of Industrial and Labor Relations.

Hodgson, Geoff (1989) "Institutional Rigidities and Economic Growth," *Cambridge Journal of Economics* 13:79-101 (March).

Holt, Stephen (1972) "British Attitudes to the Political Aspects of Membership of the European Communities," in Ionescu (1972).

Ingham, M. (1981) "Incomes Policies: A Short History," in Fallick (1981).

International Encyclopedia of the Social Sciences (1979) *Biographical Supplement*, Vol. 18. New York: Free Press.

Ionescu, Ghita, ed. (1972) *The New Politics of European Integration*. New York: St. Martin's Press.

Jagan, Cheddi (1966) *The West on Trial: My Fight for Guyana's Freedom.* New York: International Publishers.

Johnson, Harry G. (1971) "The Keynesian Revolution and the Monetarist Counter-Revolution," *American Economic Review* 61:1-14 (May).

———(1973) "The United States and the Disunited States: The Crisis of the International Economic System," in Evans (1973).

———(1976) "What Is Right with Monetarism," *Lloyds Bank Review* 120:13–17 (April).

———(1978a) "Cambridge As an Academic Environment in the Early 1930s," in Patinkin (1978).

———(1978b) "Comment on Mayer on Monetarism," in Mayer (1978).

Jones, Bill (1977) *The Russia Complex: The British Labour Party and the Soviet Union.* Manchester: Manchester University Press.

Just, Richard E.; Hueth, Darrell; and Smith, Andrew (1982) *Applied Welfare Economics and Public Policy.* Inglewood Cliffs: Prentice Hall.

Kahn, R. F. (1984) *The Making of Keynes' General Theory.* Cambridge: Cambridge University Press.

Kaldor, Nicholas. *Collected Economic Essays* 1:1960a; 2:1960b; 3:1964a; 4:1964b; 5:1978a; 6:1978b; 7:1980a; and 8:1980b.

———(1932a) "The Danubian States," *Economist* May 14, 21, 28 and June 4.

———(1932b) "The Economic Situation in Austria," *Harvard Business Review* 11:23-4 (October).

———(1934) "Mrs. Robinson's Economics of Imperfect Competition," *Economica* N.S. 1:335-41 (August).

———(1936) "Wage Subsidies As a Remedy for Unemployment," *Journal of Political Economy* 44:721-42 (December).

———(1937) "The Controversy on the Theory of Capital," *Econometrica*, July, and CEE 1:153-90.

———(1938) "Professor Chamberlin on Monopolistic and Imperfect Competition," *Quarterly Journal of Economics* 52:513-29 (May) and CEE 1:81-95.

———(1939) "A Note on Welfare Economics," *Economic Journal* 49:549-52 (September). Republished as "Welfare Propositions in Economics," CEE 1:143-6.

———(1940a) "A Note on Tariffs and the Terms of Trade," *Economica* N.S. 7:377-80 (November).

———(1940b) "A Note on the Theory of the Forward Market," *Review of Economic Studies* 7:196-201 (June).

———(1945-46) "The German War Economy," *Review of Economic Studies* 13:33-52 (September).

———(1955) *An Expenditure Tax.* London: George Allen and Unwin.

———(1956a) "Capitalist Evolution in the Light of Keynesian Economics," (Lecture delivered at the University of Peking), typescript in KPP.

———(1956b) "Characteristics of Economic Development," *Asian Studies* (November). See CEE 2:233:42.

———(1956c) "Alternative Theories of Distribution," *Review of Economic Studies* 23 and CEE 1:209-36.

———(1957) "A Model of Economic Growth," *Economic Journal* 57 (December) and CEE 2:259-300.

———(1958a) "The Growing Disparity Between Rich and Poor Countries," in Committee on Economic Development (1958).

———(1958b) "Risk Bearing and Income Taxation," *Review of Economic Studies* 25:206–09 (June).

———(1958c) "Capital Accumulation and Economic Growth" in Lutz (1961) and CEE 5:1-53.

———(1960a) *Essays on Value and Distribution.* Glencoe, Illinois: Free Press. 2nd ed. issued in 1981 as Vol. 1 of Collected Economic Essays, contains a "General Introduction" to all eight vols.. New York: Holmes and Meier.

———(1960b) *Essays on Economic Stability and Growth.* Glencoe, Illinois: Free Press. 2nd ed. issued in 1980 as Vol. 2 of Collected Economic Essays. New York: Holmes and Meier.

———(1960c) "A Rejoinder to Mr. Atsumi and Professor Tobin, *Review of Economic Studies* 27:121-23 (February).

———(1960d) Appendix in Beveridge (1960).

———(1961) "Increasing Returns and Economic Progress: A Comment on Professor Hicks's Article," *Oxford Economic Papers* 13:1-4 (February).

———(1962) "A New Model of Economic Growth," see Kaldor and Mirrlees and CEE 5 54-80.

———(1964a) *Essays on Economic Policy I.* London: Gerald Duckworth. 2nd ed. issued in 1978 as Vol. 3 of Collected Economic Essays. New York: Holmes and Meier.

———(1964b) *Essays on Economic Policy II.* London: Gerald Duckworth. 2nd ed. issued in 1978 as Vol. 4 of Collected Economic Essays. New York: Holmes and Meier.

———(1966a) "Marginal Productivity and the Macro-Economic Theories of Distribution," *Review of Economic Studies* 33:309-20 (October).

———(1966b) *Causes of the Slow Rate of Economic Growth of the United Kingdom.* Cambridge: Cambridge University Press. See CEE 5:100-38.

———(1967) *Strategic Factors in Economic Development.* Ithaca: Cornell University, New York State School of Industrial and Labor Relations.

———(1968) "Productivity and Growth in Manufacturing Industries: A Reply," *Economica* N.S. 35:385-91 (November).

———(1970a) "The Case for Regional Policies," *Scottish Journal of Political Economy* 17:337-48 (November).

———(1970b) "Some Fallacies in the Interpretation of Kaldor," *Review of Economic Studies* 37:1-7 (January).

———(1970c) "The New Monetarism," *Lloyds Bank Review* 80:1-18 (July).

———(1970d) "A Rejoinder to Professor Friedman," *Lloyds Bank Review* 98:54-5 (October).

———(1970e) "Role of Modern Technology in Raising Economic Standards of the Less Developed Countries," in Hodges and Kelly (1970).

———ed. (1971a) *Conflicts in Policy Objectives.* Oxford: Basil Blackwell.

———(1971b) "The Truth about the Dynamic Effects," *New Statesman,* March 12.

———(1971c) "The Money Crisis: Britain's Chance," *New Statesman,* May 14.

———(1971d) "The Distortions of the White Paper," *New Statesman,* July 16.

———(1971e) "The Dynamic Effects of the Common Market," in Evans (1971).

———(1972a) "The Irrelevance of Equilibrium Economics," *Economic Journal* 82:1237-55 (December).

———(1972b) "Mr. Heath's New Socialism," *Sunday Times,* October 8.

———(1974a) "Managing the Economy: The British Experience," *Quarterly Review of Economics and Business* 14:1-11 (Autumn).

———(1974b) "Mr. Heath's Road to Ruin," *New Statesman,* February 21 and March 1.

———(1975) "Economic Growth and the Verdoorn Law—A Comment on Mr. Rowthorn's Article," *Economic Journal* 85:891-96 (December).

——(1976) "A Keynesian Theory of Distribution," in Surrey (1976).

——(1977) "The Nemesis of Free Trade," *Spectator*, August 27.

——(1978a) *Further Essays on Economic Theory*, Vol. 5 of Collected Economic Essays. New York: Holmes and Meier.

——(1978b) *Further Essays on Applied Economics*, Vol. 6 of Collected Economic Essays. New York: Holmes and Meier.

——(1980a) *Reports on Taxation I*, Vol. 7 of Collected Economic Essays. New York: Holmes and Meier.

——(1980b) *Reports on Taxation II*, Vol. 8 of Collected Economic Essays. New York: Holmes and Meier.

——(1980c) "A Supplemental Personal Expenditure Tax," in Pechman (1980).

——(1980d) "The Issues," in Baumol (1980).

——(1980e) "Foundations of Free Trade Theory and Their Implications for the Current World Recession," in Malinvaud and Fitoussi (1980).

——(1981a) "Discussion," in Currie, Nobay, and Peel (1981).

——(1981b) "The Role of Increasing Returns, Technical Progress and Cumulative Causation in the Theory of International Trade and Economic Growth," *Économie Appliqué* 34:593-617 (No. 4).

——(1982) *The Scourge of Monetarism*. Oxford: Oxford University Press.

——(1985a) "How Monetarism Failed," *Challenge Magazine* 28:4-13 (May/June).

——(1985b) *Economics Without Equilibrium*. Armonk, New York: M.E. Sharpe.

——(1985c) "Lessons of the Monetarist Experiment," in van Ewijk and Klant (1985).

——(1986a) "Recollections of an Economist," *Banca Nazionale del Lavoro Quarterly Review* 156:3-26 (March).

——(1986b) "Limits on Growth," *Oxford Economic Papers* 38:187-98 (July).

——(1987) "The Role of Commodity Prices in Economic Recovery," *World Development* 15:551-58 (May).

Kaldor, Nicholas and Mirrlees, James (1962) "A New Model of Economic Growth," *Review of Economic Studies* 29 and CEE 5:54-80.

Kalecki, Michal (1942) "A Theory of Profits" *Economic Journal* 42 (June-September).

Katz, Bernard S., ed. (1989) *Nobel Laureates in Economic Sciences*. New York: Garland Publishing.

Keynes, John Maynard (Various Years) *The Collected Writings of John Maynard Keynes*. Ed. by Donald Moggridge. 28 Vols. London: Macmillan, St. Martin's Press for the Royal Economic Society. Referred to as JMK.

——(1925) *The Economic Consequences of Mr. Churchill*, First appeared in *The Nation and the Atheneum*. See JMK 19:362-453.

——(1936) *The General Theory of Employment, Interest and Money*. London: Macmillan.

Kornai, Janos (1971) *Anti-equilibrium on Economic Systems Theory and the Tasks of Research*. New York: American Elsevier Publishing.

Kubota, Koichi (1968) "A Re-examination of the Existence and Stability Propositions in Kaldor's Growth Models," *Review of Economic Studies* 35:353-60 (July).

Lawson, Tony; Palma, J. Gabriel; and Sender, John (1989) "Kaldor's Contribution to Economics: An Introduction," *Cambridge Journal of Economics* 13:1-8 (March).

Leasure, J. William and Turner, Marjorie S. (1974) *Prices, Profit and Production: How Much is Enough?* Albuquerque: University of New Mexico Press.

Leontief, Wassily (1971) "Theoretical Assumptions and Nonobserved Facts," *American Economic Review* 61:1-7 (March).

Lieberman, Henry (1956) *New York Times*, May 27.

Lipgens, Walter (1982) *A History of European Integration.* Oxford: Clarendon Press.

Little, I.M.D. (1956) Review of Kaldor's *Expenditure Tax, Economic Journal* 66:116-20 (March).

Lodewijks, John (1988) "Arthur Okun and the Lucasian Critique," *Australian Economic Papers* 27:253-71 (December).

Lutz, Freidrich, ed. (1961) *The Theory of Capital.* London: Macmillan.

Machlup, Fritz, ed. (1976) *Essays on Hayek.* New York: New York University Press.

Malinvaud, Edmond (1991) "The Next Fifty Years," *Economic Journal* 101:64-8 (January).

Malinvaud, Edmond and Fitoussi, Jean-Paul, eds. (1980) *Unemployment in Western Countries.* New York: St. Martin's Press.

Mayer, Thomas, ed. (1978) *The Structure of Monetarism.* New York: W. W. Norton.

McConnell, Primrose (1988) *The Agricultural Notebook.* 18th ed. by R. J. Halley and R. J. Soffe. London: Butterworths.

McPeak, Elynor Fay (1966) *The Theory and Practice of Wage Policy in Great Britain 1959-1964.* Master's Thesis, San Diego State University.

Mezerik, Avram G., ed. (1962) *Common Market: Political Impacts.* Vol. 8 No. 72 of *International Review Service.*

Miles, Marc A. (1983) Review of Kaldor's *The Scourge of Monetarism, Journal of Economic Literature* 21:1016-17 (September).

Minarik, Joseph J. (1989) "How Tax Reform Came About," in Colander and Coats (1989).

Miyazaki, Koichi (1991) "On the Neo-Keynesian Interpretation of the Anti-Pasinetti Theory," *Oxford Economic Papers* 43:187-94 (April).

Modigliani, Franco (1977) "The Monetarist Controversy, or Should We Forsake Stabilization Policies?" *American Economic Review* 67:1-19 (March).

Molana, H. and Vines, D. (1989) "North-South Growth and the Terms of Trade: A Model on Kaldorian Lines," *Economic Journal* 99:443-53 (June).

Monnet, Jean (1978) *Memoirs.* Garden City, New York: Doubleday.

Morishima, Michio (1991) "General Equilibrium Theory in the Twenty-First Century," *Economic Journal* 101:69-74 (January).

Moyne, Richard (1972) "The Role of Jean Monnet," in Ionescu (1972).

Mueller, M.G. (1971) *Readings in Macroeconomics,* 2nd ed. London: Holt Rinehart.

Musgrave, Richard A. (1957) Review of Kaldor's *Expenditure Tax, American Economic Review* 47:200-5 (March).

Musgrave, Richard A. and Domar, Evsey (1944) "Proportional Income Taxation and Risk Taking," *Quarterly Journal of Economics* 58:389-422 (May).

Myint, Hla (1965) *Theories of Welfare Economics.* New York: Augustus M. Kelley.

Myrdal, Gunnar (1965) *Monetary Equilibrium.* New York: Augustus M. Kelley. First published in German in 1933.

Naipaul, V.S. (1991) "A Handful of Dust: Return to Guiana," *New York Review of Books* 38:15-20 (April 11).

Nuti, D. Mario (1969) "The Degree of Monopoly in the Kaldor-Mirrlees Growth Model," *Review of Economic Studies* 36:257-60 (April).

Observer, (1964) "Men and Matters," *Financial Times,* November 1964, KPP.

Okun, Arthur M. (1981) *Prices and Quantities: A Macroeconomic Analysis.* Washington, D.C.: Brookings Institution.

Ott, D.J.; Ott, A.F.; and Yoo, J.H. (1975) *Macroeconomic Theory.* New York: McGraw Hill.

Overton, David (1983) *Common Market Digest.* London: Library Association.

Palma, J. Gabriel and Marcel, Mario (1989) "Kaldor on the 'Discreet Charm' of the

Chilean Bourgeoisie," *Cambridge Journal of Economics* 13:245-72 (March).
Parker, Geoffrey (1979) *The Countries of Community Europe*. New York: St. Martin's Press.
Pasinetti, Luigi L. (1962) "Rate of Profit and Income Distribution in Relation to the Rate of Economic Growth," *Review of Economic Studies* 19:267-79 (October).
———(1966) "New Results in an Old Framework," *Review of Economic Studies* 33:303-6 (October).
———(1979) "Nicholas Kaldor," in *International Encyclopedia of the Social Sciences, Biographical Supplement* (1979).
———(1983) "Nicholas Kaldor: A Few Personal Notes," *Journal of Post Keynesian Economics* 5:333-40 (Spring).
Patinkin, Don and Leith, J. Clark, eds. (1978) *Keynes, Cambridge and the General Theory*. Toronto: University of Toronto Press.
Pechman, Joseph A., ed. (1980) *What Should Be Taxed: Income or Expenditure?* Washington, D.C.: Brookings Institution.
———ed. (1985) *A Citizen's Guide to the New Tax Reforms*. New Jersey: Rowman and Allanheld.
———ed. (1987) *Federal Tax Policy*, 5th ed. Washington, D.C.: Brookings Institution.
———ed. (1988) *World Tax Reform*. Washington, D.C.: Brookings Institution.
———(1990) "The Future of the Income Tax," *American Economic Review* 80:1-20 (March).
Pelling, Henry (1972) *A Short History of the Labour Party*, 4th ed. London: Macmillan.
Phillips, A. W. (1958) "The Relation Between Unemployment and the Rate of Change of Money Wage Rates in the United Kingdom," *Economica* N.S. 25:283-99 (November).
Pomfret, Richard (1985) "Measuring the Economic Consequences of British Membership of the European Economic Community," *Applied Economics* 17:705-7 (August).
Reddaway, Brian (1970) *Effects of the Selective Employment Tax, First Report, the Distributive Trades*. London: Her Majesty's Stationery Office.
———(1973) *Effects of the Selective Employment Tax: Final Report*. (Department of Applied Economics Occasional Paper 32), Cambridge: Cambridge University Press.
———(1989) "Tax Reform in the United Kingdom," *Cambridge Journal of Economics* 13:141-54 (March).
Reder, Melvin (1959) "Alternative Theories of Labor's Share," in Abramovitz (1959).
Reid, Gavin C. (1987) "Disequilibrium and Increasing Returns in Adam Smith's Analysis of Growth and Accumulation," *History of Political Economy* 19:87-106 (Spring).
Riese, Martin (1988) "Raw Material Prices and Kalecki's Wage Share Theory: Reply," *Journal of Post Keynesian Economics* 10:487-88 (Spring).
Robbins, Lionel (1938) "Interpersonal Comparisons of Utility: A Comment," *Economic Journal* 48:635-41 (December).
———(1940) *An Essay on the Nature and Significance of Economic Science*. London: Macmillan. First published in 1932.
———(1970) *The Evolution of Modern Economic Theory*. Chicago: Aldine.
Robinson, Joan (1966) "Comment on Samuelson and Modigliani,"*Review of Economic Studies* 33:307-8 (October).
———(1969a) "A Further Note," *Review of Economic Studies* 36:260-62 (April).

——(1969b) *The Economics of Imperfect Competition*, 2nd ed. London: Macmillan. First published in 1933.

——(1976) "The Theory of Distribution: A Synthesis," in Surrey (1976).

——(1978) *Collected Economic Papers*, Vol. 1. Oxford: Basil Blackwell.

Robinson, Sherman (1991) "Macroeconomics, Financial Variables and Computable General Equilibrium Models," in Bourguignon, de Melo and Morrisson (1991).

Rothschild, K.W. (1965) "Themes and Variations: Remarks on the Kaldorian Distribution Formula," *Kyklos* 18:652-69 (Fasc 5).

Rowthorn, R.E. (1975a) "What Remains of Kaldor's Law?" *Economic Journal* 85:10-19 (March).

——(1975b) "A Reply to Lord Kaldor's Comment," *Economic Journal* 85:897-901 (December).

——(1979) "A Note on Verdoorn's Law," *Economic Journal* 89:131-33 (March).

Samuels, Warren, ed. (1976) *The Chicago School of Political Economy*. East Lansing: Michigan State University. See also "The Chicago School of Political Economy," *Journal of Economic Issues* (1975) Vol. 9 (December) and (1976) Vol. 10 (March).

Samuelson, Paul A. (1946) "Lord Keynes and the General Theory," *Econometrica* 14:187-200 (July).

——(1973) *Economics*, 9th ed. New York: McGraw-Hill.

——(1983) "The World Economy at Century's End," in Tsuru (1983).

——(1991) "Extirpating Error Contaminating the Post-Keynesian Anti-Pasinetti Equilibrium," *Oxford Economic Papers* 43:177-86 (April).

Samuelson, Paul A. and Modigliani, Franco (1966a) "The Pasinetti Paradox in Neoclassical and More General Models," *Review of Economic Studies* 33:269-302 (October).

——(1966b) "Reply to Pasinetti and Robinson," *Review of Economic Studies* 33:321-30 (October).

Sandilands, Roger J., ed. (1990a) "Nicholas Kaldor's Notes on Allyn Young's LSE Lectures, 1927-29," *Journal of Economic Studies* 17:1-170 (No. 3/4).

——(1990b) *The Life and Political Economy of Lauchlin Currie*. Durham, North Carolina: Duke University Press.

Scitovsky, Tibor (1941) "A Note on Welfare Propositions in Economics," *Review of Economic Studies* 9:77-88 (November).

Scott, Maurice Fitzgerald (1989) *A New View of Economic Growth*. Oxford: Clarendon Press.

Sender, John (1989) "Kaldor's Contribution to Economics: An Introduction," *Cambridge Journal of Economics* 13:1-8 (March).

Simms, Peter (1966) *Trouble in Guyana*. London: George Allen and Unwin.

Smith, V. Kerry (1990) "Can We Measure the Economic Value of Environmental Amenities?" *Southern Economic Journal* 56:865-78 (April).

Solow, Robert M. (1976) "How Constant Are Relative Shares?" in Surrey (1976).

Solow, Robert M. and Samuelson, Paul A. (1960) "Problem of Achieving and Maintaining a Stable Price Level," *American Economic Review* 70:292-93 (May).

Spinner, Thomas J., Jr. (1984) *Political and Social History of Guyana, 1945-83*. Boulder: Westview Press.

Sraffa, Piero (1926) "The Laws of Returns Under Competitive Conditions," *Economic Journal* 36:535-50 (December).

Steedman, Ian (1990) "Growth and Distribution: a Muddling Exercise," *Cambridge Journal of Economics* 14:229-32 (June).

Steel, David (1980) "Labour in Office: The Post-War Experience," in Cook and Taylor (1980).

Steindl, Josef (1990) *Economic Papers 1941-88*. London: Macmillan.
Stern, Nicholas (1991) "The Determinants of Growth," *Economic Journal* 101:122-33 (January).
Stevenson, Richard (1989) "John Richard Hicks," in Katz (1989).
Surrey, M.J.C. (1976) *Macroeconomic Theories*. Oxford: Oxford University Press.
Tang, Anthony M.; Westfield, Fred M.; and Worley, James S. (1976) *Essays in Honor of Nicholas Georgescu-Roegen*. Lexington Massachusetts: Lexington Books; D.C. Heath.
Targetti, F. and Thirlwall, Anthony P., eds. (1989) *The Essential Kaldor*. London: Gerald Duckworth.
Taylor, A.J.P. (1965) *English History 1914-1945*. New York: Oxford University Press.
Thirlwall, Anthony P. (1976) *Keynes and International Monetary Relations*. London: Macmillan.
——(1979) "The Balance of Payments Constraint As an Explanation of International Growth Rate Differences," *Banca Nazionale del Lavoro Quarterly Review* 32:45-53 (March).
——(1980) "Rowthorn's Interpretation of Verdoorn's Law," *Economic Journal* 90:386-88 (June).
——(1982) *Balance of Payments Theory and the United Kingdom Experience*. London: Macmillan.
——(1983a) "What Are Estimates of the Natural Rate of Unemployment Measuring?" *Oxford Bulletin of Economics and Statistics* 45:173-79 (May).
——(1983b) "A Plain Man's Guide to Kaldor's Growth Laws," *Journal of Post Keynesian Economics* 5:345-58 (Spring).
——(1986) "Model of Growth and Development on Kaldorian Lines," *Oxford Economic Papers* 38:199-219 (July).
——ed. (1987a) *Keynes and Economic Development*. London: Macmillan.
——(1987b) *Nicholas Kaldor*. New York: New York University Press. Referred to as APT.
——(1992) "The Balance of Payments and Economic Performance," *National Westminster Bank Quarterly Review* pp. 2-12 (May).
Tobin, James (1960) "Towards a General Kaldorian Theory of Distribution," *Review of Economic Studies* 27:119-20 (February).
——(1976) "A General Kaldorian Theory of Distribution," in Surrey (1976).
——(1989) "Growth and Distribution: A Neoclassical Kaldor-Robinson Exercise," *Cambridge Journal of Economics* 13:37-45 (March).
——(1990) "Growth and Distribution: A Reply," *Cambridge Journal of Economics* 14:232 (June).
Toye, John (1989) "Tax Reform in Developing Countries," *Cambridge Journal of Economics* 13:183-200 (March).
Tsuru, Shigeta, ed. (1983) *Human Resources, Employment and Development, Vol. 1: The Issues*. New York: St. Martin's Press.
Turner, Marjorie S. (1989) *Joan Robinson and the Americans*. Armonk, New York: M.E. Sharpe.
——(1990) "The Cambridge Keynesians and the Bastard Keynesians: A Comment on Economists and Their Understanding of the Inflationary Aspects of Keynesian Policy," *Journal of Economic Issues* 24:886-90 (September).
United States Strategic Bombing Survey (1945) *The Effects of Strategic Bombing on the German War Economy*. Overall Economic Effects Division, October 31, 1945. U.S. Government Document.

———(1987) "The Effects of Strategic Bombing on the German War Economy 1945," Maxwell Airforce Base, Alabama, 36112-5532: Air University Press.

van Ewijk, C. and Klant, J. J. (1985) *Monetary Conditions for Economic Recovery.* Boston: Martinus Nijhoff Publishers.

Verdoorn, P. J. (1980) "Verdoorn's Law in Retrospect," *Economic Journal* 90:382-85 (June).

Viner, Jacob (1950) Review of Full Employment Document, *Quarterly Journal of Economics* 64:385-407 (August).

Walker, Martin (1979) "Economists With a Mission," *Manchester Guardian* (October) in KPP.

Weintraub, Sidney (1971) "An Incomes Policy to Stop Inflation," *Lloyds Bank Review* 99:1-12 (January).

———(1972) "Incomes Policy: Completing the Stabilization Triangle," *Journal of Economic Issues* 6:105-30.

Whiteley, Paul (1983) *The Labour Party in Crisis.* New York: Methuen.

Wolfe, J. N. (1968) "Productivity and Growth in Manufacturing Industry: Some Reflections on Professor Kaldor's Inaugural Lecture," *Economica* N.S. 35:117-26 (May).

Wood, Barbara (1984) *E. F. Schumacher.* New York: Harper and Row.

Wright, David McCord (1951) *The Impact of the Union.* New York: Harcourt Brace and World.

Young, Allyn A. (1928) "Increasing Returns and Economic Progress," *Economic Journal* 28:527-42 (December).

Young, Warren (1987) *Interpreting Mr. Keynes: the IS-LM Enigma.* Boulder: Westview Press.

NK

NAMES INDEX

NK

SUBJECT INDEX

Accession, Treaty of, 86
Acorn Securities, 69
Agricultural policy. *See* Common
    agricultural policy; Farm Fund
Alienation of working class, 134
Alliance for Progress, 61
"Alternative Theories of Distribution"
    (Kaldor), 115, 116
Alternative theory of distribution, 115,
    116–17
    debate, 126–31
American Academy of Arts and
    Sciences, 141
American Committee for Economic
    Development, 136
American Economic Association, 49,
    141, 165, 173
Amoco Oil, 168
Anglo–Midland Trust, 69
Anglo–Nippon, 17
Argentina, 196*n.21*
Aristocracy, British, 177–78
Artificial intelligence, 149
Atlantic Partnership, 77
Australia, 166, 196*n.21*
Australian Economic Papers, 141
Austria, 20–21, 77, 181
Austro–Hungarian Empire, breakup
    of, 20

Balance of payments, 65, 70–74, 95,
    96–97, 99, 102
    North Sea oil, 168, 169
    See also Exports; International trade
"B and K," 69, 97
Bank of England, 101
    nationalization of, 66
Barre Plan, 196*n.26*
"Bastard Keynesians," 182
Belgium, 76, 102, 195*n.13*, 196*n.26*

Berkeley Roundtable on the
    International Economy, 141
Blueprint of Tax Reform (U.S. Treasury),
    161
BNOC. *See* British National Oil
    Corporation
BP. *See* British Petroleum
Brazil, 196*n.21*
"Bretton Woods and After" (Kaldor),
    84
BRIE. *See* Berkeley Roundtable on the
    International Economy
Brighton Conference, 85
British Association for the
    Advancement of Science, 21, 132,
    141, 144
British Guiana, 54–57, 67, 70, 192*n.25*,
    193*n.35*
British National Oil Corporation, 169
British Petroleum, 168
Brookings Institution, 44, 161, 162, 164,
    179
Bulletin (ECLA), 59

California, capital gains tax, 191*n.11*
Cambridge Circus, 26, 29, 114
"Cambridge debate," 97–98, 176–77
Cambridge Economic Policy Group,
    87, 93, 98, 100, 175, 176–77
Cambridge Economic Policy Review, 176,
    177
Cambridgeshire County Council,17–18
Cambridge theory of distribution. *See*
    Kaldorian theory of distribution
Cambridge University, 4, 11, 12, 41, 69,
    78, 84, 114, 185*n.6(ch.3)*
    Kaldor's inaugural address, 73, 82,
    137–38, 139–40
    New School vs. Old School, 97–98, 99,
    176–77

227

NK

Marjorie Shepherd Turner was educated in Texas and taught economics in Texas, Arizona, and California. Her interest in Keynesian economics was first generated in 1944 by graduate studies at the University of Texas under Edward Everett Hale who had his students struggle through the whole of John Maynard Keynes's *General Theory of Employment Interest and Money.*

While on sabbatical leave from San Diego State University she visited Cambridge University in 1963. There Turner was further stimulated by the arguments Cambridge Keynesians R.F. Kahn, Joan Robinson, and Nicholas Kaldor were having with visiting American economists Robert M. Solow and Kenneth Arrow. Her book *Joan Robinson and the Americans* highlights these differences and was published in 1989. This study of Lord Kaldor examines not only Kaldor's many contributions to economic thought but also his efforts to apply post Keynesian economic policy in the real world.

Turner divides her time between a home in the Oregon Cascades and sailing in California.